2⁰⁰/6·19

Twins and Supertwins

Twins and Supertwins

A Handbook for Early Childhood Professionals

Eve-Marie Arce, EdD

Redleaf Press®
www.redleafpress.org
800-423-8309

Published by Redleaf Press
10 Yorkton Court
St. Paul, MN 55117
www.redleafpress.org

First edition 2010
Cover design by Jim Handrigan
Cover photograph ©iStock
Interior typeset in Minion Pro and Gill Sans and designed by Michelle L. N. Cook
Printed in the United States of America
17 16 15 14 13 12 11 10   1 2 3 4 5 6 7 8

Photographic contributors: Blakely Fetridge Bundy; Lisa Dirito—Lisa Dirito Photography; Rachel Hill—Rachel Hill Photography; Jim Ramirez

Library of Congress Cataloging-in-Publication Data
Arce, Eve-Marie.
  Twins and supertwins : a handbook for early childhood professionals / Eve-Marie Arce, EdD.
    p. cm.
  Includes bibliographical references and index.
  ISBN 978-1-60554-030-6 (alk. paper)
  1. Twins—Psychology. 2. Early childhood education. 3. Child development. I. Title.
  HQ777.35.A73 2010
  306.875—dc22
            2009053177

Printed on acid-free paper

To Henry

You kept the wind in our sail

Contents

Acknowledgments

Special appreciation is due to many—family, friends, and professional colleagues. I am grateful to each one for supporting and encouraging me to inform the early childhood profession about twins and supertwins.

Numerous professional colleagues played a particularly important role. To each, I express an unending message of gratitude and much joy in our mutual dedication to acknowledging multiples.

- Pat Malmstrom, founder of Twin Services, inspired me over thirty years ago. She became my mentor when we finally met during my doctoral studies. Her commitment and enthusiasm profoundly helped me formulate this book.
- Cary Larson-McKay was my go-to colleague. Our friendship and affiliation generated wonderful suggestions. Cary's critical reviews influenced this book's application as a resource for teachers.
- Sherry Magee and the other professors in the Organizational Leadership Department at the University of La Verne supported my doctoral dissertation about twins and early childhood.
- Rachel Franklin responded to my request to read the chapter about the meaning of twins and supertwins. This was an extraordinarily generous and supportive gesture, considering her schedule as a family medicine specialist and associate professor of family and preventive medicine at the University of Oklahoma College of Medicine.

I am in debt to the researchers whose work is cited throughout the book. Four international experts established the foundation for what you will read: David Hay, Patricia Malmstrom, Pat Preedy, and Nancy Segal.

I thank them and sincerely desire that the book honors their work and meets their expectations.

The children whose photographs are featured throughout the book are twins and supertwins. I am extremely appreciative to the following families for their contribution of the photographs:

The Ager Family
The Annan Family
The Blek Family
The Bose Family
The Brooks Family
The Bush Family
The Chapin Family
The Goulet Family
The Houchin Family
The Irwin Family
The McGredy Family
The McKay Family
The Mendell Family
The Pearson Family
The Perry Family
The Rapinoe Family
The Rodrigo Family
The Simpson-Showalter Family
The Villafana Family

Children's names used throughout the book to illustrate examples are not the names of the children in the related photographs.

Personal and professional colleagues from early childhood education centers throughout the United States submitted photographs. To each, I extend a huge and sincere thank-you.

Arleen Uryu, Director, Santa Margarita Children's Center
Cecily Mendell
Clovis Unifed School District, Clovis, California
Dakota Circle Head Start Preschool Program, Fresno, California
Denise Holder
Eunice Thiesen

Kathy Ramirez, Executive Director, Village Infant/Toddler Center
    and Preschool
Liz Dacey
Lori Rodrigo
Marva Lyons, Director, Happy Town Family Child Care
Olivia Brooks
Regina Martin
Shasta College Early Childhood Education Center, Redding,
    California

Most essentially, it is my family who deserves the most appreciation. They guide my reality and encourage my work. My daughters, Cecily and Olivia, led me into the realm of twins, and my grandsons give perpetual meaning to encourage the recognition of multiples.

Introduction

W hat is it like to have twins?"
As I prepared to answer this question, I scanned the eighty
or so college students assembled in the lecture hall. The
question was very familiar, asked innumerable times during the semesters I taught child and human development courses. Would this student, this semester, want a professional response? Or was the student seeking a reply with personal insight?

Even now, I think about my responses. Most were simple, and all elicited more inquiry because I couldn't really answer the question. Students rarely missed responding to me with, "But why not? You're a mother of twins." While I confidently taught the courses, I was unable at that time to answer with enough substantiated resources and information. My bachelor's degree in child development and master's degree in human development and early childhood education had not included training about twins. Throughout my years teaching preschoolers in Head Start, publicly funded preschools, and a university laboratory school, none of the children who were enrolled were twins. My own experience as a mother of twins provided only one example of a set of twins, in one family, in one community, in one less-than-objective environment.

The college students remained curious about twins. They wanted to know about twin language, whether twins were always friends with each other, and which teaching methods would be most appropriate for twins. I realized that students intuitively recognized that twins might have particular needs.

Twins as a topic most often is addressed very briefly in child development textbooks. Generally, they are mentioned in a paragraph or two about conception. Teacher preparatory coursework and related instructional material, however, do not include content about them. For this reason, I supplemented lecture topics with whatever information I could find. Handouts produced by Twin Services were the most helpful; they established a foundation for my course content. Twin Services was founded in 1978 by an educator and mother of twins, Patricia Malmstrom, to address the lack of resources for families.

Inquiries from students and conference attendees continue. Now the questions also address triplets and sometimes quadruplets and quintuplets, called *supertwins* or *multiples*. *Multiples* is an inclusive term referring to children who are twins, triplets, quadruplets, quintuplets, and the other higher-order numbers. *Multiples* will be used interchangeably with *twins* and *supertwins* throughout the book.

The continuing questions from students, conference attendees, and teachers ask for practical information. Many wonder, "What is going on?" Teachers and program administrations are not just seeing double and triple. They are, in fact, seeing more children whose last names are the same, whose parents are the same, whose birth dates fall on the same day, and who may physically look quite similar. This is because approximately one child in every thirty is now a multiple (Hay and Preedy 2006; Martin et al. 2009).

Teachers' comments validate the escalating population and present inquiries:

"I have two sets of twins and one set of triplets."

"We have eight sets of twins in our school. We're trying to figure out what to do."

"Parents have demands. We're a co-op. None of us really knows anything about twins."

"I have a group of twelve preschoolers; eight are twins."

The extraordinary increase in the multiple population is occurring along with efforts to increase preschool programs for all children. As an early childhood educator, you know that the preschool experience influences young children. It is their first point of entry into the educational system. Inquiries about twins and supertwins from teachers suggest that the preschool experience may affect twins and supertwins differently than it does singleborn children. The baby boom of multiples poses social, economical, and educational challenges. Conscientious teachers want to know how the challenges affect multiples and what the implications are for teaching them during their early childhood years.

Many multiples begin attending preschool programs with teachers who have not received appropriate professional preparation on the developmental needs of twins and supertwins. Too often, teachers and program administrators make decisions about the care of multiples based on popular misconceptions and generalizations. The very limited references to twins in child development books usually refer to dated case studies describing unusual and extreme behaviors.

Because the public remains fascinated with twins and supertwins, popular publications contain sensational stories about them. Most books written about twins are directed to families, and the contents primarily cover prenatal and early development of multiples. Medical professionals who are parents of twins write some of the parenting references.

The population of multiple-birth children is increasing, and information about them has been limited. As both of these circumstances merge, they offer the rationale for *Twins and Supertwins: A Handbook for Early Childhood Professionals*. This book grew out of the certainty that teachers will use new knowledge to enhance their interaction with children. Inspired by this conviction, I've written this book as a practical guide for early childhood educators and child caregivers.

This book lays out my understanding of twins and supertwins based on the information that was previously available only in the research literature and in books addressed specifically to parents (birth parents, adoptive parents, and any other adult guardians of twins or supertwins). As you begin absorbing the information, you can build a foundation of knowledge for making informed decisions about the twins and supertwins attending your preschools. Having such information helps you clarify misconceptions and dispel misinformation about multiples. The details are useful for staff members working toward agreement on the care and interaction with multiples, for instance, and agreement about the appropriate terms to use when describing multiples. Facts and figures prepare you to implement programs that can have a positive impact on the health and welfare of the twins and supertwins enrolled in your programs. The information in this book facilitates your interaction with the families of multiples.

Twins and Supertwins is organized into three parts. The book starts with background information in chapters 1 and 2, including definitions for twins and supertwins, data on their increasing numbers, and commentary about popular interest in and fascination about them. In the second part (chapters 3, 4, and 5), I discuss multiples' physical, social and emotional, and learning and language development, enhancing the developmental areas with published research that is twin- and supertwin-specific. The third part synthesizes practical information for early childhood teachers. Chapters 6 and 7 introduce the unique needs of preschool multiples and the program practices that best meet their needs. These practices establish a foundation for school guidelines and prospective policies. My basic assumption is that as soon as teachers have adequate background and practical information about multiples, they will literally and figuratively make room for multiples in their classrooms.

You will find comments from preschool teachers, program administrators, and families of twins threaded throughout the chapters. I have gathered observations of twins for more than thirty-five years in varied educational settings. The names of teachers and children in all of the examples have been modified with the exception of direct quotes from adults. In the appendixes, you will find a list identifying the unique needs of twins, a list of the program practices that best meet their needs, and a Teachers Taking Action template to assist you in reviewing the needs and practices. A glossary, a list of additional resources, and references complete the book.

The groundwork for establishing the unique needs and program practices is based on a study I conducted that was specifically designed to identify the needs of twins in center-based preschools (Arce 2008). A panel of four experts reviewed and confirmed the conceptual framework. Most the foundational concepts emerged from the valuable work of David Hay, Patricia Maxwell Malmstrom, Pat Preedy, and Nancy Segal. The contributions from these four international experts provide important insight regarding multiples and their early development and education. Two additional groups of professionals, teachers, and academics contributed to the study. The teachers were drawn from the center-based preschools accredited by the National Association for the Education of Young Children (NAEYC). The sample of preschools was included because NAEYC Accreditation Academy includes the widest range of early childhood programs, including publicly funded, private-for-profit, and faith-based programs for young children. The academics were researchers, authors, professors, physicians, counselors, and children's advocates.

The needs and practices lists that emerged from my study synthesize the perceptions of experts, teachers, and academics. The wording in a few of the statements that identify the needs and practices have been slightly modified from the study findings. You will find in *Twins and Supertwins* that the changes enhance readability while sustaining the perceptions of the study participants.

Twins and Supertwins: A Handbook for Early Childhood Professionals is valuable for everyone involved in early childhood education. Teachers, program administrators, and families can benefit from the informative strategies identified to enhance the well-being of twins and supertwins during their preschool years. The information in this book can enhance your confidence in teaching twins and supertwins by helping you identify the most suitable practices for multiples. Once this knowledge finds its way into pre-service professional preparation, teachers can arrive at preschools ready to meet the needs of multiples. Perhaps then some of the questions previously asked by college students will no longer be asked. Or perhaps new questions will be raised by educators, especially by those with three, four, and sometimes seven sets of multiples attending their preschool programs at once.

Now, attendees who learn through my presentation that besides being a mother of twins, I am a grandmother of twins, regularly ask, "What it is like to have twin grandsons?"

Historical
Perspectives

PART ONE

The Meaning of Twins and Supertwins

chapter one

Teacher, what's a twin?"

How does an early childhood educator answer four-year-old Jackson's question? What indeed, is the meaning of *twin*? What is the meaning of *supertwin*?

Every profession uses its own definitions and acronyms for communicating. The definitions evolve as the discipline advances. Today that information evolves much more quickly than it did even a few years ago. Increasingly, sophisticated technologies reveal findings never before imagined; this is especially true about prenatal development. New terms are added, definitions are refined and updated, and old terms become obsolete. The changes influence relationships, procedures, and people, including our understanding of twins.

The quest to understand twins and supertwins is significant for many reasons. Most important, teachers need to respond appropriately to questions from the preschoolers attending their programs. A teacher's immediate answer may be something like this: "Your friend Max is a twin. Your friend Joseph is a twin. They are also brothers." You have opportunities to answer the children's inquiries when the twins are first introduced to the class or as the children ask questions. "We have two new friends today who are joining our group. Their names are Anna and Isabella. They are twins. They are sisters."

Older preschoolers may probe further and insist on more information to answer the question "But teacher, if they are twins, why don't they look the same?" The teacher who is informed about twins and supertwins is prepared to answer, "Twins do not always look alike. Anna and Isabella are twins. They are sisters. They were born on the same day. Ethan and Ava are twins too. Ava is Ethan's sister and Ethan is Ava's brother. They were born on the same day and they have the same mother and father."

Twinship and *supertwinship* are terms that identify the relationships between children born on the same day to the same parents. Twinship includes two children. Supertwinship may include triplets, quadruplets, or larger groups. The relationship defines a particular phenomenon— one that is normal to the pair or the group in a world in which singletons are the usual reference point (Stewart 2003).

Some parents enrolling their twins and supertwins in early childhood programs are aware and knowledgeable about the facts, statistics, and descriptive nuances of multiplehood. They are advocates for their children and have strong preferences about their children's education. Your familiarity with the information in this chapter establishes a base of knowledge for your work with multiples. This knowledge probably replicates much that is already known by their families. Equipped with similar information, you are ready to build an inventory of responses to questions about multiples and to develop materials that complement your existing preschool program policies and family education plan.

Twins and supertwins are individual preschoolers who enroll in and attend preschool or prekindergarten with one or more of their same-age siblings. Their increasing numbers may initially give the impression that their enrollment will double and triple the demands on you. They will not, because you are already prepared to work with children in groups. Even so, you may become absorbed in learning as much about the new arrivals as possible. Your need for information does not require that you become overloaded with statistics and scientific data. This chapter includes the basic facts about twins and supertwins you need.

Avoid generalized information about multiples. Just like each singleborn child, each twin, each supertwin, and each twin and supertwin family is unique. For this reason, your guidance of multiples deserves careful consideration. Most children attending preschool programs are singletons. Some singleton preschoolers may be siblings to multiples or have cousins or neighbors who are twins or supertwins. For the majority of singletons, however, preschool is their first direct interaction with a multiple-birth child. In contrast, for twins and supertwins, relationships and daily interactions with same-age siblings or other children are normal.

Twins

A twin is defined as two children born to one mother from a single pregnancy. Twins most often arouse curiosity. Some people are amazed and some just fascinated by them (Hay and Preedy 2006; Segal 2005b; Smilansky 1992; Stewart 2000). Twins have traits and special characteristics that define their unique relationship. As a social phenomenon, they create an identifiable category. People react to them and their twinness in both positive and negative ways (Stewart 2003).

A few definitions answer the most basic questions and help you frame positive descriptions. What are twins? What are multiples? What is a singleborn child, and what are supertwins?

Twins can share the same biological makeup or be as dissimilar as any two singleborn siblings. A multiple-birth child, multiple-birth children, and multiples are members of a group of two (twins) or more (supertwins). They shared the same prenatal environment. Multiple-birth children also typically are conceived at the same time, are born on the same day, and share biological makeup. A singleborn child is one child born to one woman from one pregnancy and one birth. When the term *singleborn* is used in connection with the word *multiples*, it generally refers to the fact that the singleborn does not have a twin or supertwin sibling. *Singleborn children* and *singleborn child* are terms used throughout this book.

Twin Type and Multiple Type

Twin type is a term used to explain the various known classifications of twins and supertwins. The term *multiple type* may also be used to explain the classifications. Twin type is a categorization that provides a more accurate reference to the identity of twins and supertwins. Knowing the type of twin, or twin type, is thought to be beneficial to parents because it increases their insight about the development of their children.

Twin type is a topic area of confusion as well as of interest to families of twins and supertwins. Numerous factors determine twin type, but

Related Terms

singleborn
A singleborn child may have siblings, each of which has a different birth date. A singleborn child is sometimes referred to as a *singleton child* or a *singleton*.

multiples
A multiple-birth child, multiple-birth children, and multiples are a group of two (twins) or more (supertwins) children who typically are conceived at the same time, are born at the same time, and share biological makeup. A co-multiple is a child who is paired in a twin, triplet, quadruplet, quintuplet, sextuplet, septuplet, or octuplet set.

twins
Twins are two children born to one woman from a single pregnancy. They typically are conceived at the same time, are born on the same day, and share biological makeup. *Co-twin* is the term used to identify the child who is paired. The term *twin pair* is another phrase referring to twins. Twin pair is the primary usage in this book.

supertwins
Supertwins are multiple births of three or more, including triplets, quadruplets, quintuplets, sextuplets, septuplets, and octuplets, born to one woman from a single pregnancy on the same day. Supertwins are also referred to as higher-order multiples and triplets/+. *Co-supertwin* is the term used to identify a child who is part of the supertwin group that consists of triplets, quadruplets, quintuplets, or more. The term *co-multiple* can also be used to refer to supertwins and twins.

only two classifications have become commonly used as social definitions of multiples: identical twins and fraternal twins. The terms are usually used with reference to the physical appearances of twins, although doing this is not technically correct. The two classifications continue to be used even though they do not accurately describe twins. As a group, twins are much more variable than those two types suggest. Genetic research has clarified and established more accurate descriptive terms.

The use of the term *twin type* to describe multiples downplays the tendency to reduce twins to one of two kinds (Koch 1966). Use of the concept of twin type widens the range of detailed and useful information you can gather. For example, you can ask parents, "Do you know your children's twin type? Can you tell me their twin type?"

According to Malmstrom (Malmstrom and Poland 1999), the use of the term *zygosity* may discourage common misconceptions about twins. *Zygosity* is another term used to identify twin type. Zygosity indicates whether the twins developed from one zygote or more (Guilherme et al. 2008). A zygote is the single cell formed at the moment of conception from the fusion of sperm and an ovum (Berger 2005). Learning about the zygosity of twinning is helpful because it reveals genetic information about the multiples. For example, testing to determine zygosity can explain the significantly different health conditions of twins and provides multiples and their families answers to common questions. Zygosity may explain dissimilarities in growth among multiples. Zygosity may also contribute to the formation of multiples' identities (Noble 2003).

DIZYGOTIC TWINS

Except among Asian Americans, the majority of twins are what have been commonly referred to as *fraternal*. The precise term to use is *dizygotic*. Dizygotic (DZ) twins represent about 70 percent of twins (Hankins and Saade 2005). Dizygotic twins are the product of two ova fertilized by two sperm. Of dizygotic twins, 25 percent are brothers, 25 percent sisters, and 50 percent are boy-and-girl twin pairs. Some twins are obviously dizygotic—notably different in height, size, and eye and hair color. Yet families of boy-and-girl twins surprisingly and repeatedly hear, "Oh, look at the identical twins!" Dizygotic twins can be as alike or different as any two singleborn siblings (Berger 2005).

Parenting books about multiples, as well as some research articles, use shortcuts to identify twin pairs and to communicate zygosity. Parents enrolling their twins and supertwins in preschool programs may also use a variety of acronyms. The acronym list expands with extensions such as *SS* for same sex and *f* or *m* for female and male. The acronym *DZSSf* refers to dizygotic (nonidentical), same-sex twins who are girls (Tinglof 2007).

MONOZYGOTIC TWINS

Approximately one-third of all twins have identical genes. These children are commonly referred to as *identical twins* or, more precisely, *monozygotic (MZ) twins*. Monozygotic refers to one fertilized egg, or ovum, that splits very early in its development, creating two zygotes. Half of the cluster of cells separates days after conception, early in the first week of embryonic growth (Berger 2005; Gromada and Hurlburt 2001; Steinman and Verni 2007); and the two zygotes then develop into two separate embryos. Some refer to monozygotic twins as true twins (Noble 2003). Monozygotic twins usually look similar and are the same gender. Nonetheless, rare occurrences of monozygotic twins who are of different sexes, a boy and girl, have been noted (Hall 2003; Segal 1999).

The fact that monozygotic twins are genetically identical should not diminish recognition or acknowledgment of their differences. Research proposes that monozygotic twins are highly similar rather than identical. Their similar but not identical status has practical implications for you when you are trying to understand the dynamics of their development. The birth weight, appearance, and health of MZ twins are affected by their genetics, prenatal environment, and variations in the fertilization process. Each of these influence every developing baby in specific ways.

The term *spectrum of differences* is used to describe genetically identical but biologically different monozygotic twins (Wright 1997). Although monozygotic twins may be genetically identical, they may look and behave differently. Some MZ twins are more alike than others. You, as the teacher, need to be continuously attentive to the differences as well as the similarities among twins. Some MZ twins may look alike, yet they may have different preferences, personalities, and learning styles because their genetic material has not been expressed in identical ways (Franklin 2009). "For instance," Rachel Franklin explains, "one may have a mole the other does not have, because as the skin developed, the genetic material was copied differently into the cellular structure of part of one's skin than it was in the other" (2009). One MZ twin may enjoy fruit; the other, fresh vegetables. One may prefer all bright colors and the other may respond only to primary hues.

Monozygotic multiples may or may not have the same interests; they are just as likely to have dissimilar interests. For example, Brycen's responsive active movements became evident when he was a toddler. His very similar-looking twin brother, Noah, also enjoyed tricycles, sand play, and climbing, but he was much more excited about the smaller objects he could manipulate in the sensory activity area.

Monozygotic twins occur naturally across all populations worldwide in about one out of every 250 births; in the United States, they constitute about 30 percent of the twins (Hankins and Saade 2005; Segal 2005b). This means MZ twinning occurs randomly across populations and ethnic groups in a constant birthrate of about 4 per 1,000 (Moskwinski 2002). This frequency has been understood to mean that the frequency of MZ twinning is not related to a genetic influence. The exception is among Asian Americans (Segal 1999). Although twin births among the Asian populations, including Asian Americans, are lower than among other populations, their twin births are more frequently monozygotic. In other populations DZ twinning is higher.

Not Exactly Identical

"Identical twins are not identical in every way and, in fact, show differences in virtually every trait that has ever been studied," even when they look very much alike phenotypically, explains Nancy L. Segal, director of the Twin Studies Center at California State University, Fullerton (1999, 9). *Phenotype* refers to appearance. *Genotype* refers to genetic makeup, including features and characteristics that may or may not express themselves phenotypically. Segal proposes that knowledge of twin type is important for individuals providing care for twins. The information may prevent others from misidentifying the multiples and minimizing the identity of DZ twins. Dizygotic twins may not resemble one another, yet their lives are connected extraordinarily because they are twins.

Newer Classifications to Consider

Many contributing factors affect development among genetically identical twins. As research continues, simple classification of twins as this or that type of twin will be replaced by more complete and possibly more complicated categories.

Regardless of the new acronyms and advancing research, most people remain loyal to the binary classification of twins as identical or nonidentical or fraternal. Terms used to describe twinning and supertwinning continue to be modified, and as this occurs, the dated classifications may be replaced. Current terms and definitions are introduced, replaced, and often overlapped to explain the types of twinning. It is best for you as an educator to stay aware of emerging research findings that will provide newer definitions. Be prepared to acknowledge a variety of labels and definitions about multiples in your conversations with the families of the twins and supertwins enrolled in your program.

A fitting example is the term *third-type twinning*. This concept has been used to account for the differences between the two children in a twin pair, especially when the pair do not apparently fit into the more common MZ twin or DZ twin classifications. You may hear parents refer to a third-type twin as half identical. Third-type twinning is also termed *third-phase-of-egg twinning* and *polar-body twinning*. It is theorized that third-type twinning results from an ovum splitting prior to fertilization by two sperm, resulting in the inheritance of identical genes from the mother but not from the father (Bryan 1992). Third-type twinning has been studied extensively by Charles Boklage, a father of DZ twins and a geneticist at East Carolina University. Boklage asserts that twinning, both MZ and DZ types, is the outcome of cellular events. He questions the two-ova origin that has been established as the explanation of DZ twins conceived naturally (Malmstrom and Poland 1999; Segal 1999).

The birth of a twin pair in 2007 grabbed the attention of researchers. The researchers reported that the boy-and-girl twin pair could be referred to as "semi-identical," although that may be a simplistic explanation for their genetic inheritance. The researchers suspected that the twins inherited identical genetics from their mother and only half of their father's DNA, which they claimed accounts for the physical characteristics of the twins. One of the twins was born anatomically male and one was born with sexually ambiguous genitalia, possibly because of different proportions of male and female cells (Masters 2007).

Occurrences like this are rare. Nonetheless, researchers want to understand the causes. In the attempt to define the variations in twinning, another term, *sesquizygotic,* has been suggested. Sesquizygotic is similar to third-type twinning because it refers to twins who are the outcome of an egg fertilized by two separate sperm after the egg splits. These twins can be born same-sex or opposite-sex. It is further theorized that they may inherit more genetic material from their mother (Noble 2003). *Semi-identical* is a term used to define sesquizygotic twins. Still other researchers, such as biologist Michael Golubovsky, call sesquizygotic twins *half-identical* (Boklage 2006).

With research accelerating, expect additional terms and definitions. For now, the terms *DZ twins* and *MZ twins* may be the most practical, particularly as knowledge is generated by the new science of epigenetics.

Epigenetics is looking at development and contributing new and, we hope, practical knowledge—for example, development among MZ twins and especially the differences in and exceptions to their development. We may be able to determine why twins who inherited the same genes have different characteristics and, in some cases, different diseases (Begley 2009).

Epigenetics studies heritable changes and patterns of gene regulation. It is currently demonstrating how certain genes switch on or off and direct changes in development. Zygosity testing provides a clear picture of MZ twins and verifies their same inheritance. Some will look and behave similarly. Other MZ twins are quite different, or discordant, in their phenotype—that is, in their observable features and characteristics (Bio5 2009). Epigenetics will help explain the direction or path of certain DNA codes and genes that switch off. In twins, this may happen at different times or not at all, which may explain why some syndromes and diseases affect only one twin in an MZ pair (National Geographic 2009).

One last term, *lyonization,* is proposed to aid understanding of twinning. Laura Herzing and other researchers at the Institute for Cancer Research in London have proposed a process in which one of the two X chromosomes in each cell inactivates when they implant in the uterus. This may occur only in MZ girls, and this X inactivation may create the potential for the MZ girls to have differences in traits depending on whether the deactivated X chromosome came from their mother or their father. (Male twins are not affected because they have only one X and one Y chromosome [Segal 1999].) To further explain lyonization, Segal analyzed the Dionne quintuplets as an example. The Dionne quintuplets were born in 1934 in Canada. They were identified as identical, having the same genetic inheritance, yet only two of the five were color blind (Segal 1999). Color blindness would have been expressed only if two recessive X-linked chromosomes had been inherited (Berger 2005).

Twin-type classifications, such as polar body twinning, provide definitions relating to development. You may hear the word *virtual* used to identify twins. This describes a relationship rather than development. Virtual twins are unrelated children who are the same age. They are reared together in a family as siblings beginning for many during infancy. Virtual twins, as unrelated siblings reared together, can be two adopted children without genetic relatedness or one adopted child and one biological child of the adopting family. Nancy Segal suggests that these sibling pairs in many ways replay the twin relationship (Segal 2000).

Related Terms

twin type

Twin type is a category that provides a more accurate reference and avoids the two outdated labels *identical* and *fraternal*. Twin type is also referred to as *zygosity*.

zygosity

Zygosity refers to whether the twins developed from one or more zygotes. A fertilized egg is called a zygote. Learning about the origins of twinning is helpful because it reveals something about genetics. It also clarifies twin type by referring to the type of conception. Simple tests are available.

identical, or monozygotic

Identical, or monozygotic, twins develop from a single egg, or ovum, that splits after being fertilized by a single sperm. Monozygotic (MZ) twins have the same genes and therefore are more similar than fraternal, or dizygotic, twins. One-third of twins are monozygotic. Triplets can be monozygotic, meaning all three multiples developed from the same fertilized ovum.

fraternal, or dizygotic

Fraternal, or dizygotic, twins develop from two eggs (ova) and two sperm. Two-thirds of twins are dizygotic (DZ). Triplets can be nonidentical if all develop from separate eggs fertilized by separate sperm. They would be trizygotic (TZ) (Guilherme et al. 2008; Koch 1966; Luke and Eberlein 2004; Malmstrom and Poland 1999).

opposite-sex twins

Opposite-sex twins are a twin pair—a boy and a girl. This twin pair is also referred to as *unlike-sex pairs* and *boy-girl twins*. The image of opposite-sex twins influences their twin status. (More details about boy and girl twins can be found in chapter 4.)

Identifying zygosity prenatally or at the birth of multiples is preferrable, because doing so provides important medical information early in their lives (Moskwinski 2002). The medical information may help explain the apparent physical differences of an MZ twin pair, especially a significant difference in their sizes. The information may reveal the cause of the differences, perhaps the result of a problem that occurred prenatally. A developmental or physical delay of one MZ twin may justify early intervention services. The expectation for MZ twins is that they grow similarly, both developmentally and physically. Professional literature supports early testing of zygosity to prevent potentially difficult adjustments to empirical information acquired when the children are older. Family accessibility to testing has improved in the past decade.

TESTING TO BE SURE

The social definition of twins, especially the two outdated references *identical* and *fraternal*, does not explain twin types. For this reason, experts recommend accurate determination of twin type, including genetic analysis (Segal 1999). Some believe that both MZ and DZ twins and supertwins have the right to know their twin type and that testing should be done at birth. Knowledge of zygosity is important for parents because it can influence how they care for their multiples and opens up a greater understanding of the children's development. When parents have accurate knowledge, they may be more likely to celebrate their twins' differences and similarities. Accurate identification of twin type may also clarify parents' expectations and help parents appreciate each of their multiples' characteristics and behaviors. Knowing the true zygosity eliminates guesses and allows parents to answer questions from others. Such information encourages families to enjoy the special interests of each multiple and appreciate the aptitude one may have for music and the other for the structure details of building (Malmstrom and Poland 1999). Accurate information about zygosity should be provided by health professionals when it is requested. The information may be reassuring to families (Bamforth and Machin 2004).

Chorionicity is the term used to explain twin type according to the form of placentation (the number of placentas and amniotic fluid cavities) (Guilherme et al. 2008). The chorion, the outer layer of the placenta, acts as a protective sac. Monochorionic twins develop from the same amniotic sac. Monochorionic twins are always monozygotic (Franklin 2005). Dichorionic twins develop when there are two separate amniotic (inner) sacs. The twins can be monozygotic or dizygotic. A common misconception is that only dizygotic twins have separate placentas. Dizygotic twins may have fused placentas, and many MZ twins have separate placentas (Agnew, Klein, and Ganon 2005; Noble 2003).

If it is not determined prenatally, accurate twin-type or zygosity identification can be ascertained through DNA analysis performed at specialized laboratories. The DNA sequence is usually the same for MZ twins. Zygosity can now be determined through a blood specimen or by simply swabbing the inside of the cheek to gather cells for laboratory analysis of DNA (Moskwinski 2002).

Pat Preedy and David Hay's work with multiples and their families offers interesting insight into identifying zygosity. When they asked adult twins whether they were MZ or DZ pairs, most twins' responses agreed with what formal genetic tests revealed. This was not the case, however, when the researchers asked parents about the zygosity of their multiples. A questionnaire used to collect responses from the parents included inquiries about the twins' physical features and asked whether the parents were able to distinguish their twins physically. The form also asked whether the parents thought other people could tell their twins apart. Preedy and Hay employed a statistical analysis to project the identity of the twins included in the study. They determined that parents usually say their twins are dizygotic. Preedy and Hay suspect that parents view minor differences as indications that their twins are dizygotic. The researchers also believed that some parents emphasize individuality and want to think of their twins as DZ pairs or accentuate their children's similarities to emphasize the specialness of twinship (Twins and Multiples 2006). I would add a third explanation, one without underlying motivation, which is that parents simply see, feel, and know the differences of their twins, even when the children look very much alike.

Hay documented similar results in a 1990 study that reported differences between parents and teachers in identifying the zygosity of young twins. The Australian study concluded that teachers thought more of the twins were very alike, while the parents considered them to be nonidentical.

MIRROR-IMAGE TWINS

Mirror-image twins, or mirror twins, have similar but opposite physical features. The physical characteristics may include such features as opposite-handedness and hair that whorls in reverse or opposite directions.

The prevalence of left-handedness among MZ twins may be explained by mirror imaging. Among MZ pairs, about one-third include a left-handed twin. This occurrence is twice as frequent as among non-twins. Determination of mirror-twin type can be accomplished only by observation. Mirror-image twins occur in about 23 to 25 percent of MZ twin sets, most often because the ovum splits seven or more days later than usual (Malmstrom and Poland 1999; Moskwinski 2002).

TWIN TO TWIN TRANSFUSION SYNDROME

Twin to Twin Transfusion Syndrome (TTTS) is a condition that occurs when both babies share a single placenta, causing unequal nourishment. One twin takes blood from the other baby's system through the shared vessels. The ultrasounds may reveal growth-size differences and potential heart failure. This occurs in 5 to 15 percent of twin pregnancies, is possible only in MZ twin types, and is a result of monochorionic twins sharing the same outer sac (the chorion). This condition may be related to the vanishing twin syndrome (see below). Treatments for TTTS are progressing (Franklin 2005).

VANISHING TWIN SYNDROME

Vanishing twin and *vanishing twin syndrome* are terms for spontaneous fetal reductions, meaning that one or more of the multiple fetuses fails to survive the pregnancy. This occurs because one of the gestational sacs does not develop and is absorbed into the uterus or disintegrates. The chance that the remaining twin will survive is high, although the incidence of cerebral palsy increases for the surviving twin. Elizabeth Bryan has written that a surviving twin may experience a feeling of loss (1992). Today the syndrome is more appropriately referred to as *spontaneous fetal reduction*. Early ultrasound screening within weeks of conception has shown that as many as one-third of pregnancies begin as a multiple (Gromada and Hurlburt 2001; Noble 2003). The prevalence of this condition doubles among same-sex twins (Noble 2003).

Twin-Type Summary

- Most twins look different because dizygotic (DZ) twinning is more common.
- Monozygotic (MZ) twins are about one-third of the total twin population.
- Dizygotic (DZ) twins are about two-thirds of the total twin population.
- Mirror twins occur in about 23 to 25 percent of MZ twin pairs.
- Parents are most likely to learn the zygosity of their infants before their infants are born.
- Experts recommend completing twin-type identification.

Supertwins

Supertwins are three or more children born to one woman from a single pregnancy. They are referred to as *higher-order multiples (HOM)*, having been born as a set of multiples numbering more than two (Gromada and Hurlburt 2001). A supertwin combination may be three (triplets), four (quadruplets), five (quintuplets), six (sextuplets), seven (septuplets), or eight (octuplets).

Anecdotal information provided by families of supertwins and by supertwins themselves offers important insight into their special development and experiences. Record keeping about supertwins was inconsistent before 1974. The reported statistics tended to group multiples together without distinguishing the type of higher-order multiple. This created difficulties in distinguishing numbers in each supertwin category. Information about quintuplets and quadruplets, for example, was often rolled into statistics about triplets (Multiple Births Canada/Naissances multiples Canada 2009).

The birth of supertwins is popularly considered quite a fantastic event. This super phenomenon attracts attention and commonly brings the family into an immediate spotlight. Striking evidence about being in the spotlight is reported in the anecdotes from families of supertwins, showing that support and guidance is essential for them.

Related Terms

conjoined
Conjoined twins are born physically attached in some way. They used to be referred to as *Siamese twins*.

mirror image
Mirror-image twinning occurs in approximately 23 to 25 percent of monozygotic twins. Each mirror-image twin has similar features on the sides opposite from its occurrence on the other twin—a mirror image of one another (Malmstrom and Poland 1999; Moskwinski 2002).

Twin to Twin Transfusion Syndrome (TTTS)
Twin to Twin Transfusion Syndrome (TTTS) is a condition that occurs when both babies share one placenta, causing unequal nourishment. This occurs in 5 to 15 percent of twin pregnancies and is possible only in MZ twin types (Franklin 2005).

vanishing twin syndrome
Vanishing twin syndrome is spontaneous fetal reduction, meaning that one or more of the twin fetuses fails to develop and does not survive. Early screening during the first three months has shown that as many as one-third of pregnancies begin as multiple pregnancies (Gromada and Hurlburt 2001; Noble 2003).

virtual twins
Virtual twins are unrelated children who are the same age and from infancy are reared together in a family as siblings. Unrelated siblings reared together can be two adopted children without genetic relatedness or one adopted child and one biological child of the adopting family. Nancy Segal suggests that these sibling pairs in many ways replay the twin relationship (Segal 2000).

Although information and evidence-based research about super-twins may be limited, their lack does not give us license to construct generalizations about them. For example, some information about twins does not apply directly to triplets, quadruplets, or quintuplets. You may need to use the information that is available about twins cautiously when dealing with supertwins simply because data on supertwins and the resources supporting them are negligible. Use the twin data sparingly and welcome research findings that are specific to triplets, quadruplets, quintuplets, and larger groups.

Supertwin Zygosity

When you are considering the information that is available about super-twins, you may also want to review their zygosity. Supertwins may be one of various combinations of twin types. They can be a mix of MZ and DZ twinning, or they may be just one of these types. The term *polyzygotic (PZ)* is used to explain the numerous twinning patterns of supertwins. The majority of triplets, quadruplets, and quintuplets are polyzygotic (Segal 2006).

Monozygotic (MZ) supertwins are rare. Triplets more commonly result from three separate eggs, referred to as a *trizygotic (TZ) group* (Noble 2003), making triplets similar to twins, the majority of whom develop from separately fertilized ova.

Triplets may include a set of MZ twins and one non-monozygotic triplet. You may hear the third triplet referred to as the fraternal triplet or the singleton or the singleborn one. The third triplet is not a singleborn child. The triplet combination—MZ twins and a third triplet—would have developed from two ova fertilized by two sperm, after which one of the fertilized ova split to form the MZ twins. If three ova had been fertilized by three different sperm, this would result in a trizygotic set of triplets (Noble 2003). Identifying zygosity reveals if the triplets resulted from one fertilized ovum, resulting in MZ triplets.

The most common combination of quadruplets is quadrazygotic (QZ), which results from the fertilization of four ova. A set of four girls was born in February 2000 in South Carolina, naturally conceived and monozygotic (Segal 2006). Rare examples of monozygotic quintuplets exist. (The famous Dionne quintuplets, who were born in 1934, will be discussed in chapter 2.)

Related Terms

higher-order multiples
Higher-order multiples (HOM) are children who are part of a triplet, quadruplet, quintuplet, sextuplet, septuplet, or octuplet set born to one woman from a single pregnancy. Higher-order, multiple-birth children typically are conceived at the same time, are born at the same time, and share certain biological makeup. References to them include multiples, supertwins, and triplets/+.

triplets
Triplets are the three children born to one woman from a single pregnancy. They typically are conceived at the same time, are born on the same day, and share biological makeup dependent on their zygosity.

triplets/+
The U.S. Department of Health and Human Services uses *triplets*/+ to refer to triplets and higher-order multiple births in reporting vital statistics. Quintuplets, sextuplets, and higher-order multiple births are not reported separately or differentiated in the national data set (Martin et al. 2009).

quadruplets
Quadruplets are the four children born to one woman from a single pregnancy. They typically are conceived at the same time, are born on the same day, and share biological makeup dependent on their zygosity.

quintuplets
Quintuplets are the five children born to one woman from a single pregnancy. They typically are conceived at the same time, are born on the same day, and share biological makeup dependent on their zygosity.

sextuplets
Sextuplets are the six children born to one woman from a single pregnancy. They typically are conceived at the same time, are born on the same day, and share biological makeup dependent on their zygosity.

septuplets
Septuplets are the seven children born to one woman from a single pregnancy. They typically are conceived at the same time, are born on the same day, and share biological makeup dependent on their zygosity.

octuplets
Octuplets are the eight children born to one woman from a single pregnancy. They typically are conceived at the same time, are born on the same day, and share biological makeup dependent on their zygosity.

Increasing Numbers of Multiples

The population of multiples has increased steadily for almost thirty years. In the United States, the twin birthrate increased 70 percent from 1980 to 2004. This escalating trend may have halted, because the 2006 twin birthrate has remained essentially unchanged for two consecutive years (Martin et al. 2009).

By 2006 the twinning rate was slightly more than 32 twins born per 1,000 births. This compared with approximately 19 births per 1,000 in 1980 (Martin et al. 2009). Twins represent almost 3 percent of the total population. Triplets/+ (triplets, quadruplets, and quintuplets) represent about 0.1 percent to 0.15 percent of the total population. Twins account for 94 percent of all multiples born (Beachamp and Brooks 2003).

Twin Births in the United States			
Year	Twin Births (Individual Children)	Twin Birthrate	All Births
2006	137,085	32.1 per 1,000	4,265,555
1980	68,339	18.9 per 1,000	3,612,258
Statistics record live births and explain the uneven number recorded for twins (Martin et al. 2009, 7).			

The dramatic increase in the twin birthrate has been accompanied by a soaring birthrate of triplets. Since 1980 the number of triplet births in the United States has grown tenfold. Other countries, including Australia, England, France, Belgium, Holland, and Israel, have reported similar increasing rates of triplet births (Feldman and Eidelman 2005).

The triplet birth population has been the most rapidly growing segment of multiple births. In 2006, 143,625 multiples were born. This included 137,085 twins, 6,118 triplets, 355 quadruplets, and 67 quintuplets and other higher-multiple births, or supertwins. The triplet/+ births (triplets and other higher-order multiples), which had soared for years, peaked in 1999 and decreased 5 percent in 2006 (Feldman and Eidelman 2005; Mothers of Supertwins 2009). The decline has been attributed to the guidelines published by the American Society of Reproductive Medicine in the later 1990s, which recommended limiting the number of embryos transferred through assisted reproductive treatment (Martin et al. 2009).

Some Communities' High Triplet Birthrates

In 2005 the state of New Jersey reported a high number of triplet births, thought to be the result of more women in some New Jersey communities delaying parenthood and more couples successfully completing fertility treatment. Naperville, a community of 100,000 in Illinois, also boasts sets of triplets: twenty-one sets of triplets lived in the town in 1997, all but two of the sets younger than eight years (TWINS 1997). The states of Nebraska and New Jersey reported double the national levels of triplets/+ birthrates from 1995 through 1997 (Martin and Park 1999).

Delaying childbirth and using fertility treatment significantly increases the chances of becoming parents of triplets (Nussbaum 2009).

Supertwin Births in the United States			
Year	Triplet Births	Quadruplet Birthrate	Quintuplets Plus Births
2006	6,118	355	67
2003	7,110	468	85
1999	6,742	512	67
Statistics are recorded for live births and explain the uneven number recorded for twins (Martin et al. 2009, 7).			

Social Changes Increase Multiple Population

Social changes have effectively increased the population of twins and supertwins. Natural twinning results from many factors, including a woman's heredity, age, hormone levels, nutrition, emotional state, ethnicity, race, and environment (University of Viriginia Health System 2004). Another social change, healthier populations, contributes to the increase of multiple-birth children.

Today many women wait until an older age to have children and are more likely than younger mothers to give birth to twins. Twins born to older mothers are more likely to be dizygotic. When women choose to delay having children, they decrease their capacity to conceive. This trend has led more women to seek treatment after they find their reproductive ability has declined. Ironically, women's hormones also change with age in a way that can increase the number of ova released, making the rate of twinning higher for women in their mid to late thirties. This trend and the extraordinary use of fertility-enhancing treatments are two of the primary factors in the increasing number of multiples born over the previous thirty years (Guilherme et al. 2008). Adding to these two social changes, the survival rate of multiples and premature infants has increased because of improved medical care.

Statistical reports vary, and data for twinning and supertwinning fluctuate. The date of a report, the region or country reporting, and the purpose of the research influence the outcomes. Science quickly changes what was previously thought to be fact. Research findings are quickly changing what is known about multiples, especially supertwins and the statistics related to them. The concept of supertwins became more evident when the triplet/+ birthrate escalated by more than 400 percent between 1980 and 1990. (The birthrate refers to the number of triplets, quadruplets, and quintuplets and other HOM who were born per 100,000 live births.) In 1998 the supertwin birthrate topped out at 193.5 per 100,000 births (Martin et al. 2007). Seventy-five percent of supertwins are born to mothers using assisted reproductive technology (ART). Three-fourths of all triplets and almost all quadruplets and other higher-order multiples (Luke and Eberlein 2004) or supertwins are the products of ART. As the number in the set of multiples increases, the number of girls increases, because female embryos commonly survive stressful pregnancies more often than male embryos (Berger 2005; Noble 2003).

The infertility treatments numbered among the options of ART have expanded. The variety of techniques includes ovulation-stimulating drugs, IVF, and gamete or zygote transfer (Luke and Eberlein 2004; Pearlman and Ganon 2000). The multiples resulting from ART have been termed *iatrogenic multiples* (Sutcliffe and Derom 2006). Researchers advise that studies are needed to determine the outcome of multiples resulting from spontaneous conception and from ART (Sutcliffe and Derom 2006).

Twin birthrates have been highest for women between thirty-five and thirty-nine years of age. A woman's high parity, which means having given birth one or more previous times, increases her odds of giving birth to multiples. Besides age, education seems to affect the multiples birthrate. The triplet birthrate in 1989 was two-thirds more common among college-educated women than among women of similar age who had less than a high school education. Researchers attributed this prevalence to the increasing use of fertility-stimulating drugs among this population (Family Planning Perspectives 1995).

Statistics show differences in twinning by geographical region and ethnicity of the mothers. African American women are more likely to have naturally occurring twins than other ethnic groups. Native American and Asian American woman have twins the least often. Asians commonly give birth to twins the least often. Location and even state of residence seem to influence the incidence of supertwins. As discussed earlier, triplets were delivered in Illinois and New Jersey at about twice the national rate; quadruplets and other higher-order multiples were born there at almost double the national pace. There were 1,932 sets of triplets born from 1998 to 2002. New Jersey had the nation's highest number of fertility clinics during this period, with at least twenty of the four hundred facilities located throughout the U.S. The state claimed that its population had the necessary incomes to pay for such costly services as ART (Nussbaum 2009).

Projections show that the numbers of twins and supertwins will continue to expand, although not at the record rate experienced in the previous two decades. Technical advances influence social attitudes as well as individual decisions about family planning. Economic change is another social factor that may affect the use of ART.

Twinship and Supertwinship

Twins, triplets, quadruplets, quintuplets, and other higher-order multiples interact with their birth partners in complex relationships. Their relationships are unfamiliar to the majority of individuals. Given this, professionals should be cautious about making unexamined assumptions. The relationship begins prenatally for twins and supertwins, as researchers have documented with improved imaging techniques, which permit observation of the early interactions of twins even before birth.

Twinship is considered one of the closest human relationships possible. Twinship is both single and dual existence, simultaneously; it is intimate; it is viewed with fascination; and it stimulates curiosity from some and envy or excitement from others (Segal 2005b). Although reactions and descriptions vary, the words *special* and *unique* appear consistently. Twinship identifies the social relationship between two children who were born on the same day to the same parents. The relationship is one that is normal to the pair in a world in which singleborn children are the usual reference point.

Multiplehood is a term describing the relationship among siblings who are born as supertwins. *Multiplehood* offers an alternative to describing sets of multiples other than twins, and it highlights the differences between the most familiar relationship—that which exists between singleborn siblings—and that of multiple-born siblings. The word encompasses the scope of these unique relationships.

Multiples Are Noticed

Multiples are noticed, receive attention, and are singled out because of their special relationships with same-age siblings. Parents of twins and supertwins know the drill. When you go out in public, especially when the children are babies, you become the center of attention. Authors, psychologists, sociologists, and researchers document the uniqueness of twins. An increasing number of researchers are collecting similar data about supertwins. These data will provide insight about the special aspects of these relationships, including multiples' distinct experiences as a group and as individuals. For example, at the Osaka City University in Japan, Yoshie Yokoyama has been leading research about the growth and development of triplets and their motor development. Ruth Feldman of Bar Ilan University in Israel, and Arthur Eidelman, MD, of Hebrew University in Israel, research the risks of triplet births and the affect on cognitive development of triplets. Feldman and Eidelman also explored triplets' mother-infant interactions.

Twins and supertwins may be in a class of their own. They encounter both positive and negative reactions to their twinness and supertwinness. People also react to the uniqueness of their relationship. In her child development textbook, Louise Bates Ames notes that twins as a pair are unique (1970). Twins and supertwins raise questions about the formation of friendship. (The topics of friendship and peers will be discussed in chapter 4 and as a special issue in chapter 7.)

Parents Provide Insight

Preschool teachers trying to understand the behaviors of supertwins may need to rely on the insights of parents for more specific information about multiple children's unique needs. The Mothers of Supertwins (MOST) has established a Families of Supertwins Bill of Rights. The fifth tenet ensures that each person in the families of triplets, quadruplets, quintuplets, and sextuplets has the right to be appreciated, respected, and loved as an individual for his or her unique personality, special gifts, and important role in the family (Mothers of Supertwins 2009). The tenets are applicable to twins in the same way that much of the information specific to twins is applicable, with caution, to supertwins.

Parents of triplets/+ offer credible anecdotal information. In the collection of stories *Finding Our Way: Life with Triplets, Quadruplets and Quintuplets* (Lyons 2001), families provide accounts of the special needs of supertwins. One of the parents, Oonagh Hastie, notes that "when people see triplets or quadruplets or more, I think they are so shocked they don't realize they are asking prying questions. They are just interested in finding out about such a unique and special situation" (Lyons 2001, 364).

Another parent of triplets, Lucy Carley, writes, "Their camaraderie was entrenched by the time they were crawling and then hanging onto one another for support as they learned to walk" (Lyons 2001, 389).

During their professional preparation, teachers learn the value of encouraging young children to work together as a team. In keeping with this pattern, the teamwork occurring routinely among same-age siblings in a group of two, three, and more will offer you new knowledge.

Finding Our Way's stories highlight the challenges unique to supertwins and their families. Supertwin parents comment about the inaccessibility of community programs to them and their children. Library reading time and swimming lessons usually require the presence of one adult for each child. This requirement excludes many families with supertwins from benefiting from opportunities in their communities.

Ongoing guidance, possibly transformed into family education topics, is needed. Parents need help to guide their children in dealing with others who call them "quads" instead of by their names. Families with supertwins face challenges. The majority of them welcome help from family members and community volunteers to balance their own efforts to rear their multiple children. Parents of supertwins also find joy and excitement in the special moments (Lyons 2001). Bracha Mirsky tells of her three five-year-olds excitedly describing their new friend by saying, "He's a single" (Lyons 2001, 446). Words such as *unique, special, gifted, blessings,* and *different* are woven into the supertwin stories, establishing valuable insight about closeness, interaction, and relationship.

Perspectives about Twins and Supertwins

chapter two

Myth, Fiction, and Reality

Stories about twins appear throughout history in mythology, folklore, religion, art, and literature. Multiples have been welcomed by some cultures and feared by others. In legends, myths, and stories, their presence changes stories about sibling rivalry and competition, identity and individuality, bonding ties, and reverence and hostility. At the same time, descriptions of twins disclose a continuing fascination with them. This fascination remains today.

Researchers' observations add to our knowledge about multiples. While science produces knowledge about twins and supertwins today, former civilizations created stories to explain them. The arrival of more than one baby at a time violated social expectations. As a consequence, when the unexpected occurred, cultures developed fables, customs, and narratives to justify and possibly explain the arrival of multiples.

Dual Relationships

Themes embedded in cultural narratives consistently probe the dual relationship. The positive and negative themes compared twins to traditional expectations. Societies, in the past and today, maintain one individual as the standard point of reference—that is, one child born at one time in a family. The biblical story about Esau and Jacob is an example. The Old Testament story describes competition and rivalry between the twins for a firstborn position. Firstborn status is not as much of an issue when children arrive in a family one at a time. Greek mythology describes harmonious ties between twins Castor and Pollux, the two primary stars in the constellation Gemini, which can be viewed on a clear evening. The phenomenon of Saint Elmo's fire describes two flames named for Castor and Pollux that forecast fair weather after a storm (Abbe and Gill 1980).

Travelers to Rome and Sienna observe engravings and sculptures of the brothers Romulus and Remus, twin brothers who were found by a she-wolf and raised by a flock keeper and his wife, and who founded the ancient walled city of Rome.

Numerous examples of twins appear among the divinity themes of American indigenous people. Twins rose to become the Sun and the Moon in pre-Columbian Mayan culture. The Incan civilization honored mothers of twins. Navajo and Zuni people believe that twins are divine, having been fathered by the Sun. The Mohave state that human twins come from the sky. Both Huron and Iroquois tell stories about twins who they believe founded their tribes. In contrast, a few cultures, like the Apache, feared twinning because they believed it harmed the family (Abbe and Gill 1980; Colon and Colon 2001; Stewart 2003).

The legends and myths about twins and supertwins persist in folklore, literature, and religious stories. Too often, themes and images are stereotypical. Familiar stories, especially those about rivaling brothers Esau and Jacob and Romulus and Remus, trigger a common theme of intense sibling rivalry. In real life, all twins do not experience intense rivalry. Still, this and other famously visible misinterpretations persist.

Familiar Stories, Rhymes, and Images

Twins who appear in literature may be familiar to you. William Shakespeare was surely influenced by his own children, twins Judith and Hamnet. The bard included themes of mistaken identity in his plays *The Comedy of Errors* and *Twelfth Night. The Comedy of Errors,* written in 1592 or 1594, describes two sets of identical and identically named twins. Shakespeare's insight into twinship describes separate and individual personalities cloaked by physical resemblance (Segal 1999; Smilansky 1992).

The 1937 Broadway hit *The Band Wagon* featured triplets. One of its musical numbers expresses the multiples doing everything alike and hating each other enough to want to be only one (Scheinfeld 1967).

Tweedledee and Tweedledum appeared in an anonymous nursery rhyme before author Lewis Carroll used them in *Through the Looking-Glass and What Alice Found There.* In the rhyme, the twins agree to battle one another because Tweedledee says that Tweedledum has ruined his rattle. The rhyme implies that they change their minds because one brother will not contradict the other (Parisi 2004).

The fictional Bobbsey Twins (two sets in one family) appeared in seventy-two books published from 1904 to 1979. Reference to the Bobbsey Twins is used figuratively to define one person acting just like another person. Twins Bert and Nan and Freddie and Flossie embody an image of a childhood free of family-related problems and social pressures.

The "cutesy" image of twins persisted in television commercials of the Doublemint Twins, Joan and Jayne Boyd, until 1963. The Boyds reinforced an image of alikeness while trying to convince consumers that the gum product would "double your pleasure." Some other commercial advertisers also took advantage of look-alikes to establish the value of their products. Home hair permanents became popular when consumers were unable to recognize which twin paid for professional services and which "twin had the Toni" (Cassill 1982).

Separation, discovery, and identity switching were all part of the successful Disney film *The Parent Trap,* released in 1961. Twins Sharon and Susan switch identities to trick their parents so that the twins can get them together again. The remake of the film in 1998 updated the girls' names to Hallie and Annie, but the plot remains the same: twins switching roles.

Jessica and Elizabeth are monozygotic twins who became familiar characters to adolescents who read about their relationship and adventures in the Sweet Valley High series. The series, created in 1983 by Francine Pascal, included 152 books published over twenty-five years by many ghostwriters. Another popular series, *Beverly Hills 90210,* depicts the issues confronting a boy-and-girl twin pair (Stewart 2003).

Reality and Recognition

Stories about twins often attempt to explore the mysteries and realities of dual relationships. The popularity of famous twins can be traced to a sea captain who in 1829 convinced the mother of conjoined twins to allow her adolescent sons to travel with him to Boston for public exhibition. Eng and Chang of Siam, conjoined at the base of the chest, became farmers before they were thirty and married sisters Adelaide and Sallie. Each of the twins fathered children of his own (Jackson 2001).

Some of the stories about twins attempt to solve mysteries related to two individuals born on the same day. Often the information illuminates the novelty of circumstances and relationships. Some stories, like *The Silent Twins,* feature unusual attributes of human relationships (Stewart 2003). *The Silent Twins* documents the interaction of June and Jennifer Gibbons, twin sisters born in 1964. The girls gained public attention because they communicated only with each other. Author Marjorie Wallace wrote about their psychiatric treatment, describing them as geniuses and as mentally subnormal. They were diagnosed as schizophrenic and hospitalized for eleven years. Jennifer died at age twenty-nine years. Their lives were not typical of twins, and their story projects an image of twins having antisocial behaviors and unhealthy relationships. A French opera, *Jumelles (Twins),* was based on the book about them.

Researching multiples or writing books about them can be influenced by a personal link to them. Researcher Helen L. Koch published *Twins and Twin Relations* in 1966, providing what may be the earliest study focused on twins. She dedicated the book to her mother, who was a twin.

INSTANT CELEBRITIES

The Dionne quintuplets, born in rural Canada in 1934, became international celebrities. Weighing less than two pounds each, they were considered miraculous for surviving at that time. As wards of the provincial government, the children were observed by thousands of tourists while they played until they were returned to their parents when they were nine years old. Their images and likenesses were used to endorse many commercial products. Although they performed at functions and starred in films, the sisters' commercial success was overshadowed by the release in 1995 of *Family Secrets.* The book revealed physical abuse and exploitation (Soucy 1995).

The public's access to the lives of multiple-birth children shifted in 1970, when the Kienast quintuplets were born. *Good Housekeeping* magazine awarded photography privileges exclusively to photographers who were twins, Kathryn McLaughlin Abbe and Frances McLaughlin Gill. The photographers maintained close relationships with the children and their family and were inspired to write a book about multiples. *Twins on Twins* (Abbe and Gill) was published in 1980 with photographs by the authors.

In 1977 newspapers and magazines extensively covered the story of Virginia and Grace Kennedy, seven-year-old twins celebrated for developing their own language. Their conversations were unintelligible to others when the twins were brought to the Children's Hospital and Health Center in San Diego. Their parents, who had turned their care over to their grandmother, thought they were retarded. As a consequence, the parents, along with the grandmother and others outside the family, seldom communicated with the girls. The private language was not a result of their twin status but rather of neglect by their caregivers.

The fascination with twins and supertwins escalates enormously with the birth of multiples numbering up to six and seven infants, and now eight. The McCaughey family, having produced the first set of surviving septuplets in 1997, faced both encouraging attention and negative feedback about their use of fertility treatment. By the time the children turned ten years old, the family granted only yearly stories to NBC *Dateline* and *Ladies Home Journal*. At the time the McCaughey babies were born, three of the sixty-three-year-old surviving Dionne sisters offered advice to the McCaugheys. At the sisters' request, *Time* ran the open letter. The Dionne sisters warned Bobbi and Kenny McCaughey, the parents of the septuplets, not to confuse multiple births with entertainment (Dionne, Dionne, and Dionne 1997). The television show *Jon and Kate Plus Eight* became immensely popular after Kate and Jon Gosselin allowed the media to film their daily life with their twins and sextuplets in 2007.

The degree of exposure and celebrity status of families with higher-order multiples varies for each family. Many welcome their babies with minimal national news coverage, even though the events are significant for the families and their local communities. Most of the families with higher-order multiples choose to rear their children outside of the media spotlight, desiring normal childhoods for their multiples. For example, the Fisher babies, born in 1963, were the first quintuplets to survive in the United States. Three of the Fisher quintuplets are monozygotic. The Guttensohns from Montgomery, Alabama, welcomed five boys in 1996. Since the birth of the Guttensohn boys, six other sets of all-male quintuplets have been born (Fierro 2009; Jackson 2001).

In 1993 Keith and Becki Dilley became parents of six babies born on the same day—the first surviving sextuplets in the United States (Goldblatt 2004). Three New York families became parents to sextuplets in the 1990s: the Haners in 1996, the Boniellos in 1997, and the Carpios in 2008. Four-year-old Aubrianna Headrick of Kansas became an older sibling to three brothers and three sisters in 2002 (*New York Times* 2002). A couple in Texas, Nkem Chukwu and Lyke Odobi, became the first parents of octuplets in 1998, the first group of eight babies to be born alive. Their weight ranged from eleven ounces to one pound and eleven ounces (Jackson 2001). The media amplified coverage of multiple births when a single, unemployed mother of six gave birth to octuplets in January 2009. The Southern California mother of the longest surviving set of eight negotiated business deals through several publicists. She has faced charges of child neglect (Celizic 2009).

ASSOCIATIONS, CELEBRATIONS, AND SERVICES

Organizations, institutions, and clubs promote information about multiples to multiples and others. (You'll find some of these resources in appendix D).

Edward Clink and his twin sister, Elsie, of Indiana founded the International Twins Association (ITA) in 1934. The nonprofit organization for twins and managed by twins promotes the spiritual and intellectual welfare of twins and multiples. Conventions are staged in different locations throughout the U.S. every year during the Labor Day weekend.

The annual Twins Days Festival is celebrated in Twinsburg, Ohio, a town named in honor of monozygotic (MZ) twins Moses and Aaron Wilcox. The lives of the Wilcox twins were intertwined: they worked as business partners to develop what became known as Twinsburg, married sisters, and died on the same day.

The National Organization of Mothers of Twins Clubs (NOMOTC) was founded in the United States in 1960 and is now a network that includes more than 450 clubs supporting parents of multiples with resources and conferences.

Interest in multiples is expanding in a number of countries. The International Society for Twins Studies (ISTS), founded in Rome in 1974, is a nonprofit, multidisciplinary scientific group organized to further research and education. Numerous research articles cited in this book were published in ISTS's journal, *Twin Research and Human Genetics.*

The Center for the Study of Multiple Birth was founded in 1977 by Louis and Donald Keith, MZ twins. The center leads research on multiple pregnancies and, in affiliation with Northwestern University, conducts research and archives and disseminates valuable information about multiples. The center facilitates research, education, and public service.

The twinship link is apparent in researchers' and authors' contributions. Patricia Malmstrom, mother of twins, founded Twin Services in 1978 in Berkeley, California, offering resources for families with financial support from the California and the U.S. Departments of Health, foundations, and individuals. Twinline became a national lifeline of information and services for parents. At California State University, Fullerton, Professor Nancy Segal, a twin, researches and writes extensively about multiples while directing the Twin Studies Center she established at the university.

Following the example established in Canada and Australia, the NOMOTC, the Fetal Foundation, and TWINS established Multiple Birth Awareness Month in April 2009. The Multiples Family Festival was staged in Denver, Colorado, to kick off the first awareness month about multiples in the United States. Multiples Births Canada/Naissances multiples Canada held its first National Multiple Births Awareness Day in May 2005 at the Dionne Quintuplets Museum. In Australia the celebration marked the fortieth anniversary of its first multiple-birth local clubs (Multiple Births Canada/Naissances multiples Canada 2008) with a Twins Plus Festival in 2009.

Relevant Research

Researchers have used twins extensively in studies to explore questions about development of children, but little of this research has been dedicated to understanding the growth and behavioral changes of twins and supertwins themselves. More recently, academic contributors have begun building a knowledge base that can directly enhance your recognition of multiple-birth children's basic needs and patterns of development.

Most-Studied Individuals

Attention to multiples and inquiry about them are not new. Their unique and similar makeup places them among the most-studied individuals (MacDonald 2002). Although considerable research involving twins exists, most of it has concentrated on the influences of hereditary factors and environment. Twins have been used in this research to study the contribution of nature and nurture to development. Many consider twins, both MZ and DZ, as subjects for researchers to observe, test, and document in determining the roles of genes and the impact of the environment on behavior.

Research about twins and supertwins is evolving. In recent years, improved genetic analysis, ultrasounds, and a growing interest in the development of twins and supertwins have changed the focus of research. Nonetheless, questions about the influence of nature and nurture on development continue. Because science still wants answers, the inclusion of twins provides unique opportunities for study.

In twin studies, the characteristics of MZ twins are compared with those of DZ twins. Behavioral geneticists use the twin study method primarily because MZ twins are more similar genetically than DZ twins and singleborn children. Their identified similarities can be attributed to their inherited makeup, a constant component that can be analyzed.

USING THE TWIN METHOD TO STUDY NATURE AND NURTURE

Sir Francis Galton first studied the nature and nurture question in 1876. To investigate individual differences in mental abilities, he formed what is now recognized as the classical twin method of research. Galton collected anecdotal evidence about twins and identified the two types of twins as identical and fraternal. His 1876 paper proposed that twins were perfect for examining the influence of nature and nurture on behavior, introducing the systematic use of multiples in research (Jensen 2000). The frameworks for research about twins compare either twin types MZ or DZ pairs, giving us an understanding of heredity and environment, or twins and non-twins, giving us a look at the impact of twinship on twins' development.

Fewer than thirty years later, psychologist Edward Thorndike reported that cognitive tests demonstrated twin resemblances (Parisi 2004). Twins have contributed to knowledge about cognition by providing educators and researchers with insight into human development (Segal 1999).

Numerous countries today maintain national twin registries precisely because the classical twin method provides essential information for genetic study of development (Jensen 2000). In the December 2006 issue of *Twin Research and Human Genetics,* fifty-two twin registries in twenty-three countries were reported.

REARED APART

Twins who were separated early in their lives and reared apart help researchers explore the heredity-environment question, establishing the ultimate test for answering big questions about development. Twins reared apart are nature's unique control group (Farber 1981). Monozygotic twins reared apart are rare, but they have been thought to provide perfect raw material. The first research study to also include dizygotic pairs of reunited twins is the Minnesota Study of Twins Reared Apart (MISTRA) (Segal 2003).

Careful to note the bias of a limited sample, Susan Farber conducted another study of separated twins in 1981. She analyzed the 121 reared-apart twins reported in the literature at that time and provided a glimpse of the remarkable similarities between the twins. They laughed and gestured alike, described the same symptoms, and reported similar onsets of developmental milestones.

The twin study method is not without criticism. One evaluation has questioned whether adults, especially parents, might be reinforcing the similarities among MZ twins. Could their similar behaviors and likeness therefore be environmentally influenced rather than attributed only to their genetics (Santrock 1993)? Parents and others may be emphasizing the similarities of MZ twins more than DZ twins. Automatic inclusion of MZ twins separated in infancy has been questioned, because the authenticity of their twin-type or zygosity identification may not have been scientifically determined (Jensen 2000). Determination of zygosity has often relied on parental responses to questionnaires and the placental method. The latter yields imprecise results because its accuracy depends on the medical doctor's expertise (Moskwinski 2002).

TWINS ACCESSIBLE FOR RESEARCH

Apparently twins and supertwins are accessible for research because multiple-birth families more commonly respond to invitations to participate in studies than other families (Hay and O'Brien 1983). From a practical standpoint, longitudinal studies on twins are useful to developmental psychologists as well as geneticists. Longitudinal studies follow the participants in the research over a period of time. Earlier studies established a foundation on which subsequent studies have been based, and the findings have persisted in the research literature. Many of these early findings rationalize common views about twins even though subsequent research has produced opposing findings. In one such study reported in 1932, "The Development of Language in Twins," Ella J. Day compares twins and singleborn children, reporting that the language development of twins is retarded and that the progress of twins during the preschool years is slow.

Not all early studies report negative descriptions about twins. A researcher at Northwestern University, Ernest R. Mowrer, investigated affectional adjustment and family roles by studying the interaction of twins with one another and with their family members. He suggests in the *American Sociological Review* (1954) that the study of twins provides a method to differentiate the treatment of children in a family. This particular study notes that the way a culture defines sex roles determines the relationship between the twins, the twin and parents, and the twin and the non-twin siblings.

Helen L. Koch's 1966 *Twins and Twin Relations* is often cited in journal articles and books about twins. It documents extensive findings about ninety pairs of five- and six-year-old twins. Even though Dr. Koch's investigation was a milestone in looking precisely at twins themselves, it was negatively received in a review in the *Journal of Sociology*. The reviewer criticizes Koch's selective sampling of the twins for her research and disqualifies it as a study because it lacks depth (Parker 1968). Nonetheless, Koch's findings have significant relevance for early childhood professionals, and you'll find them referenced throughout this book.

Hugh Lytton, Dorice Conway, and Reginald Sauvé from the University of Calgary wrote "The Impact of Twinship on Parent-Child Interaction" in 1977, which has profound significance for teachers of young children. Essentially, their research proposes that the language of twins is crucially influenced by the amount of speech they hear from their parents. The work of Lytton and his colleagues is covered in chapter 5 in the discussion of language development.

The Louisville Twin Study in the United States is a longitudinal study that began in 1951. The comprehensive research project enlisted twins as participants to investigate the contributions of genes and environment on development. The studies have examined many behavioral patterns, including intelligence, temperament, personality, physical growth, and individual differences. Efforts were initiated in 2008 to archive the research data and locate the twins and their families who participated in the research. Located twins will be recruited to participate in new studies about adult health.

The Twins' Early Development Study has assessed more than twelve thousand twins from early childhood through adolescence. This longitudinal study collected data at ages two, three, four, seven, nine, ten, and twelve from the participating twins in England and Wales. Significant findings about language and cognitive development have resulted in thousands of articles. The research has been funded by the Medical Council in the United Kingdom for the investigators to examine childhood behaviors (Oliver and Plomin 2007).

David Hay should be celebrated by early childhood educators for initiating studies about twins that inform educators. The La Trobe Twin Study of Behavioral and Biological Development began in the late 1970s in Melbourne, Australia. It is considered to be the longest ongoing twin research project, and important for teachers, many of the studies focus on twin development during early childhood. The study intentionally set out to learn more about twins themselves (Twin Services Reporter 1989), and the research from the longitudinal studies has contributed information about development, language, reading, and identity of twins with particular attention to the way twins differ from singleborn children. One example, *Twins in School* (La Trobe Twin Study 1991), was published by the Australian Multiple Birth Association. Hay's focus on twins now includes attention deficit hyperactivity, with particular follow-up of multiples.

The field of early childhood education boasts one honored educator who is also a twin. Lilian Katz was the director of the Education Resources Information Center (ERIC) Clearinghouse on Elementary and Early Childhood Education and is a professor emerita of Early Childhood Education at the University of Illinois. Her "Twins in School: What Teachers Should Know" (1998), notes that the research about twins and their education is limited. She summarizes a few pointers about school placement for teachers to consider until their questions can be answered by relevant research findings.

Thomas Bouchard Jr. of the University of Minnesota's Department of Psychology is renowned for spearheading MISTRA. Under the auspices of the Center for Twin and Adoption Research at the university, Bouchard completed thorough assessments of MZ and DZ twins who were reared apart because they were separated early in life (Bouchard 2009). The studies made considerable contributions to science and education about the impact of genes on personality. Photographs of two study participants, twins Jim Springer and Jim Lewis, appear in numerous human development textbooks accompanying explanations of the similarities in behaviors and traits between MZ twins—even those, like the Jim brothers, who were reared apart. The Jims were unaware of each other until they were asked to participate in the MISTRA study. Their participation in the initial study in 1979 provided the researchers with many surprising details about the twins' preferences and experiences, such as marrying women with the same names, twice, and giving their firstborn sons the same first and middle names.

Other researchers, such as French psychologist René Zazzo, became interested in twins during his studies. Zazzo was a psychology student at the Gesell Institute at Yale University. When he returned to France, he continued to work in child psychology, contributing the term *couple effect* to describe the interdependent twin relationship. The shared circumstances of the couple effect create complementary roles and functions (Smilansky 1992).

Destructive Experiments

The inclusion of twins in research has not always been productive. In contrast to research that has contributed to science, medicine, and the understanding of multiples, other research has recorded the removal of multiples from their homes and the abuse of multiples. In 1942 horrifically destructive experiments gathered twins in the sweeping *Kinderaktion* raids in Germany. The twins ended up in the death camps, where an estimated 1.2 million Jewish children, including approximately 3,000 sets of twins, were used experimentally as laboratory subjects by Josef Mengele at Auschwitz (Colon and Colon 2001).

As recent as the 1960s, researchers and social workers recommended as a matter of policy the separation of multiples who were to be placed for adoption. Professionals at some agencies assumed that inevitable rivalries would be more intense if the infants remained together, and they couldn't resist studying three identical children placed in three different homes and socioeconomic settings (Wright 1997). Robert, Eddie, and David were each placed in a different family after their birth. Although the adopting parents agreed to participate in the study, they were unaware that their sons were triplets. In 1980, a newspaper headline announced that Eddie and Robert had been reunited after nineteen years. David was given the newspaper with the headline and a photograph of two young men who looked just like him, and the three brothers subsequently met. Their childhoods had unfolded separately because an agency made a decision based on conception rather than analysis of research (Wright 1997).

Studies to Understand Multiples

Early childhood educators want to know about relationships among twins and supertwins reared together or reunited as young adults. Teachers especially welcome this information because their knowledge about child development has come from studies of singleborn children. The work conducted by David Hay establishes a credible starting point to answer teachers' questions about twins and supertwins, and the La Trobe Twin Study provides seminal information with a focus on the uniqueness of twins and the implications of twins in school. The longitudinal study involved siblings and cousins of the twins and employed detailed questionnaires with reference to biological and social problems (Hay and O'Brien 1983). Hay's findings expanded the understanding of twins' cognition. The studies also explored the stresses on families of multiple-born children and documented information about school attendance. Hay recommended in the 1983 La Trobe Twin Study that schools adopt a flexible approach toward multiples (Hay and O'Brien 1983; Hay and Preedy 2006).

Teachers may gather some answers from parents of multiples, who may be the best resource for information, according to John Mascazine. Mascazine, author of *Understanding Multiple-Birth Children and How They Learn* (2004), believes misunderstandings occur because information is poorly publicized, limiting the access of teachers and principals to timely research. Mascazine continues to study learning styles of school-age twins.

The majority of research about triplets/+ examines the risks associated with multiple prenatal experience. One study by Ruth Feldman and Arthur Eidelman determined that a triplet birth affects cognitive development. This study also looked at the mother-infant relationship. The findings emphasized the importance of postpartum parental care and management to support mothering three infants at a time (2005).

International research about twins has direct relevance for early childhood educators in the United States. One example, a study by the Support of Parents of Multiple Births, reports the speech of preschool twins near Paris and observes that no linguistic delays were seen in the twins assessed. This was the case regardless of the twin type or zygosity assessed. For language development, it appears that advantages exist for boys who are part of a boy-and-girl twin pair (Garitte et al. 2002).

But the volumes of research have not built resources and references directly about the development of multiples. It focuses instead on medical issues, pregnancy, prenatal care, and predispositions to certain diseases and conditions. In this way, twin research has contributed to many scientific disciplines, such as obstetrics, pediatrics, psychology, and genetics. Little has been documented about the unique developmental patterns of twins and their care. Even less has been established about supertwins.

Projects such as the university twin studies at Minnesota, Louisville, La Trobe, and King's College London create a foundational base of information for scientific understanding of multiples, and the findings offer sound reference material for early childhood professionals. Research specializing in gathering information about multiples is increasing. Notwithstanding this new focus, most studies are likely to continue using twins as key participants in research, and multiples will benefit from the findings as these apply to basic growth and development.

One example, the Longitudinal Twin Study of Early Literacy Development: Preschool and Kindergarten Phases, analyzes kindergarten levels of literacy and related language variables (Byrne et al. 2005). One hundred seventy-two pairs of MZ twins and 153 pairs of same-sex DZ twins who were kindergartners from the United States and Australia were studied. Their participation in this research contributed knowledge about literacy development, particularly the genetic factor in phonological awareness in preschool and kindergarten. The study included twins but was not intended to determine the impact of literacy development on twins. Nonetheless, because twins attend preschool, the study contributed information about literacy development that would benefit them as it would other children who are transitioning from preschool.

Another example of twins as research participants is Nonshared Environmental Influences on Individual Differences in Early Behavioral Development: A Monozygotic Twin Differences Study (Asbury et al. 2003). This twin differences study uses twins to establish a research population and take advantage of their similarities and differences. This particular investigation included 2,353 same-sex pairs of MZ twins about the time of their fourth birthdays. The researchers investigated the effect the environment and parenting had on children, using twin pairs to identify distinctive behaviors. The researchers found that negative disciplinary expressions delivered by the parents compromised the siblings' relationships. The affect was stronger in families of lower socioeconomic status, families that were chaotic, and ones in which mothers were depressed.

The Twins' Early Development Study at King's College London has followed twins born in England and Wales in a longitudinal study examining parenting behaviors and environmental influences. The findings have contributed globally to the field of child development rather than specifically informing preschool teachers about multiples.

Fulfilling the need for focused information about multiples, researchers in the study Perinatal and Early Childhood Outcomes of Twins versus Triplets investigated the growth and development of twins and triplets. The study looked at developmental outcomes from in utero through eighteen months of age in a population that included 141 twin and eight triplet pregnancies. The findings confirmed the higher risks to triplets during pregnancies, perinatal period, and early childhood. When triplets are compared with twins, they are found to be more vulnerable to neonatal morbidity and have lower mental and motor scores through eighteen months of age. The postnatal growth of the triplets in the study also lagged behind the growth of twins (Luke et al. 2006).

In another study of multiples, researchers at Queensland University in Australia inquired into the social development of twin children, particularly the gender effect in opposite-sex pairs. Being Opposite: Is There Advantage for Social Competence and Friendships in Being an Opposite-Sex Twin? (Laffey-Ardley and Thorpe 2006) included three- to six-year-olds. This research did not substantiate any advantages for opposite-sex twins during early childhood years, but it did identify a slight social advantage for singleborn children in social independence over twins during early childhood. The researchers' findings were based on observations provided by the parents and teachers. The sample size— thirty-six DZ opposite-sex twins, twenty-five DZ same-sex pairs, and eighty-five singleborn children of the same age and sex as the twins who had at least one sibling—may not have been large enough to detect differences. Certain distinguishing behaviors may have occurred in later childhood and so were not detectable.

Challenging Familiarity and Expectation of One Child

Multiples capture the attention of researchers and challenge the expected norm of one child in a world in which families, community members, and teachers are most familiar with the singleborn child.

Media Reports the Unusual

The media continues to deliver information about twins and super-twins. It rushes to hospitals when it learns of the births of triplets, quadruplets, quintuplets, sextuplets, septuplets, and octuplets. In *Finding Our Way: Life with Triplets, Quadruplets, and Quintuplets*, a Canadian mother of quintuplets reports that the hospital immediately scheduled and held a news conference when her babies were born (Lyons 2001). Stories in the media tend to focus on multiples' unusual characteristics and behaviors, but when focus remains on an unusual attribute such as twins communicating exclusively with one another, the public is led to believe that all twins have exclusive languages. And while a few such cases have been reported, the vast majority of twins and supertwins learn language in the same way singleborn children do: by communicating with their parents, non-twin siblings, and teachers, as well as the co-multiple. (Unique aspects of their language development are discussed in chapter 5.)

Because the public receives reports about only the unusual and uncommon behaviors of twins and supertwins, it forms opinions based on that information. Those prevailing opinions become misconceptions and overgeneralizations and begin to structure the way people think about and react to multiples. Media reports tend to stereotype; their erroneous descriptions create misinformed expectations that multiples compete for position and fight about their identity, individuality, and independence. Such distortions are detrimental to the well-being of twins and supertwins.

Clarifying Popular Myths and Stories

Accurate and carefully edited information clarifies popular legends, myths, and stories. Not all twins are close. Not all twins feud. Not all triplets exclude one from their group. The behavior of multiples is not polarized. Their personalities do not divide into good-bad, superior-inferior, and least-most. Twin children may be cooperative, or not. Or one of the twins may be cooperative while the other may need definite guidance. Supertwins may act similarly and maintain a close relationship, or they may behave differently and not interact closely. Supertwins may each exhibit a different temperament, one not divided into good or bad patterns. Multiples do not function in prescribed qualities defined by individuals unfamiliar with their growth, development, and needs.

Assumptions about multiples have been influenced by the lack of accurate information as much as by misunderstanding and stereotyping. I have heard teachers insist that there is always a dominant twin. When I ask where they acquired the information, most teachers do not say they heard about it in a college classroom or read it in a textbook or a research study. No research emphatically proclaims that multiples belong in a single category with specific personalities. As you may expect, judgmental edicts undercut accurate understanding of multiples.

Unsolicited Comments

> It's amazing to me that people always stop and say, "Wow, you must be so busy with toddler twin boys." Their tone is usually a little negative, as if somehow I drew an unlucky card with identical twin boys! I usually just chuckle and say, "Yep, it's crazy." But what I am really thinking is that I am the luckiest mom in the entire world. I have the privilege to spend every day with these amazing little people who laugh, smile, play together, and learn from each other. I stop to catch my breath sometimes. . . . I get to see the world through their four curious eyes, every single day. —Cecily, April 2009

Twins and supertwins challenge familiar paradigms of oneness, one child, and one person. Parents of multiples become accustomed to unsolicited advice from strangers, friends, and family members. Questions and comments tend to be invasive and to expose attitudes and countless assumptions about birthing issues and identity development. Parents are often barraged with questions from strangers who are so curious about multiples that they forget social mores and ask very specific and personal questions. Their questions and unsolicited advice can be judgmental.

Questions Revealing Myths about Conception and Birth
"Twins must run in your family. Right—don't they skip a generation?"
"Oh, a boy and a girl! Are they identical?"
"They can't be twins; they don't even look alike; or can they?"

Questions Revealing Myths about Identity and Behavior

"Double trouble, right?"

"Do they get along?"

"Which one is bossier?"

"Do they always know what the other one is doing, like ESP?"

"How did you bond with two babies at one time?"

Questions Revealing Negative Assumptions and Misconceptions

"Don't they have their own language?"

"They're probably rivals, aren't they?"

"Why didn't you give them rhyming names?"

"Which one's behavior is best?"

"If they are not identical, what are they?"

"How many eggs did you have implanted to have the triplets?"

Positive Change

Social changes, including medical advances and swift distribution of news events, may change attitudes about twins and supertwins. The distribution of reliable sources of information may dispel the superstitious folklore that generates and fosters uninformed attitudes and perceptions. Old language about twins and supertwins that projects erroneous assumptions and descriptions, such as *challenge, battle, stress,* and *struggle,* may be replaced by positive terms, such as *valued team, paired partners,* and *parallel interest.*

When telecommunications deliver information quickly to the public, the response is immediate. In 2009 the public reacted negatively to the detailed coverage of the birth of octuplets in Southern California. Reactions focused on the moral issues of implanting so many embryos, the economic obligations of multiple children, the health risks of multiples, and the motivation of a single, unemployed mother who already had six children under ten years of age to seek out further fertility treatment. Intensive news updates about the medically assisted conception of multiple births informs the public and may alter public views. Issues like children's right to privacy, advanced medical procedures, and the responsibility of parents generate new questions and reveal lingering assumptions and the latest misconceptions.

In response to the increase in multiples and the need for information, journal articles describing studies specifically about twins and supertwins have increased. Research is gradually establishing positive images of twins and supertwins with studies focusing on the advantages of being multiples and the specific educational needs of multiples, which differ from those of singleborn children. (You will find a discussion of the specific needs of multiples during the early childhood years in chapter 6. Chapter 7 presents program practices that best meet their unique needs.)

Sometimes educational and care decisions are made for multiples without appropriate consideration of the existing research, of the twins themselves, and of their families. Legislative campaigns working toward authorizing rights for multiples and their parents began in the United States in 2005. Since then, several state legislatures have enacted twins laws and proposed resolutions to empower parents of twins, triplets, and other higher-order multiples as the primary voices in classroom placement of their multiple-birth children (Dolan 2006).

Parents of twins and supertwins may arrive at preschools ready to inform teachers about their children's special circumstances and needs. They offer insight into their multiples' special needs. Their experiences have been influenced by the prenatal and perinatal care they received for their infants. The knowledge that parents have about their multiples may also be influenced by their participation in parents-of-multiples support groups. Some parents have read parenting books about twins and supertwins. Even so, expect families to rely on your sensitive and informed suggestions. You are their children's teacher and their source of support and guidance. You should maximize the evidence-based information about the development of twins and supertwins as more of them arrive in your programs.

Twins may be the most studied group of multiples. The majority of the studies utilize twins as research subjects. Most do not directly investigate their development. Nonetheless, the studies that include multiples contribute to scientific understanding of human development. The next three chapters include research that has investigated topics related directly to multiples and their development.

PART TWO

Development

Physical Development

When you study the development of twins and supertwins, you learn how a twin or supertwin changes as a child and as a multiple. The physical development of children follows a sequence of change in which they interact with people in their environment. For multiples, this means they sit with, crawl over, and toddle behind and ahead of others while achieving skills with at least one other same-age sibling. The physical actions displayed by twins and supertwins reveal the same physical development characteristics as those of other children. As infants, they respond to people who meet their needs. As toddlers, they express delight in achieving new goals; as preschoolers, they become unrelenting explorers.

Milestones

Milestones are the developmental levels that children are expected to achieve during a particular stage of growth. Children's heredity influences their maturation and the predictable unfolding of development and behavior. Their environment also determines the type and scope of their learning opportunities. Because the environment for twins and supertwins provides at least one same-age sibling, they acquire skills together. Together they play. Together they learn. They reinforce one another's skills and actions. As they watch each other and model actions and behaviors for one another, they reinforce the skills they have achieved and the ideas they have learned.

Twins' and supertwins' bodies grow and change as they move through the stages of physical development. These changes are quite visible. They are the visual clues that people comment on as signs of growth. Physiological changes, such as height, weight, and motor abilities, can be observed, measured, and charted. You no doubt have smiled at the eighteen-month-old toddler who runs over to you, pauses, and points while saying, "That." You enjoy engaging comments, such as a three-year-old saying, "Teacher, look at my new shoes. I'm bigger now." When you teach multiples, you are likely to hear and acknowledge similar comments from them with possible modifications, such as "Teacher, look at our new shoes. We're bigger now."

Patterns of Growth and Development

During their early years, children exhibit great variations in physical development. This principle applies to twins and supertwins as well as to singleborn children. Multiples follow the same predictable schedule of development as singleborn children. Each child within a twin pair and supertwin group has his or her own developmental map. The child's special map is one of changing patterns and variations. Each map is unique to each twin and to each supertwin individually; being born on the same day and even having the same genetic makeup does not ensure that multiples have the same appearance and developmental timetable.

On average, twins at birth weigh five pounds, four ounces. Ten percent of them weigh more than seven pounds (Noble 2003). On average, triplets weigh three pounds, eleven ounces, and quadruplets weigh two pounds, thirteen ounces. Prenatal growth of multiples differs from that of singleborn children in a few ways. First, twins and supertwins develop slightly faster and therefore are more mature at thirty weeks of gestation than a typical singleborn. The growth rate for multiples slows at about thirty-four weeks for twins, thirty weeks for triplets, and twenty-six to twenty-seven weeks for quadruplets. The forty-week gestation for a single pregnancy is uncommon among multiples. The average gestation for twins is thirty-five to thirty-six weeks, about thirty-two weeks for triplets, and about thirty weeks for quadruplets (Luke and Eberlein 2004).

Reports indicate that 7 percent of triplets weigh less than three pounds, five ounces (Noble 2003). Those birth weights contrast to the average weight of a singleborn child, who is expected to weigh slightly more than seven pounds. The conditions of prematurity and low birth weight in multiples cause measurable differences between twins and supertwins and singleborn infants. The higher incidence of low birth weight recorded for twins and more so for supertwins sets them on a developmental growth path that is theirs alone. Each developmental growth path is a bit different, including the patterns of each monozygotic (MZ) twin in a pair.

EARLY ARRIVAL AND CATCH-UP

Multiples experience what is considered to be a remarkable catch-up in their physical growth. They grow more during the neonatal period and gain weight faster in the first three months after birth than singleborn children. This rapid growth in most cases compensates for their lower average weight at birth. Their catch-up is greater than that of singleborn infants who are born full term but lighter in weight.

Twins and supertwins are smaller at birth because they are born prematurely more often than singleborn children and because their growth slows during the last weeks of their prenatal development. Some researchers suggest that when twins are compared with singleborn children, they remain slightly underweight. When their length at birth is compared with that of singleborn children, the differences are not as great as the weight deficits. The length deficits are almost totally erased by the time twins and supertwins reach eight years old (Buckler 1999). Reports indicate that male newborns weigh more and are longer than females in multiple groups, and that male neonates tend to be larger and heavier than females, regardless of the numbers of multiples in the group (Yokoyama, Sugimoto, and Ooki 2005).

Infant twin boys grow more rapidly during the first six months. By toddlerhood (eighteen months), boys are generally heavier and taller than girls (Buckler 1999). Toward the end of middle-school age, the multiples' rapid growth patterns eliminate any previously observed differences between their height and that of singleborn children (Buckler 1999). The prospect that twins and supertwins who are born early may outgrow their initial deficits is a welcome message.

Because twins as a pair are born sooner than singleborn children, they have what is called a *lower gestational age*. Gestational age identifies the length of gestation. Appropriate gestational age is the length of time expected for a full-term gestation. The expected gestational age for singleborn children is forty completed weeks of prenatal development. Researchers adjust some of the data related to gestational age of twins. The adjustment takes into consideration the gestational age of multiples who are typically born earlier than singleborn infants. In this way the researchers can attempt to determine whether differences in the milestones achieved between multiple and singleborn children actually occur. For example, one study showed that after adjusting for gestational age, the researchers found that certain, but not all, gross-motor milestones during infancy were the same for multiples and singleborn children (Yokoyama et al. 2007). This adjustment is also referred to as the *corrected age*. Corrected age is the age that the babies who are born early would have been if they had been born after a full forty-week gestation. So for twins who were born six weeks early, gestational age would be thirty-four weeks. Two months past their date of birth, their corrected age would be two weeks, while their chronological age, identified from their actual date of birth, would be two months (Agnew, Klein, and Ganon 2005; Luke and Eberlein 2004). Researchers recommend individualized growth charts rather than population-based growth charts, particularly for managing risk situations and intrauterine growth of individual twins.

Fifty-seven percent of twins and 93 percent of triplets are born preterm. Low birth weight (LBW) causes measured differences between multiples and singleborn children. Low-birth-weight babies are those who have not gained enough weight for that point of development. Forty-nine percent of twins are LBW compared with 8 percent of singleborn newborns. Twenty-three percent of all multiples are LBW; 17 percent are twins (Noble 2003). Babies who are born early and who are heavier in weight have a better developmental prognosis. By age two, their movement abilities are comparable to those of singleborn children. This is especially true when the corrected age, rather than the chronological age, is taken into consideration.

DEVELOPMENTAL VULNERABILITY

Premature infants remain more vulnerable than singleborn children to developmental problems, including disabilities. Because the majority of multiples are born early, they are more likely to have disabilities. These can include physical defects, such as cerebral palsy and other neurological defects. After genetic considerations have been ruled out, no definitive explanations exist for the incidences of higher anomalies other than prematurity and the prenatal environment experienced by multiples. Today, with improved medical care, even infants who are born less than three pounds, five ounces (considered a very low birth weight), develop without major difficulties. The pediatric specialty of neonatology provides skilled medical teams in hospitals with neonatal intensive care units and has improved the survival rate and health of multiples. Still, twins and supertwins face potential difficulties. Some of these, such as learning delays, may not become apparent until the twins or supertwins begin attending primary elementary school.

Prematurity is a condition that places triplets at risk for development during infancy and later development (Feldman and Eidelman 2005). Babies born before twenty-four weeks have a 50 percent chance of reduced abilities. It is not uncommon for one in a set of twins or triplets to be impaired. Physical growth charts have been designed to analyze the development of triplets more specifically after their birth (Yokoyama, Sugimoto, and Ooki 2005).

Research suggests that extremely low birth weight and extremely early gestational age affect growth and development after birth in triplets (Yokoyama et al. 2008).

The majority of research on triplets/+ examines the risk associated with multiples. One study by Ruth Feldman and Arthur Eidelman examined the mother-infant relationship as a factor influencing the cognitive development of triplets. The findings emphasize the importance of postpartum parental care and management to support parents who are caring for three infants at a time (2005). Support for parents awaiting the arrival of triplets/+ may replicate some of the training delivered to infant and toddler caregivers.

Characteristics of Multiples

Notable characteristics of physical development relate specifically to twins. Monozygotic twins can be genetically similar but less than identical in appearance. Their genetic material may not be expressed in identical ways. Dizygotic (DZ) twins are not expected to look alike. Their genetic material is as similar as that of any other siblings (Franklin 2005). Nonetheless, some DZ twins do resemble each other, others may look somewhat similar, and others appear so different that they do not look like siblings. The similarities and differences observed in DZ twins are similar to those observed among siblings in any family. Similarly, the physical capabilities of multiples can be alike or quite different. Monozygotic twins can also be quite different because of differences in genetic expression or the prenatal conditions (Franklin 2005).

Development is uneven when the size or capabilities of twins or supertwins differ. Uneven development does not necessarily mean that one of the multiples has a developmental deficit. If a specific condition was not identified during the early stages of infancy, especially with MZ twins, the uneven development may warrant assessment to identify causes for the differences. Each child's development is unique to that child and his or her own unfolding pattern of development.

While the typical expectation for the physical growth of twins is that they will develop within the same time frame and with identical developmental patterns, this is not realistic. Uneven development may indicate simply that their individual development is shaping up normally for each of them, and that they are not exactly alike in weight, height, and skill achievement. Consistent with research findings, the behaviors and skills of twins may unfold in closer synchrony when they are closer genetically. Monozygotic twins exhibit the closest possible patterns.

Physical development changes all children, including multiples. Their appearances change. Their abilities change. Their brains increase in size. By age two, a child's brain weighs about 75 percent of its adult weight. It increases in size and creates connections to improve speed and complexity of thinking. Growth continues to improve the connecting pathways and overall brain function. Movements occur more automatically. Children become more skilled in using their bodies, and they become much more adventuresome. Twins and supertwins, when they develop normally, in the same manner as singleborn children, are active and grow fairly predictably, their individual growth patterns influenced by their heredity and their environment.

The developmental difference for twins and supertwins is that their environment almost always includes another same-age child. For teachers, this difference means giving attention to each child as an individual and as a member of the multiple group. Make use of the children's twin type, or zygosity, for insight into their physical appearance and the similarities and differences in their physical skills. Two aspects of their development, in particular, generate questions from teachers: fingerprints and hand preferences.

FINGERPRINTS

"Do twins have identical fingerprints?" They do not. Every infant, including twins and supertwins, has his or her unique set of fingerprints. Handprints and footprints are similar, but fingerprints, even for MZ pairs, are different (Moskwinski 2002). A fetus grows skin cells during prenatal stages. The fingerprints and toe tips form during the second trimester. The environment influences the growth of the cells, creating the unique details of individual fingerprints.

Fingerprints are different, but the degree of likeness in the general populace is 40 to 60 percent. The concordance, or similarity, of the fingerprints for MZ twins is about 88 percent. Even though they may have the same genetic makeup, they do not have identical fingerprints. Physical contact during gestation and the intrauterine environment affect the differences in twins' fingerprints and toe prints. The structure of the fingerprints is determined by genetic inheritance. The form is influenced by the pressure on the pads during prenatal growth. The differences in the fingerprints among groups of multiples increase with the increasing number of multiples in that group. Within a quintuplet group, the concordance of fingerprints is 71 percent (Steinman and Verni 2007). Their fingerprints are not anticipated to be as alike as those of MZ twins but more alike than those of non-twins.

HAND PREFERENCE

Another common question from parents and teachers is about hand preference or handedness. Perhaps you've heard that almost all twins are left-handed. There is no conclusive research predicting whether a twin will be left-handed or right-handed.

Babies begin showing some preference for using one hand as early as two to three months. By six months, they may reveal a strong preference for using the right hand when reaching and grasping. The right hand is clearly the choice for most preschoolers. By the time children begin writing, parents and teachers describe the children's handedness as either left or right (Etaugh and Rathus 1995).

Preferences can be observed in the way some infants lie most often on their right sides, while others lie more often on their left sides. During the toddler and preschool years, children alternate between hands for some activities and frequently choose to use one hand for certain skills, such as holding a spoon. Often, toddlers hold a spoon in either hand. Children show hand preferences in their use of particular tools for large-motor activities, such as digging dirt. While they use their right hand for digging, they may paint with the paintbrush in their left hand. In other words, toddlers and preschoolers alternate preference for one hand over the other before establishing consistent use of the left or right hand. Children begin to show more consistency in hand preference between four and six years of age.

The relationship between left-handedness and multiples was first identified in early studies about hand preference. The first study comparing hand preference of MZ and DZ pairs was conducted in 1924 (Medland et al. 2006). The research suggested that 20 percent of twins were left-handed. Some evidence does suggest more left-handedness among firstborn twins, and reports indicate that 25 percent of DZ twins are left-handed (Segal 1999). A 10 percent incidence of left-handed children is found among singleborn children. The higher incidence of left-handedness of twins has been explained by the occurrence of mirror-image twins. Mirror-image twins generally have opposite laterality; one is right-handed and one is left-handed. Opposite laterality of twins does not confirm that they are mirror-image twins, however, and it does not identify them as DZ twins.

Charles E. Boklage, who researches third-type twinning, suggests a relationship between DZ twinning and opposite-handedness. Although research has not confirmed his figures, Boklage suggests that as many as 25 percent of DZ twins are opposite handed. A 1994 study showed a high incidence of left-handedness among the twins. A 1995 study identified left-handedness as more prevalent in opposite-sex twins than in same-sex dizygotic twins (Segal 1999). In more recent studies, the prevalence of left-handedness was found to be similar for multiples and singleborn children (Medland et al. 2006). Ninety percent of the general population is right handed. More boys are left-handed than girls, and a positive relationship exists between left-handedness, academic success, and ability in music and art (Etaugh and Rathus 1995).

Development of Physical Skills

After children, including twins and supertwins, acquire physical skills, their body movements become more complicated. Their physical skills develop in large-muscle and small-muscle groups, leading to other related and increasingly more difficult skill developments. As physical skills improve, growth contributes to development in other domains, such as social development. When toddlers become more capable of walking, they are able to enjoy the outside play area. If they are in infant-toddler care, they are able to interact with more and different children.

Skill and ease in physical development create a cycle of growth that increases large- and small-motor movements. Children's movements, including those of twins and supertwins, become refined, allowing them to do more with much more ease. Maturation, readiness, motivation, and opportunities encourage skill development, especially in the realm of physical development. Skills build upon one another. For example, when a preschooler begins climbing, options for other large-motor development open up. The skills learned in climbing activities increase the child's capability to master other large-motor activities, such as climbing up and sliding down the slide. When preschoolers develop various behaviors and skills, they can interact with others in ways that multiples may have already experienced. This interaction reinforces the development of additional physical skills. The inevitable interaction among same-age siblings may be an advantage for twins and supertwins, extending their chances for learning. Early experiences with cooperation, involvement, and participation are available to multiples twenty-four hours a day.

Children's readiness is determined by their maturity and the opportunities they have in the physical environment. Readiness is influenced by their interests and desires. When you focus on their individuality, including that of twins and supertwins, you support their learning. It is not necessary to push or drill children whose twins or supertwins may have already mastered a task. It is not necessary that each child in a set of multiples behaves and performs exactly the same. One triplet may be able to pour, one may be able to swing, and another may be more able to paint with numerous colors. Your attention to each child's distinctive patterns of development reveals the child's individuality. This will confirm that those patterns of development are rooted in each child's own inheritance and environment.

Large-Motor Development

During the early childhood years, most preschool children become more coordinated. They gain muscle control and balance as their strength improves. Children who are afforded opportunities and are physically able to participate become skilled at pedaling, pushing, pulling, throwing, jumping, and swinging.

Multiple-birth children afforded the same opportunities also improve in their large-motor skills. As they grow through infancy and toddlerhood, they engage with at least one other same-age preschooler in the home. They have plenty of chances to crawl over or on top of another toddler while their movements became more skilled.

Large-motor activities challenge body muscles and can become predictors for continued development. Physical development engages critical thinking skills. Critical thinking helps children plan an activity, evaluate what happens, and, for example, design the blanket-tent layout as a secure hiding place. A three-year-old maneuvering a wheelbarrow closer to the sand area validates the intensity of her concentration. She is working toward physical mastery. The age-appropriate activities you provide for all young children challenge their abilities while they attain large-motor skills and behaviors. And yet each twin and supertwin experiences mastery of tasks differently. Their activities in paired sets or in triad groups add interactive and cooperative dimensions to physical development.

When twins and triplets/+ experience large-movement activities in the presence of a twin or co-supertwins, each one's physical development progresses while watching one another. They model actions and acquire behaviors from one another, establishing an enhanced set of experiences that is not typical for singleborn children, except for singleborn infants and toddlers who attend child care programs or have older siblings.

Typical or not, twins and supertwins start out being together, and this affects their development. They attain early milestones together, although not always at the same time. They watch their same-age sibling or siblings work through stages of crawling, walking, and backing down steps. They may practice a skill by moving through the paces together, or together they may solve opening a kitchen cabinet. Multiples also approach physical tasks as individuals in their own styles and at their own paces. One twin may position himself to back down the two steps into the larger play area, cautiously maneuvering one foot down each step. His twin may approach the task by sliding forward with arms outstretched. Each twin's temperament, physical size, and particular ways of moving influence the way he manages movements and acquires skills.

Large-Movement Experiences Contribute to Skill Development

crawling	pulling+	galloping	walking
throwing+	skipping	jumping	hopping
running	carrying	pushing+	pedaling
swaying	catching+	throwing+	kicking+
hanging	sliding	balancing	lifting+
stretching	tossing+	wiggling+	climbing
swinging+	rolling+	leaping	bouncing

+Advantage of twins and supertwins (Arce 2000)

The presence of a same-age partner or two optimizes the acquisition of certain skills for multiple-birth children. Throwing, kicking, lifting, catching, tossing, and rolling become more engaging when an available, same-age partner is ready to play. The experience of pushing and pulling a wagon can be enhanced when another preschooler is available to play, creating opportunities to exchange a push for a ride.

You are accustomed to normal wiggles from the two-, three-, and four-year-olds in your classrooms. Twins and supertwins are likely to have experienced wiggling, jumping, swaying, and hopping with their same-age siblings long before their parents enroll them in your early childhood program. Some are ready for challenges that require their solo participation because they did not have many solo opportunities in the constant presence of their co-multiples. Bouncing a ball alone, for example, can be arranged in a special area so that one child can improve and enjoy that skill. Multiples have interacted daily with their same-age siblings in numerous large-motor experiences. These added opportunities particularly enhance such actions as pulling, pushing, throwing, kicking, lifting, catching, tossing, wiggling, rolling, and swinging.

Small-Motor Development

As an early childhood educator, you are professionally prepared to work with groups of same-age children who touch, grasp, pick up, and place almost any object in their mouths, and your preschool environment is prepared to handle these behaviors safely. Infants grab and grasp objects in their reach. Toddlers stack shapes, push buttons, and begin to clap. Preschoolers fit puzzles, hold paintbrushes, cut with scissors, pour ingredients, type on keyboards, write, and improve their whistling. Expect the same small-movement behaviors from twins and supertwins.

Young children, including multiples, become more independent when they practice new small-motor skills that improve their strength and increase their precision and endurance—for example, they can take off and put on clothes, put on shoes, and tie shoelaces or attach Velcro fasteners. When they use the muscles in their fingers to hold a marker, the muscles in their hands to unzip their jacket, and the muscles in their arms to dig in the sand, their small-motor abilities improve. As young children practice their skills, they become more dexterous.

Children's small-motor development continues to improve when they investigate your enriched early childhood environments. The potential perceptual and sensorial skills of all young children can expand when they play with materials and discover spatial awareness through movement. Their statements verify their proud confidence: "I can do it," "I want to paint another," and "It's cinnamon; I can smell it." Twins and supertwins develop dexterity, perceptual awareness, and learning through their senses when small-motor activities are available to them. Multiples express comments similar to those of singleborn children. They also make dual and triple assertions: "*We* can do it," "*We* want to paint another," and "It's cinnamon; *we* can smell it."

The facial expressions of most young children become more dramatic as small-motor abilities improve. The facial responses of twins and supertwins may offer you a glimpse into their individuality and individual preferences when you observe their small-motor activities. For instance, watching Cash skillfully pluck a raspberry from his tray using his thumb and pointer finger and pass it to Graham's plate gives you a glimpse into his food preferences as well as his insight into his brother's.

Twins and supertwins reach milestones with the same curiosity and exploratory behaviors as singleborn children do. You should expect that multiple-birth children have explored their environments and achieved small-motor skills while interacting and developing beside their twin or supertwins, watching, imitating, instigating, and reinforcing one another's behaviors. Abbie pushes the shapes into the container after watching her twin brother, Shunish, do the same, and Shunish bangs a wooden spoon on the turned-over cooking pot after watching Abbie's capable display. Long-term, ongoing interactions with same-age siblings affect the acquisition of small-motor skills. Observing and hearing Abbie whistle may encourage Shunish to pucker his lips and blow. Observing and interacting with a constant and available partner enhances the acquisition of small-motor skills for multiple-birth children.

Small-Movement Experiences Contribute to Skill Development

holding	plucking	squeezing	buttoning
fitting	zipping	pinching	steering
placing	painting	keyboarding	whistling
clapping	washing	tracing	cutting
coloring	smiling	steering	shaking
pouring	chewing	writing	typing

(Arce 2000)

Health Differences and Special Needs

Although the increase in the number of twins and supertwins is noticeable and has been documented in preschools, the media, and the community, the high rate of disabilities among multiples has not been as well documented. Multiples may be more vulnerable to disability than singleborn children because of the circumstances and conditions of their multiple gestation and birth. Undiagnosed neurological or physical problems may cause the developmental delay of one, both, or more in a multiple group (Thomas 1986–1987). Teachers who are aware of the potential health differences and special needs of multiples can improve multiples' chances for favorable developmental outcomes (Twins and Multiples 2006).

Early Identification and Intervention

Early identification, intervention, and appropriate introduction of adaptations to the preschool environment improve the developmental outcome and potential of a twin, twins, a supertwin, or supertwins.

Common birth disabilities are more apparent among multiple-birth children. Some disabilities decrease as multiples develop over time, with both of the children usually coming within the normal physical development range for their gender and age. Weight and height deficits generally disappear for healthy children by the time they are in the primary grades at age eight. However, multiples who are below the fourth percentile in weight for gestational age may face attention difficulties and lower speech and reading scores. Male multiples who are born small for their gestational age may be vulnerable to behavioral and learning problems.

Teachers should not ignore deficits that are apparent in a twin or supertwin. The child simply may not mature out of a particular deficit or delay (Rooney, Hay, and Levy 2003). Children whose behavior is delayed, compared with an age-appropriate range of functioning, should be referred for assessment—twins and supertwins included. The expectation that multiples will lag behind does not justify ignoring their behaviors. Some may be at greater risk for adverse medical conditions, some of which (cerebral palsy, for example) can be identified early by medical professionals. You should remain watchful and review slight variations outside the norm with other members of your teaching and management team. A staff review of the children's actions and behaviors can determine the appropriate expression of concern to parents.

Differing Health Status

The health of multiples in a twin pair or supertwin group may not be the same. The differences among the twins or triplets/+ can become problematic when the needs of one of the multiples are ignored. The healthy multiple child may be aware that her health is different from that of her twin's. Too frequently, the healthy multiple is compared with the less-able or less-healthy twin or supertwin. Some studies suggest that the siblings of children with special needs are more susceptible to depression and conduct disorders. The stress of having a less-able or less-healthy sibling may be problematic for all children. For multiples, the emotional burden is considered greater because of the close presence and the immediacy of comparison. The child who is healthy may feel envious enough to want an illness of his or her own (Bryan 1999).

One twin may be diagnosed with a condition that is significantly different from her co-twin's condition. One or two triplets in the group may have conditions that separate them in abilities from the third. One of a twin pair may develop within the normal growth range, while the co-twin may be identified before birth with a condition requiring spending additional days, weeks, or months in the neonatal intensive care unit (NICU) than the healthy sibling. Or perhaps both of the twins or all of the supertwins must stay longer in the NICU as a result of premature birth, a common factor with multiple births. With the help of the NICU medical staff, family members can acquire skills to bond with the children during extended hospital stays and during their early infancy and toddlerhood. Parents exhibit markedly similar approaches to their multiples, even when the twins have different abilities. However, the condition of a sibling may become detrimental to the healthy, nondisabled child. Children may become vulnerable to rejection or insecurity if they feel that they receive less attention from their parents (Shere 1956).

The core principles of early childhood education support helping parents, because doing so enhances the well-being of their children. Parents who have multiple children with disabilities especially benefit from supportive help from you and other members of the teaching staff. Parents of twins and supertwins whose multiples have differing abilities should be included in your supportive efforts. Families with one or more special-needs children benefit from child care programs and other supportive services, such as family education workshops. As a group, parents of twins and supertwins are believed to be at higher risk for depression. Their family situations are stressed by the challenges of disabilities. Research findings suggest that mothers, especially those with multiple children with special needs, need support to relieve stress (Yokoyama 2003).

Parents usually say that preparation for their new parenting role is helpful. Some find that networking with other families helps with the adjustment. Parents of multiples remind others to celebrate the happy moments when their child accomplishes a task, especially when the parents of multiples have been told their own child may never be capable of reaching that level. One father pointed out the many opportunities to teach children sensitively, such as when parents explain to the healthier twin that a sister or brother was born with a special or different need. The nonprofit organization Multiples Canada supports parents by sponsoring an awareness month. During that month, health professionals are encouraged to educate families about the risks of multiple births. In April 2009 the National Organization of Mothers of Twins Clubs collaborated with the Fetal Hope Foundation and TWINS to celebrate the first Multiple Birth Awareness Month in the United States.

Parents of multiple children with differing needs share stories about their twins. The story of twin brothers Jared and Bryce is an example. They were born in 1989. Jared was born with clubfoot and arthrogryposis, a rare disease that causes abnormal muscle development and stiff joints (Children's Hospital 2009). The parents treated the twins as individuals, without giving special treatment to Jared because of his condition. He was allowed to try anything, just like his brother, although there were consequences for his participation in some activities. The equal treatment was beneficial to the development of both boys, especially to Jared. The parents encouraged his abilities rather than focusing on his limitations (Rector 2008).

Twins' parents, including some who are medical doctors, offer informative stories. Dr. John Wood's twin sons were delivered at thirty weeks, one weighing one pound, seven ounces, and one weighing two pounds, five ounces. Twin to Twin Transfusion Syndrome (TTTS) (a condition that occurs in 5 to 15 percent of twin pregnancies, in which one placenta is shared by both babies) had been diagnosed at twenty-six weeks of pregnancy (Franklin 2005). When TTTS affected his family, Wood acted as a physician and a parent to gather more information about the condition. He offered to write an ongoing column to support other families affected by TTTS so they would know they were not alone (Wood 2007).

Attention Deficit/Hyperactivity Disorder

Public awareness of twins' and supertwins' needs may encourage greater support for research about conditions affecting young children. One very familiar condition to early childhood educators is attention deficit/hyperactivity disorder (ADHD), now considered one of the most common childhood psychiatric disorders. It results in heightened levels of inattention and/or hyperactive and impulsive behavior (Hay et al. 2007), and evidence of a slightly higher occurrence among twins exists. The elevated incidence may be associated with the language and speech difficulties that have been identified in twins. This association presents an additional concern for academic underachievement (McDougall, Hay, and Bennett 2006).

The incidence of ADHD in the general population is 5 to 10 percent (Hay et al. 2004). Family studies reveal that 30 to 55 percent of children with siblings who have ADHD also meet the ADHD criteria (N. Martin et al. 2006). Research suggests that the incidence for multiples, especially boys, is higher. Projecting the percentages of multiples affected by ADHD is unreliable because researchers have used a variety of assessment methodologies to gather data about the disorder. Study purposes vary, and application across ages, groups, and countries must be done with caution.

In addition, the criteria for identifying ADHD have changed. Twins have been participants in these studies, and because they face higher risk for the condition, scrutiny of the research may yet yield specific and informative data about them during the early childhood years. One study confirmed that growing up in the same home may have a greater affect on hyperactivity-impulsivity than on inattention for multiples, because of different parental expectations and overestimations of the differences in one twin's behavior (Hay et al. 2004). Children who are the most vulnerable for ADHD are those who are genetically at greater risk and are members of families with little organization and guidance in impulse control.

Research about ADHD reveals an association between the disorder and motor coordination problems (Rommelse et al. 2009). Attention deficit/hyperactivity disorder has been found to be related to delays in language development and reading disabilities (Wadsworth et al. 2007). The Colorado Longitudinal Twin Study of Reading Disability at the University of Colorado at Boulder is the first investigative study including twins in which the subjects were selected because of their history of reading difficulties. The study was initiated in 1982. The current research is a collaborative study with the University of New England in Australia and Stavanger University in Norway (Institute for Behavioral Genetics 2008).

Attention deficit/hyperactivity disorder has also been correlated with delayed reading abilities and associated with conduct disorder and oppositional defiant disorder (Martin, Levy, Pieka, and Hay 2006). The more frequent incidence among multiples could be in part the result of parents shifting attention from one to the other twin (Noble 2003).

The Australian Twin ADHD Project, begun in 1991, is a comprehensive investigation directed by David Hay and Florence Levy. Research continues on the genetic influence and the contribution of the family situation to impulsivity and problems with attention (Hay and Preedy 2006). Additional research on ADHD and multiple children is included in these resources:

"The Development of Hyperactive-Impulsive Behaviors during the Preschool Years: The Predictive Validity of Parental Assessments" by Nancy Leblanc, Michel Boivin, Ginette Dionne, Mara Brendgen, Frank Vitaro, Richard Tremblay, and Daniel Pérusse in *Journal of Abnormal Child Psychology*, October 2008. The study sample of 1,112 twins reveals a view of hyperactive-impulsive behaviors derived from ratings by the parents and teachers. The study supports parental assessment of hyperactive-impulsive behaviors during the preschool stage as a valid method for identifying children at risk in order to further evaluate and intervene in their lives.

"Having a Co-Twin with Attention-Deficit Hyperactivity Disorder" by Megan R. McDougall, David A. Hay, and Kellie S. Bennett in *Twin Research and Human Genetics*, February 2006. This research discusses the impact of attention deficit/hyperactivity disorder and the impact of the condition on the nonaffected twin. The study demonstrates that the co-twin without ADHD is made anxious by the affected twin's condition. Such anxiety raises questions about school placement of multiples with differing health conditions and needs.

"Does Maternal Warmth Moderate the Effects of Birth Weight on Twins' Attention Deficit/Hyperactivity Disorder (ADHD) Symptoms and Low IQ?" by Lucy A. Tully, Louise Arseneault, Avshalom Caspi, Terri E. Moffitt, and Julia Morgan in *Journal of Consulting and Clinical Psychology*, 2004a. Birth weight apparently has an effect on ADHD in school-age twins. The researchers point out the study's limitations concerning parental recall and self-expressed emotions. The study finds that ADHD symptoms may be moderated by maternal warmth and that enhancing maternal warmth may prevent behavior problems among the increasing population of low-birth-weight children.

Research about ADHD continues to be robust. The implications for you as a teacher of young children are threefold: twins and supertwins are vulnerable; you may select opportunities to influence how parents guide their children, particularly in families lacking organization and direction for managing children's impulses; and you should engage multiples in experiences that particularly enhance their language development, focusing on one multiple at a time. The research implies that children at risk for ADHD benefit from your asking them simple questions, providing them with brief directions, and engaging them in one task at a time.

Physical Development: Implications for Twins and Supertwins

Researchers, teachers, and parents continue to learn more about multiples as their presence increases in our society. Observation of multiples and interactions with them continue to reveal dimensions of their development and behavior yet undiscovered. Prior to their enrollment in preschool programs, multiples experienced their lives together, sharing space as a pair or as a group of three or more. Such experiences modify and elaborate the standard definitions of physical development. For example, a preschooler's appearance can be described by height, weight, shape, hair and eye color, and other defining physical characteristics. A multiple child's appearance includes these same defining physical characteristics but also includes look, size, and dress in relation to a co-twin or a co-supertwin. Besides appearance, other factors that add understanding to twins and supertwins include ability, appearance, birth order, and gender. Although the same factors relate to singleborn children, the significance of the topics are highlighted for multiples who develop alongside a same-age sibling.

Ability

Ability develops and becomes apparent as each child matures. Siblings in a multiple group demonstrate a range of ability levels. One girl may ride a tricycle sooner than her twin sister, while her twin may be able to cut with a pair of scissors earlier. The variations may result from differences in birth weight, differences in twin type or zygosity and therefore heredity, or differences in preferences. Differences may be the result of developmental or physical conditions or specific microexperiences in their environment.

Early assessment and intervention are recommended if one multiple's ability is outside the normal range for the child's age. Sensitive consideration of all the children in the multiple group is important to each child's individual growth and attainment of skills. As you work with multiples, you will become familiar with the physical and behavioral characteristics that distinguish each in the twin pair and supertwin group. The physical capabilities of twins may be close in achievement, or they may be quite unalike. When co-twins and co-supertwins significantly differ in their size or capabilities, their growth will be considered to be uneven. Uneven development is not necessarily negative or deficient; it may be a sign that each multiple is following his or her individual growth rate and pattern. However, uneven patterns could also be a sign of a developmental deficit if extreme differences exist between or among the multiples, especially if the parents have no explanation. Probe the issue in ways as you do for singleborn children. Is the development you observe within the expected developmental early childhood norm or range for toddlers and preschoolers? Assessment may be warranted if parents are unable to provide you with an explanation for the differences.

Appearance

Some people expect twins to look the same, and because of this, families of multiples are confronted by uninvited comments about the twins' or supertwins' appearance. The remarks also often emphasize the apparently uneven or dissimilar development of the multiples, which can be particularly upsetting to parents and certainly to children when they see their parents' reactions. As children mature during the early childhood years, they increasingly understand negative emotions and feelings. They are developing their ability to respond and react. Their behaviors are dependent on their temperament, social experiences, and communicative skills. Infants and toddlers respond to your tone of voice, facial expressions, and body movements. By three and a half to four years, preschoolers' reactions begin to change as they begin to gain control of their emotions. They will continue to need your approval and will continue to respond to your tone of voice. You naturally nurture children's emotional development in your group or classroom by accepting, valuing, and celebrating every child's individuality. Expand your acceptance of twins and supertwins by acknowledging their identities as multiples.

Because of their different appearances, DZ pairs often become invisible twins to observers who expect them to look alike. Until their sibling relationship is discovered, the identity of DZ twins often remains unnoticed when they begin school, especially if they are enrolled in different groups or classrooms. The appearance of twins and supertwins can also be affected by their dress. Dressing alike or differently is another issue related to multiples.

DRESSING ALIKE AND DIFFERENTLY

Parents of multiples have been encouraged, particularly by parenting books, to dress their twins and supertwins differently. Most parents actually dress their multiples differently because the majority of twins are dizygotic. The differences in multiples' gender and appearance prompt parents to select dissimilar clothing. Dizygotic twins, even when they are the same sex, are more likely to have different preferences in clothing.

Clothing is really more a logistical issue—for example, what clothing is available, where it can be found, and at what cost. Finding clothing in enough numbers to accommodate multiples is a challenge, particularly during the first year. Multiples grow so quickly, especially those born early, and they rapidly move from the premie to the newborn to the three-to-six-month and then the six-to-twelve-month sizes. Managing a quickly growing family with two or more children the same age limits parents' time to consider clothing details. It is easier to assemble two or three of the same or similar clothing items, regardless of the multiples' identity. Multiples receive clothing as gifts from family and friends, and those gifts often arrive in matching sets. The clothing industry limits choices. There are only a few ways to diversify jeans and T-shirts. When multiples graduate to middle childhood, they use clothing selections to distinguish their personal identities. They may achieve visible differences and be able to moderate other people's reactions to them as part of a pair or group.

Very similar-looking twins may need you to use new methods for learning their names and matching their identities with their unique characteristics and behaviors. Teachers have commented that they appreciate parents who dress their multiples slightly differently. One method that works, suggests teacher Vicki Starcevic, is dressing the twins in different-colored socks. This offers a way for teachers to initially tell them apart, especially while learning their names and fitting their names to their special behaviors. As multiples develop, their preferences change. "One boy," Starcevic says, "didn't like wearing the blue tennis shoes, so he switched to black ones like his co-twin was wearing." By that time, she says, "we knew the children because we knew who they were, and not just by the color of their clothing."

Birth Order

The birth order of children has a determining social role in families. Sometimes one's birth order establishes particular privileges or responsibilities. It can also determine how one is treated. Cultural definitions of roles, even those established by birth order, operate to define the relationship between twins, between parent and twin, and between twin and non-twin sibling (Mowrer 1954).

Personality, some researchers have suggested, correlates with birth order. Firstborn children tend to generally please adults. Youngest children tend to be more easygoing and social. The consequences of birth order among multiples are not conclusive in the research literature. Yet patterns usually ascribed to singleborn children appear in the literature and seem to apply to twins and supertwins.

Personalities may be affected by the expectations of parents. Parental attitudes about twins and supertwins and their birth order may affect the multiples' personalities. Birth order and descriptive roles can become factors in parents' interactions and expectations. Some parents view their twins and supertwins as individual children, and others consider them a group. A 1954 Northwestern University study noted that twin type and gender seem to affect behavior as it relates to birth order. Among the opposite-sex DZ twins studied, birth order made no difference in their decision making, but among the same-sex DZ twins and male MZ twins, birth order slightly affected their decision making (Mowrer 1954). Social changes and cultural attitudes about gender modify our views and expectations. Physical size may be another factor, regardless of who was born first, second, or third.

The birth of more than one child in the same family on the same day imposes some challenges to the children and the family that may not be apparent during the infant and toddler years or even the early preschool years. The importance of size and age becomes more notable once multiples grasp the notion of biggest and oldest. The position a child holds in a family is of considerable importance. The positions of multiples in a family are not the same as those of their non-multiple siblings. Twins and supertwins share status and position. They may also have status and position of their own within their group of twin pairs or supertwins. Their membership in a multiple group establishes alternative positions from the simple rank or order in a family.

Parents are confronted by issues about their multiples' date of birth. North America uses date of birth as an identifier for members in a family, for insurance coverage, for example. Occasionally, twins are born on either side of midnight. A mother from British Columbia reported twin boys born at 11:59 PM and 12:04 AM (Meijer 2007).

Parents usually make great efforts to impart equal treatment to their singleborn and multiple children. Teachers divide their time and attention among the children in their groups or classrooms. You also respond to parents who are concerned about balancing their time among their children. You advise parents to monitor treatment of their children in age-appropriate ways. You also encourage them to respond to and encourage the individual needs and preferences of each child—an extremely important recommendation for families of multiples that does not contradict responses to individual needs or invalidate providing twins and multiples with comparable objects and experiences. Tricycles for all three of the triplets are common gifts for their second birthday. The design, color, and accessories can be different. Assure parents that their multiples have common interests because they are the same age, are in the same range of development, and may have similar, inherent preferences. Fairness may be more readily achieved by responding to the individual tempo, needs, and preferences of each multiple. Equal treatment is a matter of focusing on each child within the multiple group rather than concentrating on equalizing every reaction, comment, opportunity, and experience (Segal 2000).

Gender

Gender has a special impact on twins and supertwins, especially when the pairs or groups are mixed gender. Among all children, there are maturity differences between boys and girls, especially in their rates of physical development and physical development milestones. Girls mature earlier.

Gender-role development may also be affected by the makeup of the twin pair or supertwin group. Research suggests that the social behaviors of twins may be influenced by their shared environment. Socialization also has an influence on gender-role behavior. Influences on behavior emerging from the shared environment of multiples determine gender-related interests and activities more than personality traits. Personality traits are affected by inherited tendencies for characteristics, such as temperament (Iervolino et al. 2005). Researchers have found that girls in different-sex twin pairs tend to be more adventurous and to process spatial information more typically like boys (Blum 2008). Studies of adolescents show a social advantage in different-sex twin pairs, while another study suggests that this advantage may not be apparent during early childhood (Laffey-Ardley and Thorpe 2006).

All children have a basic right to reach their potential. Their physical development is influenced by many factors, including their status as a twin or supertwin. Whether it is their birth order, physical differences, or opportunities that they share in common, they are affected by the ongoing presence of their membership in a twin or supertwin group. Later in the book, I will discuss identity and individuality further. A section in chapter 4 focuses on girl-and-boy twin pairs, or opposite-sex twins.

Social and Emotional Development

Individuality is one the most apparent characteristics of any child. A twin has a characteristic individuality. A supertwin has a characteristic individuality. Each of these children has another trait that is unique to his or her status: each is a multiple. The characteristics of each child and the characteristics of his or her multiple group shape the outcome of social and emotional development during the early childhood years.

Guillaume offered ready smiles to the teachers the day he began attending the child development center when he was two and a half years old. Every day that he and his monozygotic (MZ) twin brother, James, attended, smiles from James appeared after morning snack. Guillaume characteristically approached an activity if other toddlers were participating and involved. James characteristically moved toward the activities that were teacher guided. Both toddlers adjusted easily to their enrollment at the center. They each interacted with the teachers and the other toddlers. Each interacted in his own individual manner.

Teachers are more familiar with singleborn children because the majority of preschoolers enrolled in early childhood programs are singleborn. The enrollment of a singleborn child is the norm, and consequently, your expectations for enrolling preschoolers are likely based on the characteristics and needs of singleborn children. Familiarity with singleborn children continues to dominate school policies, curriculum, and guidance strategies.

Milestones

As a teacher of young children, you learned concepts about child growth and development through formal college coursework and in-service training. You have enhanced those basic concepts by attending conferences, observing children, and talking regularly with your colleagues.

Looking at a photograph of newborns may influence your thinking and potentially modify your perception about growth and development. For example, an experienced teacher looks at a photograph and remarks, "Someone definitely posed these two babies for this photograph, or the babies wouldn't be lying so close to one another. It looks like they are snuggling, but they're too little to maneuver themselves that much."

The photo shows twin boys lying in a hospital layette. They are both facing left with their hands similarly placed close to their faces. Striped sock hats cover their heads. The cuffs on their nursery gowns are folded to fit their tiny arms.

My reaction to the photo is quite different from the teacher's. The babies are only sixteen days old and healthy enough to begin sharing the same layette for the first time since their birth. No one has placed them in that position. No one has posed them for the photograph. They have moved themselves together, perhaps in reaction to their reunion, tiny brothers together again.

Multiple- and singleborn newborns reveal behaviors and preferences similar to those demonstrated by the sixteen-day-old twin boys in the photograph. Family members and others outside the family respond to an infant's behaviors. When people react and respond to the behaviors, they influence the infant's development. But even before babies are born, their distinctive and individual characteristics are noticeable. Individual characteristics of temperament have been documented through observation of intrauterine behavior. The observations demonstrate that multiples, even monozygotic twins, do not behave identically (Piontelli 1999).

Some infants and toddlers experience others outside their families in family child care homes and child development centers. By the time young children begin attending preschool at three and a half or four years of age, they have progressed through the infant and toddler stages of social and emotional growth. Each preschooler has formed significant attachments and worked through separation from parents, siblings, and caregivers. The quality of parenting and caregiving influences their sense of trust and feelings of security. Children, including multiple-birth children, who have experienced closeness and quality time together with others are more likely to achieve healthy social skills and emotional well-being.

Most young children manifest characteristic behaviors that are their own; usually, but not always, these behaviors appear after the children have adjusted to the school setting. Some preschoolers run excitedly, smiling, to an activity. Others step forward cautiously, easing into an activity. Some preschoolers remain excited, active, and smiling all day.

When you observe the behaviors of young children, you notice individual traits and manners. The movements and expressions reveal distinct temperaments, assorted emotions, and varied personalities. The behaviors of twins and supertwins are similarly assorted and varied, even for MZ twins like Guillaume and James. Guillaume and James's infant-toddler teachers observed immediately that the boys looked very much alike, something they had expected because they were told that Guillaume and James were MZ twins. The teachers also acknowledged, once they became familiar with the toddlers, that their behaviors expressed their own characteristic individualities.

Most young children, including multiples, acquire social skills as they mature. They become less centered on their own needs and thoughts and recognize their own development. Josh commented to his teachers on the first day of preschool, "I sit in a booster seat now." His twin brother, Owen, finished Josh's thought by announcing, "Both of us have booster seats 'cause we're in preschool." Their expressions confirmed their expanding recognition of themselves.

Preschool attendance expands children's social participation with others. Preschoolers enroll with a maturing sense of self and independence. Their temperaments influence how they approach new people and activities. Their personalities have been influenced by their gender, ethnicity, family structure, faith, environment, and social expectations. Their status as a twin or a supertwin influences the development of their personality and affects the manner in which they express social behaviors and emotions. They learn to fall asleep while their twin remains awake and babbling. They watch their twin or co-supertwin cry after a fall. Sometimes they feed each other bites of food from their own high chair tray.

Social and Emotional Skills

Preschool experiences provide young children with opportunities to continue their social development. For twins and supertwins, the preschool experience offers opportunities to enhance many social skills they may already have developed. They have been interacting with at least one same-age sibling since birth, and their continuing acquisition of desirable behaviors and social skills, such as using empathetic words and gestures, facilitates their interactions with other children. Twins and supertwins have had many opportunities, through choice and through necessity, to cooperate with one another. They may already have had many opportunities to participate with others in a group, just as they did when, for example, they began morning toddler classes on Tuesday and Thursday at the parent cooperative education center.

In their home setting, triplets Nelson, Bennett, and George were accustomed to waiting. And for some activities, their patience was observable. They would stand, remaining still and watching, while their father placed a tiny squirt of toothpaste on the finger toothbrush, one at a time, for each of them. When Nelson, Bennett, and George were enrolled as toddlers in the child development center, the teachers immediately commented on their ability to wait by the door until the other toddlers were ready to go outside. Their continuous time together gave them the advantage and the chance to leap ahead in some social skills. They already had considerable opportunity to practice using empathetic gestures, cooperating, and participating in a small group.

Social Development Skills

Using empathetic words and gestures+
Making appropriate choices
Cooperating+
Participating with others in a small group+
Learning about their community
Respecting differences

+Advantage of twins and supertwins (Arce 2000)

Children's development of social skills continues throughout the play years. The emotions of young children also go through changes. Their temperaments and individuality continue to direct the behaviors they display. Twins and supertwins acquire added skills as they mature emotionally. They have already played, rested, and interacted together in routine activities. They have had many opportunities to accept limits, establish self-regulating behaviors, and develop trust. These positive and negative experiences have enabled them to receive immediate feedback whenever they expressed their feelings. This also helped them begin to recognize their personal abilities.

Emotional Development Skills
Accepting limits+
Establishing self-regulating behaviors+
Expanding or achieving a sense of trust+
Appreciating pleasurable experiences
Expressing and clarifying feelings positively
Recognizing personal abilities

+Advantage of twins and supertwins (Arce 2000)

Identity and Individuality

The presence of more emotionally healthy twins and supertwins creates more positive awareness of them. Positive public awareness may, in turn, change attitudes about multiples' identity development. The pattern of their identity development is similar to that of singleborn children. Throughout the socialization process, children adapt their behaviors to gain attention, regard, and reward. They modify their behavior to please the adult from whom they desire attention. Multiple-born children seek attention but must vie for it with at least one other same-age sibling. The responsiveness and capabilities of their parents and caregivers affect the children's socialization process. The temperament and personality of each child in the multiple group determine whether one twin or two of the triplets talk louder or patiently wait. Early interactions affect their evolving self-images as well as their evolving images as members of a group.

The process of establishing a sense of identity begins in infancy. The reciprocal interaction between most infants and their mothers, fathers, and other primary caregivers establishes the foundation for social and emotional development. Infants respond to gentle, tactile contact, soothing voices, smiling faces, and watchful eyes. Each infant's responses are distinctive.

Each infant's maturational tempos are distinctive. The child's affectionate bonds with parents and caregivers are distinctive. Responsive and sensitive parenting and caregiving contribute to strong attachments and trust. A strong attachment to a significant other and a clear feeling of trust contribute to the infant's future ability to establish a confident identity.

Reciprocity operates similarly during the earliest stages of socialization for twins and supertwins with this exception: parents' time is divided among more than one baby. The participation of fathers in caregiving activities for their twins and supertwins has been reported to be higher than in families with only singleborn children. Whether out of necessity or desire, the increased participation by fathers eases the pressures on mothers and contributes to a greater quantity and, potentially, quality of caregiving.

The amount of time spent with an infant is not the determining factor for healthy socialization. Rather, parental sensitivity strongly determines positive outcomes. The *quality* of the time is most valuable, especially when parents are responsive and sensitive. High-quality parenting requires responsive reactions to a baby's temperament. This is particularly significant for the parents of twins and supertwins, because their time for each infant may be reduced. Reduced time does not inevitably result in the infants' inferior emotional development, because high-quality parenting offers consistency, sensitivity, and responsiveness to each infant's unique characteristics. When this type of parenting occurs in stable and predictable family environments, twins and supertwins, like other children in similar settings, develop emotionally healthy behaviors.

High-Quality Care for More Than One

High-quality care is equally important in infant and toddler care centers, where more than one baby's needs are met by one caregiver. Professionally prepared caregivers have been shown to effectively meet the needs of infants and toddlers and to do so without interfering with the children's attachment to their mothers. Mary Ainsworth and Silvia Bell (1970) reported that secure attachment leads to more confident and independent behaviors. Jerome Kagan (1979) validated this observation and discussed it in his work on maternal and caregiver attachment. He found no differences in the attachment behaviors of mothers and infants attending child care and mothers and infants who remained at home. Both the mothers and the caregivers met the babies' needs.

Strong attachment was achieved by mothers because their behaviors and interactions were expressively vested in their children; the mothers experienced highly emotional times of joy, praise, and discipline with their children. In agreement and in contrast, Jay Belsky and Laurence Steinberg concluded that infants' attendance in high-quality child care in the first year does not disrupt their emotional bonds with their mothers. Their 1978 data also indicated that children reared in child care interact with their peers negatively and positively. Their evidence suggests that children who attend child care for an extended time display increased aggression toward their playmates and adults.

Without specific studies about twins and supertwins and their behaviors in the home and in child care, the full significance of this research, which is based on singleborn children, is conditional. Yet the data raises questions, suggesting that future research about twins and supertwins may clarify unsubstantiated conclusions about the care of more than one baby at a time. Being with other babies does affect an infant's development, but parenting more than one same-age infant does not automatically disrupt attachment. No evidence exists to demonstrate that parenting multiple babies breaks the initial attachment formation. Research about infants has concluded that the bond is not broken because infants spend time away from their mothers. Attachment is influenced by parenting styles, including the responsiveness of parents to the needs of an individual infant. Twins and supertwins do attach to their parents. Essential factors likely to establish quality parenting and affect attachment include knowledge about development and readiness, the circumstances of the family, and the quality of child care and help provided for the families with multiples.

Attachment among Multiple Siblings

Understanding the dynamics of attachment helps you better understand identity and individuality development. Twins and supertwins form attachments to their co-twin or co-supertwins. The emotional attachments among multiple children influence the development of their individual identities.

The emotional attachments of a twin or a supertwin with multiple siblings contribute to feelings of security, trust, and a future ability to establish confident identities. When Geoffrey, a seven-month-old twin boy, woke up from his nap, teacher Moises carried him into the playroom after he was changed. Within a few seconds, Geoffrey called out,

"Gaaah," when Moises walked him to the outdoor toddler play area. Moises responded, "Yes, Geoffrey, Garrett is still asleep; he is not in the playroom now." Geoffrey used "Gaaah" to refer to his brother when he realized Garrett was not in the playroom or outdoors. He was not stressed. Rather, his communication resembled an inquiry about his brother's whereabouts, his way of acknowledging his brother's absence. His awareness demonstrated an emotional attachment.

Developing Language Reveals Identity

The language of young children provides insight into their social and emotional development. Emma clarified her identity by saying, "I'm Emma, not Kayla." She understood who she was. She understood that she was separate from her sister, Kayla. She learned the response by listening to others distinguish her from her sister and was probably prompted by her parents and older siblings. Emma's and Kayla's experiences prior to attending preschool contributed to their identity formation.

The concept that twins act as a couple has been proposed in psychological literature to explain the twin relationship and the roles twins assume in their relationship. As a couple, or as partners, twins are individuals who interact cooperatively. The genetic relatedness of MZ twins directs them to be potentially more cooperative and communicative than any other siblings. The twins as close partners may be intuitively sensitive to one another. This ability creates a relationship filled with mutual motivation, encouragement, and protection. The twins and supertwins as couples and partners assume different and sometimes complementary roles. When their behaviors are mutually satisfying, opportunities emerge to make sure that whatever tasks face them can be worked out together.

The developing language of young children defines their growing self-identities. Learning language in a partnership, as a couple, a trio, or more, influences the type of words and word combinations produced. A study about twins' language acquisition reports that the girls combined their names with a single intonation pattern to produce Kelda-Krista or Krista-Kelda. However, neither Krista nor Kelda used the team name to refer to herself as an individual. The girls dropped using the double name when they were two years and three months old, at which time they began using plural nouns and pronouns. By three years and two months, the double name was no longer used (Malmstrom and Silva 1986).

Parents of singleborn and multiple children use first-name combinations to address their children, often calling all names in order. Parents of twins may more frequently use the first-name combination. Four-year-old Trent asked teacher Shu-Chen if he could be the next one to use the sand table. Then he asked if Trent-Trina could sign up for a turn. Trent's language demonstrated a developing sense of self and of himself as part of a unit. He included his twin sister, Trina, perhaps because he wanted both of them to play at the sand table or perhaps because he was accustomed to hearing both names together. Children who hear their own names communicated separately from those of their co-twin or co-supertwins abandon the use of both names as they mature.

Changing Views about the Multiple Relationship

Studies and anecdotal information from parents and teachers have not erased lingering assumptions about twins as children with merged identities. Some research about twinship and twins' identity development has been based on adult twins who were mentally ill. The reported data from volumes of research has too often overgeneralized the entire population of twins and supertwins. Common assumptions define the twin dynamic as one that leads to psychological problems—for example, extreme competition, ambivalence, and confusion about their identities. This view will progressively change because the number of multiples is increasing and their psychological development is generally within the normal range of personality characteristics.

The identity development and individuality of twins and supertwins remain topics of research. Multiples express different degrees of particular personality characteristics. For example, one twin may appear to be happy, while the co-twin appears to be sad. If particular distinguishing traits are consistent over a period of time, the differences are referred to as *polarity*. Polarity can be the result of parents and teachers exaggerating minor differences between twins and supertwins. While exaggerating minor differences can serve as a method of distinguishing the children apart from one another (Segal 1999), polarity becomes a concern when the children become labeled with extreme identities, such as noisy and quiet. Labeling children, singleborn or multiple, inhibits their development. You should discourage parents from imposing fixed labels on their children, especially multiples. Instead, provide descriptive, favorable words that avoid polarity.

Undeniable Member of the Group

Outsiders may view multiplehood as a burden or a pleasure, but the children who are part of the group do not have a choice in their participation. Twins are identified as individuals and as members of a pair. Likewise, supertwins are identified as individuals and as members of a group. Sharing a common multiple identity does not prohibit each member from an individual sense of self. Sharing almost all early experiences within the same environment does not automatically threaten personality development. Personality development depends on many and varied contextual layers, including family, health, environment, and available resources. Twins and supertwins may be no different than other children in the external sources of their identity.

Some academics, however, describe the acquisition of self-identity among multiples to be complex and full of psychological confusion (Ainslie 1997). Multiples spend a great deal of time together. Their similar appearance has an impact on their identity development, and so does their dissimilar appearance. Their roles may be exchangeable, but they are not interchangeable as individual children. Twins are individuals with the additional identity of a multiple. Status as a multiple on its own does not inhibit multiples from successfully separating from their mother during infancy. As with each individual singleborn child, each multiple is capable of reacting uniquely to the people and circumstances in his or her environment. Although MZ twins may be expected to display the same reactions, each twin can react differently to family circumstances (Torgersen and Janson 2002).

Ideally, you support a multiple child as an individual and as a member of a group. This requires attention to the child's individual differences. Twins and supertwins may have differences in their ability to adapt to new situations. Their intensity, mood, and distractibility may be different. As an early childhood teacher, you are a careful observer and notice differences among children. For example, Yvonna, one child in a trio of four-and-a-half-year-olds, quickly approached the guinea pig's cage and swung open the door. Paulo waited until the class pet was placed on the carpet to touch it. Bianca stood back and watched, seemingly more interested in the music coming from the outdoor classroom. The three preschool-age triplets were members of a multiple sibling group, yet they showed their different personalities in the ways they reacted to one particular experience at preschool.

Behavioral development and its expression is an evolving process. Although there are consistently more similarities in development among MZ twin pairs than among dizygotic (DZ) twin pairs, developing as individuals in either twin pair is not significantly different from developing as singleborn children. Identity, individuality, and group membership evolve as children develop. Yet the stages for multiples are additionally influenced by their names, genders, and participation in interdependent and independent interactions.

Name Identity

Children's names are their first possession. They contribute to their sense of self. Children usually arrive at preschool able to identify themselves by their first and last names. Some preschoolers recognize the printed version of their name, and some are capable of writing their own name. Some multiples recognize and possibly print their own name and that of their co-twin or co-supertwins as well. A name represents family ties, culture, faith, and parental styles. Some parents of multiples select names for their children that are alliterative or sound alike to establish or identify the children as a group. Sometimes families select alliterative names for singleborn children, too, but this goes less noticed in school because the children are enrolled in different grades. The alliteration among multiples' names is apparent more often. Rhyming names, especially those with the same cadence, such as Larry and Barry, make it more difficult for you and other members of the teaching staff to initially distinguish between twins and supertwins.

The Social Security Administration reported 106 of the most popular names of twins born in 2005. Jacob and Joshua for boys and Faith and Hope for girls topped the list. In 2006 the most popular names for twin girls were Emma and Ella and Jacob and Joshua for boys.

Most school-age children hear their names rhymed and changed into chants by playmates. Depending on the names their parents select, twins and supertwins may hear manifold variations. They may also hear themselves referred to as *twin, twinsie, twinny, two-fer, carbon copy, Pete and Repeat, cycle and recycle* (Cassill 1982). Multiples may also hear or see written a new reference to their status: *cut and paste*.

Young children react to a new sound or name with a giggle, a surprised look, or a question. They may react with surprise to the presence of two children who look very much alike, especially if they have not interacted with multiples previously. You may avoid disruptive behavior and negative teasing by taking preventive actions. Introduce new children, including multiples, into the classroom or group. Share information about their names, where they live, and their families. For multiples, this involves more than one step. You may want to introduce the multiples as individuals and then together, as members of the same family. Introductions of new children are a fitting time for clarifying your expectations about acceptable behaviors. One developmental guideline appropriate for young children is that negative words about someone else's name are not acceptable in your school.

A Boy and a Girl: Opposite-Sex Twins

Bundled up in matching blankets, a boy-and-girl twin pair are indistinguishable to people outside the family, but as they mature beyond the infant stage, they begin to project a different image of twinship when their genders become more pronounced. Other terms for *boy-and-girl twin pair* are *opposite-sex twins* and *unlike-sex pair*.

Most children become aware of their biological identity as early as two years of age. They say, "I'm a girl" or "I'm a boy." Children's awareness of physical differences does not necessarily imply that they understand gender. Culture, family, society, and faith establish standards, including behaviors, for boys and for girls. Between four and five years of age, children begin to strongly identify with their gender. Preschoolers overemphasize their gender identity. They insist on wearing clothing that identifies them as a boy or a girl and playing with toys and costumes that reflect social divisions between male and female roles. Preschoolers, and some children as young as two years, begin to show preferences for playing with children who are their own gender. Older preschoolers play with groups that are more gender specific. For example, boys band together to defend the fort, trying to exclude girls from entering. Exaggerated behaviors appear in families and schools that encourage equitable and unbiased treatment of boys and girls as well as in ones that don't. Preschoolers are working toward a consistent understanding regarding their gender identity.

Gender, or sexual identity as a boy or a girl, is a significant aspect of self-concept. Being an opposite-sex twin or supertwin affects children's twin status differently than being an MZ twin or same-gender DZ twin. As boy-and-girl twin pairs grow through infancy, parental expectations and reactions to them from others begin to change. People often forget that maturation for boys and girls is different. Girls can be expected to achieve developmental milestones earlier than boys. Parental expectations, and possibly their differential treatment will influence the socialization of their boy and girl multiple. Their experiences as opposite-sex multiples become more similar to those of DZ twins who do not look alike. Once they emerge from infancy, they will be less recognized as multiples. Opposite-sex twins and supertwins share a prenatal space, have the same birthdays, and usually begin school together. Like same-sex DZ twins, however, they often remain invisible as twins to others (Segal 1999).

Gender identity becomes confirmed when parents reward children for their particular behaviors and actions. Parents communicate and model desirable actions and provide children with clothing and toys that influence their gender identification. Parents rate twin boys as more active, impulsive, and sociable than girls (Stewart 2000). This rating is consistent with parents' reports about singleborn boys.

Differing physical progress between the children in opposite-sex twins influences their identity. Opposite-sex twins are particularly susceptible to comparisons of physical size. When the boy twin and the girl twin are very unlike in size, this can become an issue if parents, family members, and strangers compare the children.

Negative reactions and inappropriate evaluation of the children—too often in their presence—adversely affects their self-esteem. Differences in children's physical sizes may also lead to disparate timing in achievement of developmental milestones. Not every partner in a twin pair, a triplet trio, or a quad group begins riding a tricycle at the same time. Distributing information about physical development timelines to parents can equip them to respond appropriately. For example, parents of opposite-sex twins would benefit from findings like those based on sample populations in Australia, the Netherlands, and the United States (Medland et al. 2008).

A normal expectation for all children is that girls mature earlier than boys. A boy in an opposite-sex twin set may be developing normally but receive unnecessary evaluative feedback from people who compare him with his sister, even though physical size and developmental timing differences should be expected.

Boys and girls in opposite-sex twin pairs usually develop physically and psychosocially like singleborn children, as do multiples who include children of both genders. Twin girls with boy-twin partners, though, outscore twin girls in same-gender sets on assessments of certain abilities.

The twin girls in opposite-sex sets display heightened abilities in spatial tasks and risk-taking behaviors. Spatial tasks and risk-taking behaviors are typically more common behaviors among boys. These girls' increased competence in tasks not generally expected of them does not signify that girls with same-age brothers are more masculine. Helen Koch's classic 1966 study of twins (1966) demonstrated that twin boys of opposite-sex pairs were more responsible, more cooperative, and less active than singleborn boys.

The twin relationship changes over time, particularly with certain characteristics such as dominance and submission. Behaviors and actions change and become more equal. A study focusing on twins' mental health showed that the boys in opposite-sex twin pairs displayed depressive and nervous complaints. The researchers found that the boys who were submissive seemed to be affected by depressiveness and nervousness. The girls did not show similar symptoms of depression and nervousness when they were submissive to their co-twin brothers (Ebeling et al. 2003).

In another study, researchers found that mothers encouraged exploratory behaviors in the boys while encouraging helping behaviors in the girls. The seven mothers observed in the study reinforced the boys' aggression and the girls' aggression almost equally. Even so, the mothers were aware that they may have treated their male and female infants differently (Goshen-Gottstein 1981). The outcome of this study closely replicated the findings of Susan Goldberg and Michael Lewis (1969), who studied singleborn infants and their mothers. The researchers noted that the mothers treated their infant sons differently than their infant girls in a standardized free-play scenario. The mothers responded to behavior patterns that the infants presented early, possibly reinforcing the sex role–appropriate behaviors. Boys were independent and exploratory. Girls were more dependent and less exploratory.

In same-gender twin pairs, girls often become best friends with one another. Being best friends also leads the girls to become slightly more competitive. Still, twin girls enjoying best-friend interactions meet each other's needs with help and companionship. Twin girls have also been found to enjoy a comfortable relationship with their fathers.

Another distinguishing difference among boy and girl twins is the condition of attention deficit/hyperactivity disorder (ADHD). As mentioned in chapter 3, ADHD is slightly more common in twins than in singleborn children. Boys are more vulnerable to this condition (Hay 1999).

Interdependence and Independence

Early childhood educators view close connections and interdependence during the preschool years as worthy attributes. Interdependence supports two abilities: dependence and independence. Interdependence supports actions for giving and receiving. Through giving and receiving, children begin to acquire skills that strengthen their future abilities to collaborate and negotiate. They learn to become successful and cooperative members of a community. Early collaborative and cooperative action contributes to healthy, interdependent behaviors. The process is moderated by the circumstances and conditions of children's homes, families, and health. Dependence requires the ability to accept, accommodate, and negotiate.

HEALTHY INTERDEPENDENCE

Twins and supertwins automatically have opportunities to acquire positive interdependence. You can observe their interactive behaviors and see that their relationships are typically healthy and happy. Their interdependence, when viewed as a positive attribute, may alter negative descriptions about them. The multiple relationship has often been described, particularly from a psychological viewpoint, as negative, turbulent, challenging, and conflictive. Some research has emphasized the social disadvantage of twinship, assuming that multiples are deficit in their abilities to become independent because of their close relationship with their co-twins. Society's insistence on independence devalues the benefits of interaction and, at least for twins, discourages their closeness. Nonetheless, the interdependence of multiples can be beneficial.

BALANCING INDEPENDENT BEHAVIORS

Interdependence contributes confidence and helps build independence. As independent behaviors evolve, the individual needs and desires of each multiple emerge. Balancing the different needs and desires becomes part of the relationship for multiples. They soon recognize their social category—that of a twin or triplet. One study reports that the children describe their views about their twinness with insight into their relationship as twins. They describe their identity as a member of the pair (Danby and Thorpe 2006).

As the behaviors of multiples emerge and evolve, you notice that multiples exchange roles—characteristics sometimes shift from one child to another. One of the twins or supertwins may be the apparent leader on one day, yet within a few days or weeks, another assumes leadership. Most children seesaw or zigzag in the process of achieving socialization and independence. The exchange of roles becomes apparent because you may have initially distinguished the multiple by a specific behavior or role now being exchanged. When multiples exchange these roles, becoming a leader and then a follower, a communicator and then a reflective listener, their individual temperaments and previous experiences influence the ways in which they display the behaviors. For example, Trent consistently presented himself in a tone of voice that was mellow. It didn't matter if he was chasing or following. Trina's voice was consistently more pronounced. When she entered a room, she did so with stomps. As DZ boy-girl twins, Trent and Trina took turns leading and following, whether mellow or pronounced. Their changing balance of power did not necessarily diminish their sense of identity. Their realignment of roles contributed to their achievement of independence.

You are familiar with competition among young children, especially a group of preschoolers who vie for your time, attention, and approval in the classroom. It is not possible to be fair all the time. It is not possible to be completely equitable. You work to provide equitable opportunities by guiding children to wait and use materials in turn. Twins and supertwins have vied for blankets, toys, snacks, and their parents' time. Twins and supertwins have negotiated with one another and their parents to be the first to select a book, to open the front door, to hold the dog's leash, and to sit on their mother's lap. By the time they enroll in preschool, they are aware of their multiple existences and the necessity to share. The challenges of waiting, sharing, and giving are familiar to twins and supertwins.

Relationships and Emotional Competence

The relationship of twins and supertwins is considered to be very close in the earlier years. Infant multiples actively seek out one another. They can be observed moving toward each other when placed in the same crib. They exchange soothing touches, listen to each other's cries, imitate each other's sounds, and begin playing hide-and-seek and chase when they are crawling. Twins may react to separation from one another in the same way they react to separation from their mother (Sandbank 1999).

Children's lives and their relationships change when they begin attending child care and preschool programs. They separate from their parents—it is a time of transformation. They begin to expand their social groups. Usually, when multiples begin child care or preschool, they do so with their twin or their co-supertwins. Like other preschoolers, they acquire new skills in the infant and toddler programs and in preschool. They also practice skills they have already acquired through interaction with their co-multiples. Multiples begin interacting with other children, gain a mastery of their emotions, and begin developing friendships outside their multiple group.

Enrollment for twins and supertwins adds new dimensions to their usual interactions with their same-age siblings. They have more and different playmates. They gain opportunities to increase their sense of autonomy from their multiple siblings and from their parents. They have chances to become more independent in pursuing actions they may have previously completed only as a twin pair or supertwin group member. Twins and supertwins develop independence.

Some multiple children initially prefer to remain in contact with their co-twin or co-supertwins. Expectations are that most children who know one another well prefer to remain in close proximity. This preference is consistent among children who are singleborn or multiples. Their readiness for the experience and their previous experiences help children adjust to the new setting. Singleborn children's readiness to separate from parents varies. Multiple-born children's readiness to separate from their parents also varies. The comfort and support of a co-twin or co-supertwins eases the adjustment for multiples who begin new experiences together.

Every multiple group is different. Pat Preedy of Great Britain has developed a model for assessing the twin relationship. She identified three categories of relationships among multiple-birth children: closely coupled, mature dependent, and extreme individual. The descriptions are helpful for parents and for you when contemplating the children's readiness for group experiences. Consideration of Preedy's three categories may reveal the multiples' readiness to engage in independent activities.

Closely coupled twins behave as a unit and may not be able to function without each other. They may have few other friends, respond to the same name, adjust their levels to each other, and have their own language.

Mature dependent twins have the ideal relationship because they enjoy one another and are happy with the relationship. They are able to operate with one another and their peer group. They may compete in a healthy way with each other and can make their own effective choices.

Extreme individual twins may dislike their twin relationship to the degree that they resent their twin. They may try to dominate one another, feel jealous, or remove themselves from a situation in which their twin is more capable. The children in this group can and do move between closely coupled and extreme individuals as they attempt to establish their own identities (Hay and Preedy 2006: Twins and Multiples 2006).

Families

Children create a type of family. They initiate and change the dynamics of an existing family. Twins and supertwins significantly affect family dynamics and relationships. The presence of more than one same-age child affects the quantity and quality of time parents have. How well the family adjusts to the addition of twins or supertwins is determined by the family's circumstances. Supportive help for the family contributes positively to adjustment. The self-confidence of the parents also affects the family's adjustment. Adjustment is significantly eased for mothers of multiples when, for example, they are informed that they are capable of bonding with more than one baby at a time.

The family experience for multiple children is one of sharing. The children share a prenatal environment. They share parental time. Caring for two or three or four babies is more demanding for parents. The caregiving tasks are multiplied. The multiplied tasks may become taxing for the parents and frustrating for each infant, whose needs simply must be met. Mothers may become more taxed caring for more than one baby at time, particularly when the infants have different temperaments and needs. Researchers have observed that reduced interactive behaviors between parents and their multiples may negatively affect the cognitive abilities of the children. Understanding the importance of interactive behaviors, or synchrony, between infants and caregivers justifies additional support for families of multiples. Rearing three infants simultaneously is not the same as caring for twins. It is definitely not the same as caring for a singleborn infant (Feldman, Eidelman, and Rotenberg 2004).

The financial burden on families increases with the increasing number of children, and limited resources can harmfully affect the children's socialization by reducing the opportunities a family can provide for multiples. The early expenses for the children's basic health and care are extraordinary. Costs, including preschool tuition, vacations, and daily expenses, weigh seriously on the families with multiples. The family environment is filled with challenges, and life stressors produce unexpected consequences. One study has shown that MZ twins react differently to stressful events and factors. Environmental factors seem to have an individualizing effect on siblings, indicating that multiples, like singleborn children, can experience the same event in the same family yet respond in different ways. Certain events—particularly stressful ones, such as divorce—affect children differently. Like singleborn children, MZ pairs act upon those events and experiences differently, even though the twins are genetically the same (Torgersen and Janson 2002).

The challenges facing families of twins and supertwins may be offset by feelings of pride. Relationships within a family may be modified from those expected in families with only singleborn children. The presence of twin boys has been found to affect the traditional father-son relationship. Unlike the more apparent competition in the traditional father-son relationship, in families with twin boys, competitive behaviors were reduced, with twin boys experiencing closer relationships with their fathers (Sandbank 1999).

Families with twins and supertwins have children who belong to an exclusive group. They make up only 3 percent of the population. Families become more assured and confident in their ability to care for multiples as the infants mature into toddlerhood. The attention that others give to multiples may help the adjustment in families and increase parents' sense of confidence. Sharing the child care workload is an important factor. When both parents are engaged in child caring, increasingly positive outcomes occur for the multiples during infancy and the childhood years (Trias et al. 2006). Research studies are contributing information and clarifying the specific involvement of parents of multiples.

- Mothers adjust to having two babies in their own ways, which are not specific to the infants' twin types, or zygosity. The mothers provide collective treatment of the infants, demonstrating the process of triadic motherhood. The triadic relationship is created with the mother and two children, the twins, forming a group of three (Robin, Corroyer, and Casati 1996).
- Mothers who display highly individualized rearing behaviors view their twins as two distinct individuals (Robin, Maner-Idrissi, and Corroyer 1998).
- Parental attitudes, particularly the expressed emotions of the mothers, influence the behavior of their children. The behaviors are affected by the emotional attitudes toward the children and can be correlated with antisocial behavior problems. Mothers in one study were found to treat their twins in MZ pairs differently, which further influenced the behavior of their children (Caspi et al. 2004).

SIBLINGS AND MULTIPLES

Siblings influence each other's socialization. In fact, they can be more influential than parents on each other's socialization. The sibling of a twin or supertwins experiences a different pattern of interaction with her sisters and brothers than the one normally observed among singleborn siblings. An older sibling's adjustment to the presence of two, three, or more infants determines whether the infants feel acceptance within the family, while intense focus on the multiples may lead an older sibling to feel apart from the family or neglected. A child with multiples as older siblings adjusts differently than a singleborn child with young multiple siblings.

Even when siblings generally enjoy each other's companionship, at times they may become combative over a toy or special possession. They may also dispute routines, such as feeding the dog, and privileges, such as whose turn it is to select a book to read. Siblings, including twins, supertwins, and non-twins, have insight into one another's behaviors. Their relationships and potentially enduring friendships require guidance from adults because children have strong and differing opinions. Yet most siblings, including singleborn children, form groups when threatened by children who are outside their group. Twins and supertwins begin as units. In their units, they are joyful and conflictive while resilient as a team.

In families with multiples, sibling rivalry may be exaggerated because of the potentially intensified competition for parents' time. Parental perceptions of gender and family birth order may also affect a singleborn child's reaction and adjustment to multiple siblings. A sibling's placement in the family, the preparation before the birth of the multiples, and the length of the hospital stay influence a child's reaction and tolerance for the added family members. The spotlight that focuses on twins and supertwins may create rivalries for the singleborn child in the same family. Guidance for self-esteem and identity building may benefit the singleborn sibling of multiples.

Peers, Play, Friendship

Preschool expands most children's social contacts and circles of interaction. Children begin interacting by first playing side by side with other preschool children, and then they work together. They identify who is allowed to play in the group and who is not allowed. Cooperative play engages their imaginations. Their pretend play becomes more complex and inclusive of other children.

The interaction of twins and supertwins with their peers in the preschool setting is more varied than that of a singleborn child. Children usually interact more with familiar playmates in preschool settings. Multiple-born children, in the same way, interact with those who are most familiar—their co-twins and co-supertwins. A study confirms that children with secure attachments, including multiples, are able to independently explore their environments. They are able to interact with one another and with others, such as new playmates and peers, who may be unfamiliar (Vandell et al. 1988).

Multiple-born children's situations also present different implications for friendship development than singleborn children's. A twin or supertwin negotiates friendship with prior experience of a sustained relationship with another same-age child. Twinship or supertwinship necessitates more interaction with a same-age child or children. The experience expands the multiples' opportunities to negotiate, share, and take turns (Thorpe 2003). You can guide twins and supertwins further in developing relational skills. Their interaction with same-age singleborn children outside their multiple group may begin in the preschool experience.

Enrollment in infant and toddler care and in preschool programs expands children's access to peers and friendships. Research on friendship and playmate preferences offers insight about multiples. Children's early peer relationships can positively influence social development in quality preschools. Children's imaginative and dramatic play may be enhanced when they interact in beginning friendship relations. Social competence increases, further developing social development and competence in social peer settings.

Monozygotic twins have been shown to be more cooperative with each other and have more similar interests. Their play behaviors are also more alike because they are genetically more similar than DZ twins and non-twin siblings (DiLalla and Caraway 2004). On the other hand, researchers testing children in a play lab within two months of their fifth birthday have determined that twins display greater inhibition during free play than do singleborn children. The researchers attribute this inhibition to twins' lack of experience in playing with children who do not look like them (DiLalla and Caraway 2004).

Guiding Emotional Competence

Preschool programs that plan for the developmental needs of young children help them achieve emotional competence. You foster the children's security and trust by helping them understand their own feelings. Some children can separate from their parents, and some cannot. Some are able to join group activities. Some need your gentle guidance, including quiet time to be held, and time to adjust.

The infant, toddler, and preschool experiences offer specific activities to assist young children in clarifying their feelings. You can help most children resolve typical emotional stresses related to separation from their parents. You can guide children's behaviors to wait, share, listen, and interact in socially acceptable ways. Preschoolers learn how to join other children in activities as they play, first side by side and then cooperatively. Their interpersonal relationships develop as they engage in self-selected activities and teacher-directed experiences. Twins and supertwins, having already interacted with more than one same-age child, learn to join children who are not part of their own groups. They learn to handle their emotions with a maturing competence resulting from their experiences as multiples. As they achieve emotional competence, their self-esteem and concept of themselves are enhanced.

CLARIFYING FEELINGS AND CELEBRATING CLOSENESS

Twins and supertwins have the opportunity to express their feelings within their multiple groups from birth. They receive empathy or rejection from their twin or co-supertwin. They acquire skills in the steady give-and-take interactions. Their partnerships provide opportunities that influence their attitudes and actions about conflict and resolution. Their behaviors have been reinforced by their co-twin or co-supertwins before attending preschool.

The bond between twins and among supertwins begins developing immediately. Behaviors demonstrating their attachment are apparent in the way they seek out one another, show distress when their co-twin or co-supertwin is not present, and look at their partner before exploring. Their co-multiple provides a secure base in the same way that parents provide a secure base for singleborn infants who are beginning to explore. The closeness experienced by multiples evolves into special relationships during their toddler years.

The relationship experienced by multiples promotes positive social and emotional skills, such as sharing and taking turns. Their early close proximity permits an increased awareness of each other, allowing reciprocal behaviors of seeing, hearing, and touching one another. The constant presence of another creates an environment of comfort and support. This elevates their feelings of confidence and security. The children in twin and supertwin groups have opportunities to compete, practice negotiating skills, work through competition, cope with comparison, and cooperate. Multiples have the security of at least one other playmate with whom they share a bond. The built-in network offers deep closeness. The thread that connects them may compensate for some of the extraordinary work required to grow up in a group.

The relationship of twins and supertwins should be celebrated. During early childhood, connectedness and closeness are meaningful and valuable for young children. As twins and supertwins develop, their relationships with one another change. What does not change are the security and support of the network, because these establish strong and lasting foundations for healthy well-being.

RESPONDING TO CUES FROM MULTIPLES

Infant and toddler programs, including those in which twins and supertwins are enrolled, implement plans and routines. A predictable and flexible plan establishes a sense of security. The teacher who arranges the environment with maximum flexibility can respond to the cues of the youngest attendees in the early childhood programs. The babies begin to show their sense of independence as they move into toddlerhood. Their developing movements empower them to explore their environment.

Because toddlers' language is just beginning to develop, their actions serve as their primary form of communication. They do not have the language skills to readily communicate their desires and needs. They may grab an object from a nearby toddler or push another toddler off the wooden rocker. Unable to say what they want, toddlers may reach over and bite the closest arm—that of another toddler. Biting occurs more often among multiple-birth toddlers, and their parents will ask you about it. Among multiples, biting happens because there are more toddlers who are interacting in the same area and generally interested in the same object, and their frustration may be expressed physically. You can discourage multiples from biting by using the same appropriate methods of guidance you use with singleborn children. Redirection, a word expressing hurt, and a tone of voice that projects disapproval are strategies that help toddlers develop social skills and self-regulation. Offer care for the injured toddler. Model empathy, and you establish a sense of trust.

Toddlers are capable of communicating discontent by stiffening and extending their bodies. Multiples may have used this expressive position at home and watched their own twin or supertwin sibling express a similar action. At school, you can respond early and gently to the physical expressions of protest. This gives toddlers the greatest opportunity to grow emotionally. Toddlers respond to you when you soothe them and offer them options. They rejoin the activity when they are able and ready, or they can be redirected into another activity. During your guiding actions, you may be in the presence of a co-twin sibling or of several supertwin siblings, who may stare, appear interested in what is happening, and perhaps show empathy for their multiple. You may have triplets Natalie and Vivienne ask you, "What did Angela do?" Acceptance of emotions, soothing of tensions, and redirection for toddlers are practices that allow them to begin understanding limits.

As an early childhood educator, you set limits on certain behaviors by encouraging the children to use words to communicate their needs. Your communication ideally should identify unacceptable behaviors— for example, "Hitting hurts." An adult's displeasure and disapproving facial expression are powerful, because children respond to favorable attention and affection from teachers and caregivers.

Studies have been conducted in which the emotional and behavioral problems of twins were rated separately by parents and teachers. The teachers rated multiples as having greater emotional and behavioral problems. Reasons for the differences were not identified; possibly, twins were perceived by the teachers to have inherent problems because of their multiple status. (Program practices best suited to meet the needs of twins and supertwins will be discussed in chapter 7.)

Understanding the behaviors of twins and supertwins requires that each situation be evaluated within the context of each twin's actions. "My mother says that I do not have to nap!" Michael announced as he stood on top of the loft, arms folded across his chest. Michael could have been labeled as disruptive. The child development center teacher listened to him and provided options for him. His four-year-old twin sister, Megan, agreed to nap without protest. Megan sat on her rest cot and glanced at a picture book. She was tired. She generally enjoyed a midday rest. The teachers did not compare the four-year-old twins; rather, they considered their individual needs and characteristics.

Experiencing Loss

A teacher at a conference workshop selected the workshop because she was trying to deal with the loss of a child at her preschool. She was searching for ways to help a surviving two-and-a-half-year-old boy whose twin had recently died. The twins would have developed a close relationship, and the loss is a permanent separation for the surviving child. Sensitive guidance is important for his well-being.

The closeness of twins or supertwins compounds the stress of a loss; the effects of a loss would be greatest for multiples who have not experienced any separation from their co-multiple. Twins have reported feelings of fearfulness that they would lose a co-twin. Such a loss alters a child's status as a multiple, at least as it would be perceived by the people outside the family, and it may influence or alter a child's identity (MacDonald 2002). With the loss of a co-twin, a twin confronts unique challenges to the twin relationship, ones that counselors and surviving siblings need to understand (Withrow and Schwiebert 2005). Support and access to professional services influence how a family handles its bereavement and how the surviving child adjusts.

Healthy twins should be informed about the illnesses of an unhealthy twin or supertwin, particularly if the sick child is hospitalized. You may need to work with parents who indicate that they do not want a healthy twin to know about a co-twin's failing health. Handouts about loss and grieving are important resources and can be obtained through such organizations as the National Organization of Mothers of Twins Clubs (NOMTC) and Multiple Births Canada/Naissances Multiples Canada (MBC). An example of a specialized group for families is Loss of Multiples Support Network (loss@multiplebirthscanada.org), which provides opportunities for grieving families to connect. Professionals recommend preparing the family and children for separation and potential permanent loss.

Young children are unable to grasp the finality of death. They often feel responsible for changes in their family status and environment, including the absence and loss of people. A British pediatrician who is an expert on twin development wrote about a young toddler who stopped talking when his twin suddenly died. The boy's reaction to a mirror elicited an immediate happy response, only to be followed by gloom when he realized the reflection was not his missing twin brother. He became increasingly withdrawn and aggressive (Bryan 1999).

Your role with families experiencing a loss or losses is to support the parents and surviving children and remain sensitive to their needs. You are important in creating the environment the children in infant and toddler centers and preschools need: a stable, caring environment that contributes to optimal social growth and development of twins and supertwins.

A recent study reveals that fathers of multiples believe they themselves should be able to cope with their loss, regardless of grief. They were not encouraged to express their grief emotionally. Some evidence suggests that the mothers in the study turned to spiritual support. They recalled experiencing more grief (Swanson et al. 2009).

Parents affect their children through the emotions they express. They also influence their children's evolving process of growth and development. The social and emotional growth of young children is at the core of their development. Throughout this process, toddlers begin to become aware of their feelings. Preschoolers begin to regulate their emotions. As they mature, their emotional regulation supports their play and interaction with others. They become less reactive and more responsive. Experiences in the early childhood setting contribute to their learning and language development. Multiples expand their interaction beyond their ever-present multiple group and learn to cooperate with others as individuals and as members of a twin pair or a supertwin group. Prospects for learning that positively affect their language and communication development increase for twins and supertwins. Learning and language development are discussed in the next chapter.

Learning and Language Development

The correlation between children's learning and language development is well established. Less well-known is the association between learning and language acquisition among multiples. This has not prevented the common use of inexact concepts, such as twin language, also referred to as *idioglossia,* to label the developing speech and communication of twins. Some multiples do exchange their own sounds and words. At times, they may communicate primarily with their twin or supertwin siblings. Nonetheless, private language among multiples is rare. The association between twins' and supertwins' language development and their intellectual abilities invites closer scrutiny of the communication and the affect of language development on their cognitive development.

The experiences you offer all young children during the early years directly affect their learning and intellectual functioning. These same activities in quality early childhood programs provide numerous opportunities for multiples to learn and develop their language skills. Preschool experiences for multiples are particularly beneficial if they have not interacted with children outside their family or if language delays have been identified.

Experiences that are exciting for young children usually satisfy their curiosity and encourage them to play. Curiosity also creates the ideal circumstances for enhancing twins' and supertwins' understanding about the world. Twins and supertwins are accustomed to playing with one another. In quality preschools, they enjoy enriching and playful opportunities to expand their interaction with other children while developing their language concepts through discovery and exploration.

Milestones in Learning

Healthy infants are born with the capacity to learn, including learning their family's language. Observation of infants reveals that they can perceive, react, respond, interact, and actively influence their environments. They develop a growing awareness of others, of objects, and of themselves. The same milestones apply to multiples. Twin and supertwin infants, toddlers, and preschoolers gather information through their senses, movements, and environments. They become capable of performing increasingly complex tasks. Accomplishing more difficult tasks leads progressively to memory development. With the development of memory, many more opportunities open for twins and supertwins.

As multiples grow, their brains (like those of singleborn children) mature rapidly throughout the early childhood period. Early sensory experiences are important, as are interactions and events that are free from overwhelming stress. The young brain is flexible, active, and capable. The potential for healthy brain development is best ensured for children when they interact with sensitive adults (Thompson 2008).

As twins and supertwins progress, they acquire cognitive skills. Eventually they are able to classify items, such as trucks, compare outdoor and indoor play equipment, and organize picture books in the reading area. The interactions they have with you in the early childhood program are essential to developing their cognitive skills. Casual and planned communicative exchanges with you encourage multiples' language development. This chapter documents how their language development differs from those of singleborn children. As twins and supertwins communicate with you and with other children in your early childhood program, they improve their abilities to answer questions, express their feelings, and repeat a familiar rhyming fingerplay, such as "Five Little Speckled Frogs."

Learning during Early Childhood

Infants respond to touch. Infant twins and supertwins respond to the touch of their parents and other intimate adults in their environments as well as to the touch of their twin or supertwin siblings. By the time they are four months old, multiples, just like singleborn infants, are aware when their mother or other primary caregiver has left the room. By six months, they begin showing an increasing awareness of themselves. Twins also show an increasing awareness of their co-twin, fellow triplets, or other multiples.

As infants' mobility increases, they roll over and then eventually crawl toward an interesting object. As multiples begin to roll and scoot, they end up in close proximity to one another. Parents of multiples attest anecdotally that their twins and triplets purposefully move closer together. The babies crawl over one another, sometimes responding to the squeals of their sibling, sometimes ignoring the reactive, pushing movements below them. Their movements become more independent, and independent movement expands their opportunities to touch, taste, hear, and learn. They become more aware of their surroundings.

Twins and supertwins immediately have play opportunities with another same-age sibling. Whether they belong to a group of two, three, or more, their early play experiences are different from those of single-born children. Always having another same-age playmate around requires a team approach. Learning team behaviors at an early age influences the dynamics of play at home and at school. A watering hose becomes an object for giving and receiving and, naturally, wetting someone else and becoming wet. A twin can enjoy holding the hose and spraying the water nozzle while her twin efficiently positions the watering can to be filled. When at least two playmates cooperate, a garden hose can quickly be turned off by one while the other or others are spraying or watering. Multiple children form inventive plans together. As a team, they stack pillows and push furniture to reach heights unattainable by one child alone. Behaviors like banging spoons turn into a rhythmical game when more than one child participates.

The environment that supports young children's curiosity with sensitive social interaction is the one that ideally supports their learning opportunities. Infants, toddlers, and preschool children repeat experiences that are pleasurable for them. Twins and supertwins have enriched opportunities to practice new skills, and as they do, their memory, logic, and problem-solving abilities become progressively enhanced.

Value of Imaginative Play for Cognitive Development

Learning during the early childhood years requires imaginative play. Children spontaneously enjoy unrestricted time to play alone or with others, though securing unrestricted time to act alone may be challenging for multiples. On the other hand, multiples have open-ended opportunities to expand imaginative play because of the availability of one or more cooperating playmates. They gain information and progressively and creatively use the knowledge in different ways. This is cognitive development. When children pretend to be a dog or a grocer or a river rafter, they practice skills that will be important throughout life. They problem solve, gain self-control, retain information in their minds, and begin to attend to relevant cues. These skills, necessary for children to develop higher-order thinking (Thompson 2008), form early and are practiced through pretend play. Imaginative play for all children builds confidence because children can make choices and find doing so satisfying because it builds self-regard and emotional competence.

IMAGINARY PLAYMATES

About midway through the preschool years, many preschoolers have imaginary playmates. This is a normal aspect of their developing imagination. Often the imaginary playmates are given names. Sometimes they are pets. Sometimes they are objects. Often they are called sisters and brothers and friends. They are real to the children. Imaginary friends provide social benefits for preschoolers in the same way that reciprocal friends do (Gleason and Hohmann 2006). Some twins and supertwins have their own imaginary playmates. They actively interact with the playmates and do so even when their twin or supertwins are in the same room. The availability of same-age siblings as playmates does not deter a three-and-a-half-year-old from creating and playing with an imaginary friend.

An imaginary playmate provides opportunities for any preschooler to carry on conversations at any time with a ready partner. An imaginary playmate allows a child to make decisions, collaborate, and deflect the blame for a lost tennis shoe or broken sand bucket. An imaginary playmate in the life of a twin or supertwin provides the same opportunities. A preschooler's relationship with an imaginary playmate does not signify that the child is lonely or uncommunicative. A multiple who remembers playing with an imaginary friend does not necessarily report later in life that his relationship with his twin was emotionally unstable.

Twins and supertwins, like other preschoolers, talk with their imaginary friends.

Imaginary playmates seldom appear during the busy hours at preschool, yet they interestingly reappear when children dictate stories to you or when a preschooler needs someone powerful to settle a dispute over who is in charge of the fort. By the time children are ready to attend kindergarten, imagined friends almost always disappear.

Intellectual Abilities

The participation of twins in research has contributed to the study of human development, particularly to knowledge about intelligence. Researchers have explored the genetic and environmental effects on cognition. By comparing the cognitive functioning of twins, both monozygotic (MZ) and dizygotic (DZ), researchers have been able to examine the interaction of nature and nurture to identify factors in development. The research has shown that intelligence is highly influenced by an intrinsic genetic plan, yet the qualitative conditions of the family situation contributes to predicting IQ scores (Wilson 1983). Research has also provided some insight into the intellectual abilities of multiples.

Twins and what is referred to as *the twin situation* have been explored to learn more about intelligence. Researchers have confirmed findings from earlier studies about the relationship between intelligence scores and biological relatedness. Children who are more closely related biologically and have been reared together have more similar IQ scores (Etaugh and Rathus 1995). A higher correlation of IQ scores exists among MZ multiples who grow up together than among those who are reared in different homes by different adults. This holds true even when the twins' academic achievement is assessed independently by different teachers (Walker et al. 2004). Genes have a direct effect on cognitive abilities and on similarity in performance (Oliver and Plomin 2007). Although their zygosity is unknown, in 2008 quadruplets were welcomed into the freshman class at Massachusetts Institute of Technology, each having met the rigorous entrance requirements (Segal 2008).

SIMILARITIES AND DIFFERENCES

Researchers have noted differences in the intelligence test scores of multiples and singleborn children. Some findings report disadvantages for twins when compared with non-twins (Deary et al. 2005). Others indicate that the deficits may be implied rather than observed (Post-huma et al. 2000). In an early study (Koch 1966), five- and six-year-old twins produced lower performance scores than singleborn children on intelligence assessments; the scores were lowest on vocabulary abilities. Data from the 1981 La Trobe Twin Study show a distinction among multiples, with the boys achieving lower scores (Hay and O'Brien 1983). Hay's research reported in 1989 that twin boys who participated in the study were behind the twin girls and singleborn children on expressive language and verbal comprehension.

The same study indicated that differences between twins and single-born children depended on the task. For example, the twin boys in the study did as well as the other groups of children on the block design test. The data in a 2005 study from two population surveys showed a similar difference of about five IQ points between multiples (lower) and single-born children (higher).

Subsequent studies have refuted the initial findings about lower performance. Data from one study revealed that the twins who participated were not universally delayed intellectually, and as a group they performed no differently than singleborn children on IQ tests (Posthuma et al. 2000).

Comparisons of intelligence scores will no doubt continue, and the scores of multiples and singleborn children are likely to show variability. Some multiples will score higher than singleborn children, and some will score lower, notwithstanding the reported differences (Segal 1999).

Earlier research citing the intellectual disadvantages of twins was often based on analysis of twins when they were children. A study by Posthuma and colleagues analyzed twins as adults and compared them with their non-twin siblings. The findings showed no identifiable cognitive performance differences in the adults, particularly when twins were compared with their non-twin siblings (2000). Children from the same family generally score about the same.

In one study, triplets were found to be at higher risk for cognitive delays during their first two years. The report indicated that the greater incidence of prematurity of triplets places them at risk for developmental problems. A second factor that places triplets in a precarious position cognitively is the quality of mothering. Basically, it is more stressful to provide mothering to three infants. The implications of the research suggest it is important to establish policies to promote prenatal and postnatal maternal support (Feldman and Eidelman 2005).

PREFERENCES AND ENVIRONMENTAL INFLUENCES

Twins and supertwins usually share environments. This means their living conditions are the same, and they are likely to attend the same schools. Sharing environments does not always result in similar outcomes. After all, there will be some experiences the children do not share or have in common, and parental treatment can vary for each or some of the children in the multiple group. Each child's predisposition interacts with her environment, shared and nonshared, effectively resulting in varied outcomes (Asbury et al. 2003; Koeppen-Schomerus, Spinath, and Plomin 2003).

Studies have shown that MZ twins view the world in similar ways. They perceive and respond to people, places, and events more similarly than do DZ twins. This is expected because of the MZ twins' identical genetic makeup. Anecdotal data substantiates MZ twins' similarities: Adult twins living in different cities purchase identical beach towels, plan similar camping trips, mail identical holiday cards, and select the same restaurant entrée. Research has documented occurrences of twins marrying individuals who coincidentally have the same first name. In the preschool setting, an MZ twin pair both may prefer a red carpet square to sit on during group time. Monozygotic girls both may choose trike helmets with the same rainbow designs as a result of their genetic similarity, and MZ twins may select the rainbow because it's trendy and available. On the other hand, DZ girls or non-twin girls may also all select rainbow helmets, more likely based only on the availability and trendiness.

Environmental circumstances, including prenatal and birth circumstances, affect the development of multiples and their cognitive functioning. Studies have shown that twins and supertwins experience poorer neurological outcomes than do singleborn children. Babies with extremely low birth weights and who are small for their gestational age experience a higher rate of learning difficulty that increases with age. Research studies document that multiples experience more long-term health issues and poorer neurological outcomes than singleborn children (Sutcliffe and Derom 2006). Cognitive functioning and social behaviors may be negatively affected if a multiple has a developmental disability. Families with children whose behaviors are not typical benefit from support and guidance. This support is especially beneficial for parents of multiples to help them anticipate the pressures of rearing children the same age with differing needs and developmental abilities. Guidance offering specific information about individuality in performance is recommended. An understanding about individualized developmental time lines will also be helpful to families.

Researchers continue to explore intellectual development to determine how it correlates with family situations and heredity. Such findings inform educators. Your role is to effectively use the information in a practical manner to benefit the children. Here are six relevant points summarized from research findings about the intellectual functioning of twins and supertwins.

1. **Intellectual Functioning:** Twins and supertwins function intellectually as well as singleborn children (Posthuma et al. 2000). The influences of genetics, health, home setting and circumstances, and environmental opportunities affect the children's intellectual abilities. Interaction and involvement with family members also influence the outcome of assessment scores. It appears that home influences do not affect each child in the same way, even MZ twins. Although MZ twins have identical genetic makeup, they may not always perform in identical ways.

2. **MZ and DZ Twins:** Research studies consistently show that over time, MZ twins become similar intellectually, with greater IQ similarity (Segal 1985; Hayiou-Thomas, Oliver, and Plomin 2005; Resnick, Corley, and Robinson 1997). The cognitive capabilities of DZ twins do not necessarily become similar over time.

3. **Expected Catch-up:** When multiple-born children show delays during early childhood, they can be expected to catch up to the levels of cognitive development for all children. The multiples' cognitive development generally stabilizes by school age, and the children then follow a normal pattern of spurts and lags. Recent research downplays the differences between twins and supertwins and singleborn children that early studies about intellectual abilities identified (Garitte et al. 2002; Kovas et al. 2005; Luke et al. 1995). One longitudinal study has reported that by age sixteen, group differences in cognitive achievement no longer exist. Preterm twins were compared with full-term twins, and boys were compared with girls. This 2003 study indicates that the twin born at higher risk reaches the same level of functioning as the lower-risk co-twin (Alin Åkerman and Suurvee 2003).

4. **Verbal Differences:** Reportedly lower cognitive abilities and performance records for multiples than for singleborn children have been based primarily on verbal abilities. More recent reports

show no differences on the general measure of cognitive skills (Koeppen-Schomerus, Spinath, and Plomin 2003). However, twins scored lower on some abilities. Those measures may be related to the verbal performance that was assessed as the measure for testing intelligence. Reduced language opportunities during critical periods of language development may cause multiples to score lower than singleborn children on specific tests of intelligence. Early reporting of test results of cognitive difficulties helps parents and educators facilitate multiples' language acquisition. Early reporting may also help multiples avoid depressed functioning as they progress through school. Intervention and family support throughout development are recommended (Thorpe 2006; Dale et al. 2003).

5. **Vulnerability:** The prenatal environment and the birth experience may affect cognitive functioning (Lytton, Conway, and Sauvé 1977). More multiples are born prematurely, with low birth weight, and are therefore more vulnerable to impairments and developmental delays. Educators would benefit from more detailed and unbiased data related to twins' and supertwins' prenatal and perinatal development. Low birth weight has been an indicator associated with lower scores on some developmental abilities. Besides birth weight of the multiples and the sensitive responses from their mothers, social and economic factors will influence multiples' intellectual performance (Feldman and Eidelman 2005).

6. **Family Circumstances:** The close relationships twins and supertwins experience during the early childhood years synchronize their routines, celebrations, and family events. The first time they experience places and people and activities, they do so together. They probably check out their first library book together, hear a lion roar for the first time in the zoo together, and receive their first tricycles together. The timing and participation in the same events form similar patterns of reaction, response, and understanding. The same and similar experiences create a closer connection and closer awareness of each other's needs, behaviors, and preferences. Non-multiple siblings who are close in age share similar stories. The experiences of twins and supertwins may be extra intense, especially for MZ twins, who have identical biological heredity.

Extra Perception

The topic of twins and supertwins and their cognitive abilities brings forth questions regarding extrasensory perception (ESP). You may have inquired about the existence of ESP or looked for an explanation of the extraordinary powers that many believe exists between twins. Popular references to ESP include extra perception, extraordinary communication, telepathic relationship, mystic tie, mental link, and psychic power. Twins and supertwins do share extraordinary relationships. They have amazing connections. Their relationships establish unique modes of communication. All the same, science has not yet officially recognized ESP or telepathy among multiples.

When twins and supertwins reach adolescence and adulthood, they share memories about incidences of extraordinary communication with their twin or supertwin siblings. They recount occurrences in which they felt, sensed, or just knew what was occurring with their twin. Their stories describe the way in which they predicted each other's plans and how they anticipated each other's movements.

Language during Early Childhood

Language proficiency during early childhood builds capacities for learning. Long-term educational success is determined by language abilities during early childhood. Skills in communication, including oral language, listening, and early literacy awareness, help all children gain knowledge and construct understanding about other people and their surroundings. Differences in abilities among and between multiples and singleborn children can be observed as language acquisition progresses. Learning and language development undeniably overlap in experiences and ability outcomes. Accordingly, the way in which multiples acquire language may affect their cognitive skills and performances.

Milestones in Language

Language development is an amazing and rapid process. The language acquisition of multiples attracts the attention of researchers and educators because multiples acquire their communication skills under social conditions differing from those of singleborn children. Multiples develop language in a social situation that provides them opportunities to hear each other coo, squeal, and babble. Brian was startled by his own squeal before his twin, Whit, reacted to the noise. Brian squealed over and over. Whit began imitating Brian's squealing sound. It was clear that squealing, hearing each other's squeals, and repeating the sounds evolved into playful activity for them both.

Most infants, including twins and supertwins, move from squealing to babbling. They mix sounds to imitate what they hear. Unless a developmental or environmental condition negatively affects their development, multiples coo and babble just like other children. When children reach toddlerhood, they begin producing words to identify people and objects in their environment. "Rmmm" is a sound that labels the dump truck and "rfff" refers to grandmother's dog. Two-year-old toddlers combine words to communicate their needs. Each experience provides another opportunity to add words and extend knowledge. Remember that baby talk is normal for all children developing their language. Twins may develop a more complex version of baby talk (Malmstrom and Poland 1999). The children's steady flow of whys creates enormous opportunities for you to reward their curiosity. Learning moments contribute to thinking and extend language learning. Children answer questions, express their needs and feelings, and listen to other children, you, and music. They name objects observed through their senses, recall events, and repeat rhymes.

The communicative capacity of preschoolers, including multiples, varies. Some children use specific words, while others can use several sentences to communicate their needs. Preschoolers' language reveals both inquisitiveness and illogical thinking, particularly when they talk about abstract concepts like size and time. Even so, research studies have consistently noted that twins exhibit later language development than singleborn children (Tomasello, Mannle, and Kruger 1986; Thorpe 2006). A print-rich preschool environment encourages early literacy awareness for all preschoolers and will benefit multiples. Conversations with you and with other teaching staff members, as well as opportunities for listening, create the optimal situations for language development. Children become more capable communicators as they mature and participate in activities. As they mature, they can think about more than one aspect at a time, such as following routine directions to join other children while finding their name tag on their own cubbyhole. They can recreate an image they saw yesterday by telling you about the matching puzzle. They can dictate a story about a new family pet and watch you write each word. They can direct a friend other than their twin or super-twin sibling to return the magnifying glass to the precise position on the science table where the words *magnifying glass* are visibly labeled in manuscript. Each twin and supertwin shows individual signs of readiness for literacy experiences.

The preschool environment sets up new communication opportunities for multiples. Sharing time and sharing space are two basic realities for twins and supertwins. Their continuous interactions and time together produce an early awareness of someone other than their mother or father. Activities at school significantly expand experiences of time and space for multiples. They see, hear, and touch new objects and talk to teachers and new friends.

Acquiring Language Together

Many factors influence the language development of all children. These include genetics, health, and family circumstances. Language development of twins and supertwins is further influenced by their constant proximity to one another as well as to their group, which is a major socializing factor that influences their language acquisition. Group membership determines the quantity and quality of communication between the siblings and their parents. Constant proximity with siblings and constant group membership create differences in language learning.

Twins and supertwins who are healthy progress through typical developmental stages for language acquisition. As they mature through the stages, continuously interacting with one or more same-age sibling, the interaction defines their socialization and creates distinctive characteristics in their acquisition of language. They acquire skills while waiting, taking turns, and sharing parental time. They hear what their parents say to their twin or supertwin siblings and what their twin or supertwin siblings say to their parents. They communicate with non-multiple siblings, grandparents, and other adults, most often in the presence of their twin or supertwins.

SHARING PARENTAL TIME

Multiples experience proximity and closeness long before their birth. From birth on, twins primarily relate in a dyadic relationship with each other. The two relate in triadic routines with their parents or primary caregiver. Supertwins also experience dyadic and triadic relationships. The interaction depends on whether the group includes a twin pair or triplets composing a triadic relationship. The relationship and type of group interactions expand and change with the number of multiples and the availability of adults. What differs for a multiple is that one-to-one interaction with a parent, most often the mother, does not occur in the way it does for a singleborn child. A singleborn child will likely experience the dyadic relationship directly with his or her mother.

Parental interaction with multiples must be divided between or among two, three, four, or more same-age children. Dividing time may adversely affect language learning. The effect of continuously sharing parental time may account for some of the reported language development difficulties identified with multiples. The number of children in a family apparently affects singleborn children. In larger families, lower verbal intelligence has been consistently documented (Rutter et al. 2003). Twin language development has been reported to be quantitatively and qualitatively different from language acquisition in singleborn children. For example, the language of twins has been reported to be less mature. Because they spend so much time together, twins and supertwins model speech to one another and learn a great deal of their language through interactions with each other. Because the twin and supertwin siblings are in the same language-learning stage, they hear an abundance of immature communication (Thorpe 2006). Twins have also been found to reinforce one another's mistaken words and sounds (Tymms and Preedy 1998). Talking primarily to each other may inhibit multiple-born children's pronunciation and word usage (Thorpe, Rutter, and Greenwood 2003).

As they learn language, in addition to mimicking each other's words, multiples at times complete each other's sentences. Sharing time means they often talk at the same time while trying to communicate with one another and their parents. Singleborn children also routinely vie for parental time and attention. The competition for parents' attention is balanced by birth order of the children. Older children communicate more capably and may therefore direct more of the conversations. They may pause and give a younger child a chance to speak—or not do so. Without deference for age, multiples adapt their communication to the circumstances and their parents, with their same-age siblings most often present. The language development of twins and supertwins is therefore affected, because they must share parent time (Thorpe 2006). Not unlike parents of singleborn children, parents of multiples direct questions and directions to all the children at the same time. If a parent asks a set of triplets, "Do you want a cup of water?" before one or two or all three children respond, the parent may hand cups to all of them; the parent may not wait for an answer from one or more of the children, or the parent may receive an answer from only one of the triplets. Typically, the multiple-born child who persistently talks the most or asks more questions than her twin or supertwin sibling may be the one who receives the majority of direct conversation from the parent.

Irrespective of shared time, twins and supertwins have options during language exchanges unlike those of some singleborn children. Twins and supertwins can choose to respond to their parent's question or comment, or not respond, perhaps with less pressure than one singleborn child feels. The singleborn child has his parents' exclusive attention and most likely their direct eye contact during a conversation. A multiple-born child can wait to take a turn to speak, or not, because at least one other same-age sibling is present and able to respond to the parent.

LESS DIRECT COMMUNICATION

Adults fulfill a significant role in young children's language acquisition. Twins and supertwins share what is said to them by their parents and other adults. Multiples must also share the time that a parent allows for them to respond. The shared time affects their language development because a multiple may or may not receive a direct response from the parent. Parents of multiples are less likely to provide individually focused time for each child (Thorpe 2006). Parents may or may not respond directly to an individual child's expressive sounds, gestures, or comments.

Parents deliver fewer verbal interchanges to multiples, including directions, such as commands or suggestions. They may also provide fewer rules and justifications, and less praise and approval (Lytton, Conway, and Sauvé 1977). The reduced communication from parents to their multiples is understandable considering the demands on parents to respond to their children in the same stage of maturity. Parents of multiples most likely are unaware that their communication may differ from parents of singleborn children.

Parents of multiples adapt their interactions with their children to the group's needs. One study analyzed mothers of twins and mothers of singleborn children. Mothers of twins communicated with their children as much as mothers of non-twins. However, although the mothers of twins did not limit their verbal communication or interaction with the twins, they communicated less frequently with each child as an individual. The mothers of twins were also more directive in triadic, or three-way, mother-twin interactions (Tomasello, Mannle, and Kruger 1986).

The communication exchange for a singleborn child is in a dyadic relationship between one parent and one child. Parents' interactions become altered with the multiples, and the patterns may create a disadvantage for language development (Thorpe, Rutter, and Greenwood 2003).

The triadic language exchange changes the type of language experiences. Mothers of twin toddlers have been documented to be less responsive to their children's cues. They use fewer words to focus on each toddler and ask fewer questions. Mothering more than one toddler at the same time increases the complexity and demands of caregiving (Butler, McMahon, and Ungerer 2003). Less direct parental time in which to give and receive responses may result in the children producing less complex sentences and grammar. Parents of multiples have been reported to respond with shorter answers, engage in less dialog individually with each child, and omit pausing to modify the child's mispronunciations. The structure of the conversations is affected, including pragmatic aspects of the linguistic and nonlinguistic communication expected from the parent and the child (Tomasello, Mannle, and Kruger 1986).

While parents adapt their communication to the multiple group, the children also adapt their behaviors to the parents' cues. Multiples are required to quickly understand the message that the parent delivers to the group. Often multiples are required to understand the nonverbal communication from the parent and from their twin or supertwin siblings. Growing up together, multiple-birth children know each other well. Their familiarity with one another may explain their reliance on nonlinguistic communication with each other. They can and do interpret each other's immature words that are, with the majority of children, appropriately related to the culture and home (Thorpe 2006). The twin situation may in fact prolong the use of immature speech because the need for multiples to produce speech is reduced (Bishop and Bishop 1998). Shared understanding is not exclusive to multiples. Private language has been reported by parents of singleborn children, although less often (Thorpe 2006). As multiples adapt to the opportunities available in a group for learning language, they adjust their behaviors to win the attention of their parents. Interestingly, they acquire the use of the word *I* relatively quickly (Resnick, Corley, and Robinson 1997).

A GIRL AND A BOY

Language differences can be observed in opposite-sex twin pairs. Twin girls in opposite-sex groups have been shown to progress sooner in speaking skills, just as singleborn girls are more linguistically advanced than boys. Since boys generally have a greater risk for language delay, opposite-sex twin groups may be particularly advantageous for boys (Thorpe 2006). The interaction provides the boy twin with opportunities to progress within a language-rich environment. His sister may afford him a positive language tutoring relationship. The girl benefits from the opportunity to guide her brother's language learning, thereby reinforcing her own language skills and comprehension of the information shared (Garitte et al. 2002).

Vulnerability, Delay, and Improvement

Researchers have studied the language of twins by conducting individual and group studies. In the group studies, in which twins were compared with singleborn children, the findings often report twins acquire language later. The jargon, or immature speech, may appear to be a language of their own. It is not. Rather, it is the early form of communication that seems to persist with twins because they can relate to one another. Their familiarity allows mutual understanding, not a display of a different language (Thorpe 2006). Although the vulnerability tends to diminish as twins mature, the findings continue to cause concern for parents and professionals, according to speech and child development specialist Kay Mogford-Bevan of Newcastle University in Great Britain (1999).

Ella Day identified language delays in twins. Day's study shows that the learning of language progresses more slowly for twins than for singleborn children. However, twins are less egocentric in their responses and dramatic-imitation behaviors. Excelling in these behaviors may be the result of the interaction advantage available to twins (1932). Environmental contributions and conditions should not be discounted when consideration is given to studies in which twins have been participants. Those studies show a genetic influence on language development. If there is a language disorder, MZ twins are both more likely to have the disorder than a pair of DZ twins. It also appears that the same genes contribute to both language and cognitive problems and may affect normal and abnormal language development (Trouton,

Sinath, and Plomin 2002). The twins with the severest early language difficulties were not necessarily those whose language deficits continued (Dale et al. 2003).

Helen Koch (1966) pointed out that twins model inferior speech to one another. This explains the reported difficulties that some twins experience more than singleborn children in learning certain elements of speech such as articulation and basic syntax. René Zazzo suggested in 1960 that delays are apparent because of what he referred to as *the twin language* and because of the type of testing (Bishop and Bishop 1998). (Zazzo's discussion of twin language and other popularized terms are discussed in the next section.)

PRIVATE LANGUAGE

Famous case studies about the language acquisition of twins, such as the Kennedy twins, created an expectation that all twins communicate in a private or secret language. While differences between the language acquisition of multiples and singleborn children have been noted, do not expect twins to communicate in an exclusive manner.

You will hear several different terms in reference to the language of twins. *Autonomous* has been used to refer to communication only to one another; *idioglossia* to a private, invented language; and *cryptophasia,* a secret language understood only by the pair. Use and definitions are not consistent, even in the academic literature. Reports credit Zazzo with the term *cryptophasia,* which he used to refer to the communication between the pairs before they acquire communication skills similar to those of others in their environment. Zazzo suggested that twins' "secret language" causes a developmental delay in their language acquisition. His concept of a secret language exclusive to twins became a popular notion and often is used interchangeably with *private language, twin talk, idioglossia, autonomous speech,* and *twin language* to describe the early communication of twins (Mogford-Bevan 1999).

Researchers question the validity of the terms used to describe the language development of twins. As mentioned, there are inconsistencies in the definitions and lack of research conducted about twins during their early stages of language acquisition (Koch 1966). The so-called secret language is misleading because it implies an intention to obscure meaning of the communication, whereas twins who communicate using immature speech may understand one another. Their understanding is similar to siblings closely spaced in age who interpret immature speech for the parents (Mogford-Bevan 1999). This explanation cancels the notion that the twins are inventing a language and secretly communicating.

Actually, autonomous language is an incomplete form of communication. Autonomous language occurs among children in all families. It has been suggested that 40 percent of twins develop autonomous language because they model immature language to one another. Nonetheless, popular use of these concepts continues. Immature speech of twins, and especially twins who communicate with others outside their twin pair, does not equate to a private, secret, or idiosyncratic language (Mogford-Bevan 1999).

Private language between twins is not common. In fact, it is rare. It is not, however, unusual for some twins to use idiosyncratic words and communicative expressions at some point in their early developmental stages. Speaking to each other with special words may not be an issue as long as their special words and communicative expressions do not exclude their parents, other siblings, teachers, and playmates. A referral for a developmental speech assessment is warranted if multiples do not communicate with others.

When the question of private language was framed using the term *secret language,* parents indicated in a research questionnaire that their twins spoke a secret language. Parents reported a higher incidence for their twin sons. However, when studies collected data about the language of twins without introducing the term *secret language,* the data showed a reduced reporting of secret language by the parents. Parents have also reported a higher incidence of twin language for children who were actually identified as having speech-language impairments. Researchers have suggested that what was described as twin language was more likely to have been immature or deviant communication between multiples (Bishop and Bishop 1998). A higher correlation for twin language has also been reported among multiples who engage in nonverbal play beyond the typical period expected during toddlerhood (Hayashi et al. 2006).

EARLY CATCH-UP EXPECTED

Studies in the past fifteen years have substantiated some differences between linguistic abilities of twins and singleborn children (Deary et al. 2005). One study in particular reported that an early catch-up can be expected for twins with delays in early language milestones. Low language performance really means that twins may be late talkers. The findings showed that language performance was resolved by the time the twins were three to four years old. Although the study showed that a positive outcome can be expected for late talkers, some multiples continued to have persisting issues at age four (Dale et al. 2003; Kovas et al. 2005).

Because twinning has been associated with language delays, it is noteworthy to reiterate that delays in twins' language are generally resolved during preschool years and that the majority of twins progress naturally in language learning. Some conditions of language development may require specific referral to a specialist, but the outcome for multiples who have early language delay is good. Some late talkers may have problems that persist throughout the preschool years. Teachers are advised to address these delays rather than viewing them as normal and expected. Multiples, just like late-talking singleborn children, can show improvement, but this is not a reason to ignore persistent problems. Multiples deserve the same attention singleborn children receive for language assessment and intervention (Dale et al. 2003).

Many potential threats to language development can be remedied. Studies indicate that parents are generally unaware that limited interaction with them may negatively affect their multiples' language development (Thorpe, Rutter, and Greenwood 2003). Preschool attendance can contribute positively to the development of language for twins and supertwins (La Trobe Twin Study 1991). The parents of multiple-born children with older siblings and multiples who attend preschool programs are less likely to report that their children have developed a secret language.

Speech and language difficulties should not be an expected part of twin and supertwin development. You should, however, review atypical communication for possible assessment and remain attentive to differences in twin and supertwin speech that is outside the expected norm for language learning.

Referral for speech evaluation is standard if a child does not seem to be within the range of normal development. When you suspect a neurological or physical reason for delay or difference in communication, you should inform the parent and then, with approval, make a referral for assessment. If multiples exchange language in what might be considered a jargon, they may be at a greater risk for later language difficulties (Bishop and Bishop 1998). If twins or supertwins speak to each other in unintelligible phrases or wordlike expressions, you should recommend referral. Or, if their vocabulary is good and they understand what you are saying but their speech is poor, a speech impairment problem may be possible (La Trobe Twin Study 1991).

Speech of multiple-birth children that significantly varies from the norm may not be caused by a language delay but instead may be an early indication of a potential impairment (Bishop and Bishop 1998). At the preschool level, utterances of multiples should be more distinct than baby talk and comprehensible to adults. Multiples should be able to name objects, declare their needs, identify themselves, and respond verbally to a request. An inability to produce understandable words and sentences could place them at higher risk for future language difficulties. Most of the same language and literacy practices that support singleborn children will enhance communication skills of multiples. In a study that included quadruplets, teachers modeling core vocabulary with gestures and verbal responses increased the rates of word learning (McGregor and Capone 2004).

Applicable Research Highlighted

Six points clarify some of the conditions of language development in twins and supertwins.

1. The sequence of language development of multiples can be expected to proceed similarly to the language development of singleborn children.
2. The social circumstances of twins and supertwins influence their language development. They acquire language in the presence of same-age siblings.
3. Multiples develop their language while sharing parental time.
4. Twin or supertwin status does automatically correlate with delayed language development. Biological variables and environmental circumstances affect vulnerability to language deficit. For mild delays, catch-up in language delays is possible during the early childhood years.
5. The preschool experience is beneficial for the language learning of twins and supertwins.
6. Awareness of the language acquisition of twins and supertwins assists parents in enhancing their multiples' communication.

Opportunities for Communication and Early Literacy

Children naturally pose questions, explore materials, and discover new ideas when adults welcome their communicative efforts. This is an optimal strategy for children to master tasks and become ready to accomplish others, especially when they are engaged in rewarding, hands-on experiences. A major developmental task for children during the preschool years is to use and extend comprehensive language. In quality early childhood settings, you can help children by accepting their verbal expressions and establishing secure beginnings for their language development. Children develop valuable language skills when you invite them into meaningful conversations, offer early literacy materials, and reward their attentive listening. Twins and supertwins, in fact all children, have increased opportunities for interaction and verbal play while attending preschool programs.

Children learn language best when they have opportunities to directly communicate with adults. Because twins and supertwins potentially experience less direct communication with their parents, they benefit from participation in quality preschools (Hayashi et al. 2006). The best-suited preschools are staffed by adults who consistently and responsively interact with the children. Quality interaction provides time for teachers to engage young children in conversations that involve speaking, listening, and extending their language capabilities.

The direct, one-to-one conversations you have with each twin and supertwin are especially beneficial in promoting their individual language development. Multiples acquire language skills while sharing parental time with their multiple siblings. Their experiences at preschool, both spontaneous and planned time engaging directly with you, offer multiples opportunities to ask questions of their own and to respond to comments you direct exclusively to them.

You have opportunities in the preschool setting to enhance language learning while contributing to the children's social and emotional development. Planned and spontaneous opportunities can be offered without imposing scripted learning. Teachers in quality preschools already incorporate many of the following experiences into their daily routine. These opportunities for direct communication with teachers are advantageous for twins and supertwins while their language progresses during preschool attendance.

- Listen to each multiple as an individual child.
- Engage each multiple in one-to-one conversations. Establish intentional experiences for each child to listen and to talk.
- Use complete sentences when communicating directly with each multiple. Model speech using examples relevant to the child and the family.
- Respond directly to the twin or supertwin who asks the question. Then ask each of the other multiples for questions or comments. Encourage each child to express ideas.
- Encourage language from the twin or supertwin who generally relies on other co-multiples to ask and answer questions.
- Ask questions and state comments that engage and motivate each multiple and the multiples. "Josephine, the magnifying glass is ready for you on the science table. Do you think you will be able to find the seeds in the pinecone with the help of the magnifying glass?" "Roxanna, you seem interested in the emergency helper costumes. Which would you like to try?" Avoid asking questions that elicit yes and no answers. "Ammee, your jacket looks new. Who gave you your jacket? When did you receive it?" "Naomi, I see you have a new jacket on. Tell me, when did you receive your jacket?"
- Accept the language that the child provides. Expand comments from each child or from three or four in the multiple group with extended statements—for example, extend the sentence and add vocabulary. When Gabriel says, "Ya, okay," you can nod and say, "I understand, Gabriel, that you would like to read the new book about trucks. Tell me if that is what you want."
- Use the guidance strategies that are appropriate for young children, directing communication to each multiple individually rather than to all multiples at the same time. When Ammee interrupts your conversation with Naomi, you might say, "Ammee, right now it is Naomi's turn. She and I are talking. You can ask me a question as soon as Naomi is finished."
- Share research information with parents about the influence of the family environment on language learning. Suggest positive communicative behaviors for parents to model to their multiples, such as speaking directly to each child and providing ample descriptions and explanations during their language exchanges with each child.

The twin or supertwin situation affects language development, but it is not predictive of long-term linguistic delay. Language development closely aligns with cognitive development. Because language proficiency predicts learning and educational success, intentional focus on the particular needs of twins and supertwins can have a positive impact on their communicative processes and learning outcomes. In the following part, you will be introduced to the unique needs of multiples and the practices that best accommodate them in the early childhood setting.

Needs and Practices

PART THREE

The Unique Needs of Twins and Supertwins

At the same time you are welcoming more twins and supertwins into your programs, greater support is available for prekindergarten and universal preschool. Preschool attendance is an important milestone for young children. Attendance is especially valuable for twins and supertwins because they have unique needs related to their identity as multiples.

The increasing enrollment of multiples has prompted teachers to seek information about them. You want to know about their development, what fosters an appropriate school experience for them, and how to answer questions from parents. The enrollment of multiples is expected to continue increasing in the next few years, as the following projected enrollment table shows. Your familiarity with the unique needs of twins and supertwins is especially imperative to ensure the optimal development of multiples during early childhood.

Projected Enrollment 2010–2014*		
Early Childhood Programs (Nursery School, Preschool, and Kindergarten) Three- to Five-Year-Old Twins, Triplets, and Higher-Order Multiples**		
Year	Twins	Triplets and Higher-Order Multiples
2010	238,217	11,372
2011	244,541	11,091
2012	250,654	10,807
2013	256,920	10,530
2014	263,343	10,261

*Projections by the author are based on data applying a factor of 58 percent enrollment of all three- to five-year-olds in the United States, Annie E. Casey Foundation Kids Count Data Center. Accessed March 3, 2009, at www.kidscount.org.

Average percentage change in twin births and triplets and higher-order births for years 2002 through 2006 as presented in National Vital Statistics Reference Data (Martin et al. 2009). Births: Final data for 2006. National vital statistics reports 57 (7). Hyattsville, Md.: National Center for Health Statistics.

**The projected enrollment is individual twins and supertwins.

Identifying Unique Needs

Twins and supertwins have unique needs related to their status as multiples. In this chapter, a list of needs particular to multiples is provided and thoroughly discussed. The applicable knowledge offers you information about the needs of multiples to help you guide twins and supertwins during their early childhood years.

Unique Needs Relate to Multiple Status

The especially close relationships between most twins and supertwins are the consequence of their maturing together. Their camaraderie and team dynamic form early and influence the relationships they have with their parents, siblings, extended family, and acquaintances. Consequently, their close relationships and their status as multiples further shape the unique aspects of their development.

Treating twins as special and unique has been challenged by some educators. They believe multiples are just like other preschoolers and expect twins and supertwins to develop according to anticipated norms. Teachers of young children predictably contend that every child is unique. They insist that all children are special and that each child is individual. Undeniably, these attitudes are accurate. Every child is unique. Each has his or her own individuality.

True as this may be, a distinction nonetheless exists between single-born children and multiples. Twins and supertwins have their own unique individuality *and* needs that are exclusive to their status as multiples.

Most people's perception of self is based on their sense of being a single person. The majority of people, approximately 97 percent, are singleborn individuals. Because social and cultural expectations have been established from the perspective of the singleborn individual, educational core principles are based on the singleborn's knowledge and needs. The foundations for early childhood education are commonly oriented toward one child, from one family, enrolled in school without a same-age sibling.

Teachers Ask Questions

As a consequence of the increasing enrollment of twins and supertwins, teachers now pose questions and comments that reflect insightful understanding about the possible differences between multiples and single-born children.

"We have six sets of twins in our program now. What should we do differently?"

"Are there special approaches for triplets? I have not had three children from the same family in my classroom before."

Teachers also submit questions during workshops that mirror their assumptions about the development and behavior of twins and supertwins. For instance, one teacher asked,

"Isn't it true that one twin is always dominant over the other?"

The unique needs of twins and supertwins during the preschool years need to be identified so that teachers' questions may be answered. Researchers and academics have documented the distinguishing characteristics of multiples and their relationships, but their findings have not been integrated into early childhood education doctrine, references, and textbooks. Some of the research findings appear in books for families about multiples, but most of the parenting books cover just the early physical development of multiples, particularly the prenatal period and the first few years of infancy and toddlerhood. That material has not been transmitted to early education professionals.

Multiples Merit Acknowledgment

Informed professionals offer meaningful experiences for multiples, and twins and supertwins merit early childhood programs that acknowledge their unique needs. The background, perceptions, and research findings about the development of multiples in the first two parts of this book provide you with the characteristics that distinguish multiples. In this third part, you will learn specific methods that will help you incorporate this information into your practices. To ensure favorable outcomes, you will afford each twin and each supertwin attention as an individual and provide each with attention as a member of an extraordinary group.

The majority of multiples are twins. Nearly all of the research about multiples has specifically studied the twin relationship. The questions teachers ask about the development of triplets are no less important than those about twins. In the absence of definitive data about triplets and other supertwins, I have used findings about twins to identify the unique needs of all multiples. Throughout this chapter and in chapter 7, I qualify the application of twin-specific information to ensure recognition of the special qualities and behaviors particular to supertwins. For example, caution has been taken to refer to twins when research findings are specific to them only. As more supertwins attend preschool, observations made by early childhood professionals will document their behaviors and interactions, and these observations will add experiential knowledge and establish insight into their development.

A List of Needs Unique to Multiples

The Unique Needs of Preschool Twins (UNPT) that follows is a resource developed to offer clarity about multiples during early childhood without intent to discount the needs of other children enrolled in early childhood programs. The developmental and behavioral needs of singleborn children are well documented in early childhood education textbooks, program policies, and guidelines developed for teachers and preschools. The references to the needs of twins that the UNPT sets forth intentionally emphasize multiples even though some are also applicable to singleborn children. My aim is to increase awareness and sensitivity of teachers to the special circumstances that define twinship and supertwinship.

Teachers who acquire more information about multiples will be ready to extend the program activities and experiences to meet the specific needs of multiples. Unique Needs of Preschool Twins expands the information provided in the previous chapters and condenses it into a practical reference for teachers.

RELEVANCY FOR ALL PRESCHOOLERS

Several items listed in the UNPT are relevant to all preschoolers. For example, the third need, "recognition and encouragement of individuality," is important for every young child. The item is included on the list of unique needs for twins and supertwins to encourage the treatment of multiples as separate, individual children. You recognize the importance of individuality because you have been professionally prepared to regard each child as special. Anticipate some families being unaware of the importance of individuality. It is likely that you will encounter a parent saying, "The twins are so alike; they're just one person and two bodies."

Another need relevant to all preschoolers is "independence as the child is ready." The significance of this need for twins and supertwins concerns their interaction and interpersonal activities. Twins and supertwins are accustomed to being together, and that togetherness creates security. When children are secure, they develop skills for independent behavior. Yet too often their close relationship is viewed as a threat to independent actions. The need "independence as the child is ready" prompts you to honor each child's individuality and relationship to her co-multiples, especially when you think about her in the context of the developmental stages.

INTENTIONALLY ACKNOWLEDGING NEEDS

Teachers can begin by intentionally acknowledging that multiples have unique needs. The UNPT establishes a reference guide for teachers to use for policy development, family education, classroom interaction, and curriculum development. The needs are divided into three defining categories. The first category, communicational, includes needs related to preschool teachers' acknowledgment and recognition of twinship. The second category, programmatic, relates to the preschool enrollment and operational plans for twinship and supertwinship. The third category, relational, includes concepts about the interaction and interpersonal activities of twins and supertwins during their preschool experiences.

The twenty-two needs on the UNPT list are not prioritized. The twenty-second need may be as important for a particular multiple as the first need is for another. Refer to the list and use any or all of the needs related to the development of the multiple children enrolled in your preschool. The information provided in the UNPT is intended to enhance your knowledge about multiples so that you can effectively and positively influence their development.

A Resource for Teachers

The UNPT provides clarity about multiples. Three concepts summarize the UNPT:

- Acknowledge individual and collective needs.
- Recognize special and situational needs by offering flexible school placement policies and being responsive to the parents.
- Encourage opportunities for interaction among multiples while supporting their developing independence and special interpersonal relations.

This resource can effectively enhance inclusiveness at your school by addressing the particular needs of multiples.

Unique Needs of Preschool Twins (UNPT)

The needs in this list are not prioritized in any order of importance, value, or benefit. They are categorized and numbered for practical referencing. The terms *acknowledge*, *recognize*, and *respect* are used interchangeably to introduce concepts focusing directly on the multiples and their participation in early childhood programs.

Communicational
Communicational refers to the preschool teacher's acknowledgment and recognition of twinship. Each twin enrolled in a preschool program has a unique need for the following:

1. Acknowledgment and encouragement both as an individual and as a twin.
2. Recognition of individual and collective needs.
3. Recognition and encouragement of individuality.
4. Recognition and understanding of twin type.
5. Recognition and encouragement of the child's differences without emphasis.
6. Recognition of potential for developmental delay without exaggeration.
7. Recognition of gender differences in maturational stages of a boy-girl twin pair.
8. Attention to the child's unique medical history, home life, and interaction with children outside the twin relationship.

Programmatic
Programmatic refers to the preschool's enrollment and operational plans regarding twinship. Each twin enrolled in a preschool program has a unique need for the following:

9. Policies and practices recognizing twins as a special group with unique family circumstances.
10. Flexible school and placement policies accommodating the twins' situational needs.

11. Principals and teachers receptive to acquiring current twin research and information.
12. Added consideration in preschool admission.
13. Parent conferences and placement procedures sensitive and responsive to twinship.
14. Reevaluation of school practices, such as mandates for classroom separation.
15. Periodic (no less frequent than annually) consultation to review group and room placement.
16. Description of performance and progress related to the child's peer group.

Relational

Relational refers to twin-specific interactions and interpersonal activities. Each twin enrolled in a preschool program has a unique need for the following:

17. Freedom from comparison with the child's co-twin.
18. Encouragement to make individual friends as the child matures.
19. Independence as the child is ready.
20. Opportunities for individual participation in activities.
21. Opportunities for self-responsibility adjusted to each co-twin's level of maturity.
22. Remaining together as long as the twins want or seem to benefit.

The UNPT is ready for you to use in your program because the basis of the list conforms to early childhood foundational practices. To best use the information provided in the list, take these steps. First, review your existing school philosophy, guidelines, and policies, and align actions and plans for multiples with the school's operational and curriculum framework.

Second, apply fundamental theories and principles of child growth and development. The UNPT integrates those basic principles. You will recognize basic premises that apply to all children and special variations that are particular to multiples. For example, great variations in the physical development of young children are observable. A time line for achieving certain milestones presents extensive variations; similarly, variations in physical development exist between and among multiples. This applies to monozygotic (MZ) twins as well. They are genetically alike, but they are not perfect copies.

Finally, use the content of the UNPT to support principles of early childhood education. Quality principles balance curricula with age-appropriate and child-centered activities. Play and discovery are hallmarks of child- and teacher-directed activities. The experiences that promote their emotional development will also encourage twins and supertwins to achieve social skills. In quality programs, children, including multiples, will experience safe, healthy settings in which imagination is a reliable link to learning and reasoning. The theories and principles will be particularly valuable when new situations involving twins and supertwins surface.

The UNPT offers an auxiliary reference for you. You are most effective as educators when you depend on the prevailing good educational practices for young children. Good practices encapsulate the values that will guide your decision making, methods of teaching, and strategies of interaction with multiples and their families. You become even more effective when you use additional information, such as the UNPT, to gather specialized knowledge about multiples.

After your systematic review of guidelines, principles of child development, and the tenets of early childhood education, the UNPT can be distributed in family newsletters, handed out during staff in-service sessions and meetings, utilized as promotional material for your school, and posted visibly on a bulletin board.

Three Goals for Twenty-two Needs

The goals of the UNPT are threefold:

- Increase professional awareness of the unique needs of twins.
- Promote sensitive and practical use of the list of unique needs.
- Benefit the twins enrolled in the preschool program.

Acknowledging and Recognizing Communicational Needs

The communicational category of unique needs calls for acknowledging the individual and collective needs of twins. The eight communicational needs acknowledge twinship and encourage teachers to appreciate the differences and similarities of multiple-birth children. The needs encourage you to nurture the growth and development of multiples by acknowledging their social circumstances and integrating their needs into practices that will benefit them.

In the first category you will be given tips regarding the communicational needs of multiples, as for example, recognizing their maturational stages in opposite-sex twin pairs. The statements of need alert you to certain characteristics related to multiples. For instance, recognizing maturational stages in opposite-sex pairs will help you facilitate their experiences as individual preschoolers and as members of a twin pair. You will be reminded to remain alert for potential special needs; to give special attention to the unique circumstances of multiples; and to give careful attention to each child's medical history, family circumstances, and interactions outside the twin relationship.

The social situation of multiples makes observations of family and sibling relationships more complex. For example, Emma, a twin, has an older sister, Corinne, a singleborn child. Emma has another sister, Kayla. Kayla is Emma's twin sister. The concept of "sister" to a twin can have more than one meaning. Teachers can acknowledge the unique social circumstances of multiples and introduce practices that will benefit the communicational needs of multiples.

You will find that the eight communicational needs promote acknowledgment and recognition of the specific needs of twins. Use discretion when applying concepts to supertwins; information and evidence-based research about them is limited. Data about them has been inconsistent, as noted in chapter 1 and this chapter.

I. ACKNOWLEDGMENT AND ENCOURAGEMENT BOTH AS AN INDIVIDUAL AND AS A TWIN.

The first item, "acknowledgment and encouragement both as an individual and as a twin," indicates that every child who is a twin has a need to be acknowledged by teachers as an individual preschool-age child. Treating children as individuals is a common and acceptable teaching strategy. Enhance this strategy by also acknowledging each twin as a member of a twin group. Fulfilling the intent of the need, you will also encourage staff to acknowledge twins as both individuals and multiples.

2.   RECOGNITION OF INDIVIDUAL AND COLLECTIVE NEEDS.

The second need in the communicational category suggests that for multiples, the "recognition of individual and collective needs" is valuable. A twin has needs as an individual preschool-age child as well as ones related to his membership in a group, either a twin group or supertwin group. Multiples have collective needs. Emma likes that she can participate in Teacher Jim's classroom by herself in the afternoon, and she also likes to participate in the morning in Teacher Elena's class, because then she has time to play with her twin sister, Kayla.

3.   RECOGNITION AND ENCOURAGEMENT OF INDIVIDUALITY.

The third need emphasizes the importance of recognizing and encouraging the special characteristics of each child. "Recognition and encouragement of individuality" means that the professional teaching staff purposefully accepts and supports multiple-born children as individuals. Their individuality can be encouraged in ways similar to the support given singleborn children to guide their sense of identity. For instance, Teacher Ginger notices that Mara arrives with a paper bag. She also notices that Mara's twin sister, Celia, arrives without a paper bag. Teacher Ginger is particularly pleased, because she and the girls' parents have discussed ways to encourage each girl's individuality. One idea suggested by Teacher Ginger was to rotate the days that the girls brought special items to share so that the focus could be on one girl at a time. To honor the girls' need to share and enjoy their twinship, Teacher Ginger then suggested to the parents that both girls also bring special items to share on Fridays.

4.   RECOGNITION AND UNDERSTANDING OF TWIN TYPE.

"Recognition and understanding of twin type" says that teachers as well as twins will benefit from recognition and understanding of the children's twin type, or zygosity. Knowing that twin pairs are dizygotic may assist you in understanding their preferences. Monozygotic twins have more similar, but not exact, preferences than dizygotic (DZ) twins. Understand the zygosity of the multiples enrolled in your classrooms without burdening your impressions by fixed expectations for certain behaviors from them. Knowing twin type may explain their interests, behaviors, and development, but it does not predict formulaic behavior. Rather, it provides another clue to understanding the development and relationship of multiples.

5. RECOGNITION AND ENCOURAGEMENT OF THE CHILD'S
    DIFFERENCES WITHOUT EMPHASIS.

Teachers meet children's needs in numerous ways. You can contribute
to the well-being of multiples by meeting their needs for "recognition
and encouragement of the child's differences without emphasis"—the
fifth communicational need. You can distinguish differences between
children without overemphasis. Twins Hayden and Avery are opposite-
sex twins who sometimes wear the same T-shirts but who are still easily
distinguished by the teachers. "Hayden, you have a red shirt with stripes
on today." A teacher's recognition of Hayden and of Avery remains as
important as distinguishing alike-looking twins and singleborn children. There will be times when attention to the T-shirts on twins may
be advantageous, particularly immediately following the enrollment of
twins, such as MZ twins Miles and Mathew. "Miles, I like your blue-
striped shirt." Turning to Mathew, the teacher says, "And Mathew, I
like your green-striped shirt." Recognition and identification can be
provided without comparing Miles with Mathew or Mathew with
Miles. The teacher then glances at the parent, who is writing the time in
the attendance sign-in log, for an approving nod because the boys have
been correctly identified. Parents of twins and supertwins are accustomed to others asking for help in correctly identifying their children's
names. Most parents appreciate well-intended efforts to identify their
children, especially during the early days of school attendance. You,
in turn, appreciate parents who dress their same-sex MZ twins and
closely similar DZ twins in different-colored clothing, especially for the
first few weeks of preschool attendance.

6. RECOGNITION OF POTENTIAL FOR DEVELOPMENTAL DELAY
    WITHOUT EXAGGERATION.

"Recognition of potential for developmental delay without exaggeration"
is the sixth communicational need. Twins as a group of children may be
vulnerable to delays because of their higher incidence of early births and
continuous association as a member of a multiple group. Remain alert to
the children's needs without exaggerating negative expectations. Children born before thirty-one weeks may have received early screening and
intervention services prior to enrollment in preschool. It is also possible
you may be the family's first contact with professional staff in a position
to identify a need for referral.

7. RECOGNITION OF GENDER DIFFERENCES IN MATURATIONAL STAGES OF A BOY-GIRL TWIN PAIR.

As the seventh communicational need, "recognition of gender differences in maturational stages of a boy-girl twin pair" encourages you to acknowledge the characteristics of opposite-sex twins that may create different experiences for them. Girl-and-boy twin pairs are more than just siblings born on the same day. Twins Charlotte and Nate have experienced events together. They have been one another's constant companions. Their parents may have heard inquiries from others asking whether the siblings are twins. Opposite-sex twin pairs may be different in size and may vary in some developmental abilities and skills. The girl generally matures sooner and therefore achieves certain milestones earlier than her twin brother. Child-oriented preschool program settings will accommodate the developmental differences in some boy-girl twin pairs.

8. ATTENTION TO THE CHILD'S UNIQUE MEDICAL HISTORY, HOME LIFE, AND INTERACTION WITH CHILDREN OUTSIDE THE TWIN RELATIONSHIP.

Last, each child in a twin pair needs "attention to the child's unique medical history, home life, and interaction with children outside the twin relationship." Intake interviews for preschool programs establish the preliminary background data about the children that is valuable to teachers. The interviews are most informative for you if parents are asked additional questions about the prenatal development, births, and early experiences of the multiples enrolled. Understanding their interactions with other children further explains their relationship and provides insight into the children's readiness for the preschool program as well as the period necessary for their adjustment.

Programmatic Needs Related to Enrollment and Operational Plans

The programmatic category includes the needs related to preschool enrollment and operational plans related to twinship. Teachers and program administrators meet the programmatic needs of twins and supertwins by implementing flexible school and placement policies. Twins and supertwins also benefit from their teachers and administrators remaining current on research about multiples. Program staff members are encouraged to be responsive to families about conferencing and placement procedures.

Program administrators face challenges when parents of multiples request enrollment for their children, particularly in relation to placement and scheduling needs. These challenges escalate with families of triplets, quadruplets, or more. The needs within the programmatic category of the UNPT are descriptive of administrative and managerial actions. Program administrators and teachers in preschools support the unique needs of multiples during their preschool experience by considering those that can be best implemented in their programs.

9. POLICIES AND PRACTICES RECOGNIZING TWINS AS A SPECIAL GROUP WITH UNIQUE FAMILY CIRCUMSTANCES.

The need "policies and practices recognizing twins as a special group with unique family circumstances" suggests that policies and practices meet the needs of twins and supertwins by being flexible and including accommodations for the multiple-born children and their families.

10. FLEXIBLE SCHOOL AND PLACEMENT POLICIES ACCOMMODATING THE TWINS' SITUATIONAL NEEDS.

The need "flexible school and placement policies accommodating the twins' situational needs" is important because families with twins and supertwins face challenges when seeking child care and preschool experiences for their children. The more children in one family who need accommodations, the more difficult it is to secure requested placement in a preschool—particularly because families generally need and request the same attendance time for their multiples.

11. PRINCIPALS AND TEACHERS RECEPTIVE TO ACQUIRING CURRENT TWIN RESEARCH AND INFORMATION.

Twins have a need for "principals and teachers receptive to acquiring current twin research and information." Current information includes research study findings that directly focus on multiples, their development, their relationships, and their behaviors. Increasingly, research focuses on them. Investigation of their development and behavior will directly benefit multiples, their families, and systems that support their growth and learning. In addition, as the number of supertwins entering early childhood programs increases, research findings may identify needs specific to their development and education.

12. ADDED CONSIDERATION IN PRESCHOOL ADMISSION.

"Added consideration in preschool admission" suggests that more atten-tion to the challenges facing families with multiples is needed. Chal-lenges increase for them in communities with limited child care and preschool options, and the options for families with multiple children further diminish if the available programs are age-organized rather than offered in groups with cross-age placement. A preschool with a multiage classroom, such as three- to five-year-olds, may be more accommodating for the family of quadruplets than a program requiring all three-year-olds to be placed in one classroom or group. Another worry for families of multiples is paying the fees and tuition for the preschool enrollment of more than one child at a time.

13. PARENT CONFERENCES AND PLACEMENT PROCEDURES SENSITIVE AND RESPONSIVE TO TWINSHIP.

14. REEVALUATION OF SCHOOL PRACTICES, SUCH AS MANDATES FOR CLASSROOM SEPARATION.

15. PERIODIC (NO LESS FREQUENT THAN ANNUALLY) CONSULTATION TO REVIEW GROUP AND ROOM PLACEMENT.

These three needs concern preschool program operating procedures. Multiples have unique needs for "parent conferences and placement pro-cedures sensitive and responsive to twinship," "reevaluation of school practices, such as mandates for classroom separation," and "periodic (no less frequent than annually) consultation to review group and room placement." You and other staff members best meet the needs of mul-tiples by recognizing that their families face extraordinary challenges in managing the schedules of multiple children. Teachers have frequently asked questions about the classroom placement of multiples, particularly about separation. Parents have strong opinions about placement. Either they believe that their children should be in the same group, or they believe that they should be in separate classrooms. Debates about place-ment have led teachers to inquire about the practices that would best meet the children's needs. This topic is specifically covered in chapter 7.

16. DESCRIPTION OF PERFORMANCE AND PROGRESS RELATED TO THE CHILD'S PEER GROUP.

The last programmatic need is "description of performance and progress related to the child's peer group." Children, including children in twin pairs and supertwin groups, vary in their development. When you assess their development, you gain insight into their particular needs. This can be most effectively accomplished by reviewing their development in relation to that of other children in the preschool or to the normal and expected behavior of children in their age range rather than to their twin or supertwins. Using expected developmental norms as reference points of developmental milestones respects the needs of the individual multiples and avoids unnecessary comparisons between twins and among supertwins. It delivers a broader, more descriptive view of a twin's or supertwin's development so progress can be identified.

Relational Needs Relating to Interaction and Interpersonal Activities

The relational category of needs refers to interaction and interpersonal activities. Interaction and interpersonal activities define relationships for multiples during their early childhood years. As developmental readiness allows, preschoolers progress toward independent behaviors, but these independent behaviors do not negate the close relationship that describes most multiple children's status during early childhood. When they are ready, encourage them to make individual friends, enjoy opportunities for individual activity participation, and achieve self-responsibility adjusted to their own maturity. Also allow them opportunities to remain together as long as they want to or seem to benefit from doing so.

The relational category of needs places emphasis on actions and behaviors familiar to you. Early childhood educators are accustomed to encouraging children's play with others and providing opportunities for individual activity. You can provide guidance for these actions and behaviors in ways that facilitate preschoolers' positive development. You can modify acceptable preschool practices to meet the specific needs of the multiples while acknowledging their individuality and their membership in a group. The relational area of unique needs outlines interactions among the multiples in a group and the activities and experiences that they may share, as well as their separate needs.

17. FREEDOM FROM COMPARISON WITH THE CHILD'S CO-TWIN.

Twins and supertwins have the right and, at times, the need to be free from comparison with one another. Preschoolers become increasingly aware of others and of the comments and opinions others may have about them. Multiples have been exposed to more uninvited comparison than singleborn children and may be more sensitized to comments than singleborn children. The comparisons of multiples are especially exaggerated because twins and supertwins almost always share the same space, creating a constant point of reference to one another. Preschool teachers in principle prohibit comparisons of children, aware of the potential harm of evaluation and judgment. Because the frequency of comparison may be more prevalent for multiples, teachers' awareness of this issue is important.

Children's readiness to associate with other children actively in play is linked to their individual development and experience with relationships. The progress of friendship among young children is dependent on their readiness and the program's opportunities to engage actively with other children. Twins and supertwins may have had previous opportunity to interact with other children, but that experience may have been limited to their co-twins or co-supertwins. (Friendship among young children will be discussed in more detail in chapter 7, Focused Issue: Friendship.)

18. ENCOURAGEMENT TO MAKE INDIVIDUAL FRIENDS AS THE CHILD MATURES.

Multiples mature at different rates and approach interactions with others having already experienced a close relationship with their twin or supertwin siblings. You have opportunities to observe the maturing of the multiples that provide you with insight into their readiness for developing friendships with others.

19. INDEPENDENCE AS THE CHILD IS READY.

20. OPPORTUNITIES FOR INDIVIDUAL PARTICIPATION IN ACTIVITIES.

"Independence as the child is ready" and "opportunities for individual participation in activities" offer specific guidelines for ensuring that the needs of twins are met. You can encourage independence by inviting a twin or supertwin into separate activities as he or she shows individual readiness. Another way to support a growing independence is to organize small-group times in different areas of the classroom. Inviting children (this includes singleborn children) into small groups establishes a way to provide space for two children who have difficulty sitting and listening to a story in the same area at the same time. For example, inviting Charlotte into one group area and Nate into another area may offer each of them opportunities to enhance their growing sense of independence. Multiples who remain in close proximity while experiencing a solo activity, such as listening to a brief story, continue to mature individually and independently.

21. OPPORTUNITIES FOR SELF-RESPONSIBILITY ADJUSTED TO EACH CO-TWIN'S LEVEL OF MATURITY.

22. REMAINING TOGETHER AS LONG AS THE TWINS WANT OR SEEM TO BENEFIT.

The last two relational needs are "opportunities for self-responsibility adjusted to each co-twin's level of maturity" and "remaining together as long as the twins want or seem to benefit." One suggests that self-responsibility is related to a level of maturity, and the other, that teachers and program administrators allow children to remain together in groups and in classrooms for as long as they need to be together and seem to benefit from doing so. You can assess each multiple to determine her maturity and readiness to take additional steps. (Because views concerning readiness are subjective, additional information about remaining together and apart will be addressed in chapter 7's Focused Issue: Together and Apart.) Research has not proven that rushing children toward maturity is beneficial. Mandated policies for separating twins and supertwins in group placement during the early childhood school years do not necessarily or automatically benefit them.

A Resource to Inform Parents

The Unique Needs of Preschool Twins is a resource that can be shared with parents of multiple-birth children. Some parents of twins and supertwins have parented children previously. Some have read parenting books about giving birth to and rearing multiples. Even so, specific information about the needs of multiples can clarify questions and assumptions about multiples' development and education and equip parents to better advocate for their children.

Because people remain curious about and fascinated by multiples, parents of twins and supertwins find it helpful to be prepared with considerable applicable knowledge about their children. Parents who are prepared can respond to most questions, even one from a four-year-old who asks, "Why are there two cakes?"

"Why are there two cakes?" A four-year-old attending a birthday party did ask a mother of twins this question. The celebration, complete with Curious George decorations and favors, was to honor the first birthday of MZ twin brothers. One four-layer cake with white frosting was placed on the decorated table. As parents hovered behind the table and chairs of the ten children who gathered for the party, the boys' aunt placed another cake, a chocolate one, in front of them. "Why are there two cakes?" the four-year-old asked a second time. The mother of the twins responded, "Well, there are two cakes because both boys are having their birthdays today, on the same day, because they were born on the same day. They celebrate their birthdays together, on the same day, because they are twins."

Expectations, even about birthday parties, are based on what parents and teachers perceive as regular, familiar, and normal. The four-year-old attending the birthday party was perplexed by the appearance of two birthday cakes. He expected just one cake to be placed in front of one child who was celebrating a birthday. The mother of the birthday boys capably answered the preschooler's questions. After all, she was accustomed to inquiries, stares, and questions: she herself was a twin. The majority of parents of twins and supertwins are not twins themselves and do not have background knowledge and experience that prepare them to explain twinning.

Most parents of multiples need precise answers and detailed insight into the development and behaviors of multiples during the early childhood years. Parenting books primarily concentrate on prenatal development and growth during infancy. Parents depend on, and usually welcome, the knowledge of the professional staff and their abilities to provide references and guidance.

Teachers agree that families need information. They want to know how to help parents and how to respond. Some teachers comment, "Parents ask questions, and none of us really knows anything about twins. We're trying to figure out what to do." On an introductory level, teachers ask for information about development first. Second, they request information identifying the experiences that best nurture the positive growth of the increasing population of multiples in early childhood settings. The UNPT offers a foundation for providing information to the parents of multiples. As the basic foundational questions are addressed, more specific and specialized questions about twins and supertwins will surface. The topics of competition and comparison take on different meanings when two or more children from the same family participate in the same preschool group. Gender differences require a more elaborate description when the needs of multiples are considered. As one parent commented, "Mixed-gender birthday parties can take on a totally different spin."

Supporting Families with Education

Early childhood education programs that promote best practices for young children integrate supportive actions for family education. The partnership between home and school begins with respect for the continuity between children's family and school. When schools support family education, they build partnerships with families. The family is acknowledged as the child's first teacher.

Family education does not just happen. It unfolds in response to the mission and goals of early childhood programs. Your actions help determine how families are welcomed and supported. The direct value for the children begins with their ease of adjustment to the preschool setting. Children adjust more quickly when their parents are present and involved in their preschool activities. The preschool years usually offer ideal opportunities for family education and experiences. These can be especially important for distributing information to parents of multiples that is specific to their children and their children's education, and that is unavailable in parenting books.

Benefits of Family Education for Parents of Multiples

Fosters respectful views about multiple children and their families.

Links families to community resources.

Supports families to become advocates for their multiple-birth children.

Encourages networking with other parents of multiples.

Creates opportunities for input on school guidelines.

Establishes inclusion of the needs of multiples in the school environment.

You can purposefully support families of multiples in numerous ways. Invite parents to volunteer in classroom activities, attend parenting classes, and participate on advisory boards. Preschool programs that integrate the needs of twins and supertwins into their operations do so by offering collaborative activities for them and acknowledging their special circumstances. For instance, informal contact during arrival and departure may require extra time for the parents of twins or supertwins. During this informal contact, teachers can listen to parents and invite their input. Collaboration with parents takes place formally during planned conferences and informational meetings. You can help by offering the parents of twins and supertwins conference times scheduled back to back for their multiples.

Another way to support and expand parent education is through a family bulletin board. Expand the existing communication boards with extra side panels for posting information and news specific to parents of multiples. The UNPT list can be a permanent part of the supplemental panel, and you can focus on different sections of the list throughout the school year.

Other beneficial aspects of family education include a well-planned family education program to improve parental confidence. Confidence helps parents guide their children's development and educational progress. Through formal and informal contact with the professional staff, parents become more knowledgeable about their children's growth, development, and health, and more aware of effective methods for facilitating their learning. Parents of multiples become more knowledgeable about their children's uniqueness. Information based on research findings may dispel assumptions about twins based on myths and folklore found in popular culture.

LINKING FAMILIES TO RESOURCES AND ADVOCACY

Family education fosters supportive, respectful views of twins and supertwins and their families, and links families to resources and agencies in their communities that offer support and services. (A partial list of supportive associations providing specific information to parents of multiples can be found in appendix D.) It encourages family members to become advocates for their children and connects parents of twins and supertwins to networking groups that can offer emotional support and updated information. Advocacy development is particularly beneficial for parents of multiples because elementary school administrators have not received much information about the development and needs of multiples. Finally, family education encourages schools to create rich environments that demonstrate understanding and acceptance of multiples.

Program Practices to Meet Unique Needs

chapter seven

"None of us really knows anything about twins."

"We're trying to figure out what to do."

"How can we answer the questions about twins that keep coming from the parents?"

As their preschool teacher, you want to be able to provide appropriate experiences for the multiples enrolled in your program, and you want to be able to answer the questions their parents ask you. The Unique Needs of Preschool Twins (UNPT) presented in chapter 6 increases educators' awareness about multiples by providing specific information based on research findings. It brings sensitivity to the special circumstances facing multiples and benefits them during their enrollment in early childhood programs.

One inventory of program practices correlates directly with the UNPT. The Program Practices to Meet the Unique Needs of Preschool Twins (PPUNPT) builds on the same research-based findings used to shape the UNPT and substantiates the goals set out for it. Both the UNPT and the PPUNPT increase professional awareness about multiples, promote sensitive and practical use of the information about them, and benefit multiples in early childhood programs. Linking the two resources enhances early childhood core concepts with focused findings about multiples and their preschool experiences.

An Inventory of Program Practices

The PPUNPT is formulated to meet the needs of multiples during their preschool experiences and offers a practical framework for early childhood educators. It functions in two ways: it correlates with the UNPT, and it presents accessible and functional strategies for teachers who are working with multiples. Hereafter, I refer to this inventory of thirty-six practices as the PPUNPT, or simply *the practices*. The practices are organized into three categories and are numbered without priority placement like the UNPT.

Twins represent the majority of multiples, and therefore most research has been focused on them. Throughout this chapter, the application of twin-specific information is carefully applied to supertwins when research findings are specific to them. As you anticipate more specific information about supertwins, you can carefully apply the available findings about twins and their unique needs.

Program Practices to Meet the Unique Needs of Preschool Twins (PPUNPT)

The practices are not prioritized in order of importance, value, or benefit. They are numbered for practical referencing and categorized into three areas.

Communicational
Communicational refers to the preschool teacher's acknowledgment and recognition of twinship.

1. Respect the twins' bond and relationship while encouraging the individuality of each child.
2. Value parental input prior to enrollment and throughout the children's participation in the program.
3. Recognize individual needs of each child and his or her mutual needs as a member of a twin pair.
4. Remain receptive to acquiring information and understanding about the development of twins, including their physical maturity, learning readiness, language acquisition, and social-emotional behaviors.

5. Capitalize on the twins' mutual support to facilitate their transitions in early childhood programs.
6. Integrate guidelines for twins into the program enrollment policy.
7. Assess each child to determine individual developmental abilities and potential delays.
8. Utilize the preschool experience as an essential resource for early intervention, as needed.
9. Focus on guiding the twins' development rather than on separation and placement issues.

Programmatic

Programmatic refers to preschool enrollment and operational plans about twinship.

10. Develop flexible policies and procedures sensitive to the special circumstances of families with twins.
11. Consider the needs of each pair of twins.
12. Review enrollment, space, and placement issues that may create challenging conditions for twins and their parents.
13. Regard no rigid policy as applicable to all twins.
14. Attend to each relationship and situation as a cooperative decision with parents.
15. Welcome conversation with parents about preschool-age development, highlighting twin information.
16. Respect individual progress of each twin and advance both twins as long as they are within the same developmental range.
17. Establish and maintain a flexible approach to placement.
18. Discuss separation/keeping-together issues with parents, advising them about research findings on the impact of separate placement on twins.
19. Advise parents that no substantial evidence exists for an absolute policy of classroom separation for twins to develop as individuals.
20. Schedule periodic consultations to liaison with parents about program placement.

21. When appropriate, develop procedures for group and room separation, taking into account the circumstances of each twin pair and their family.
22. Reverse a placement decision if it seems stressful for the children.
23. Review supportive methods with parents before reversing placement.
24. Place twins in comparable group settings, subject to the developmental needs of the twins who are placed in separate groups or rooms.
25. Support twins who are placed separately by arranging access to each other and introductions to each other's teachers and to the other children in the group or room.

Relational

Relational refers to twin-specific interaction and interpersonal activities.

26. Interact with each twin as both an individual and a multiple, respecting differences between them and accepting similarities.
27. Acknowledge the characteristics, preferences, abilities, and strengths of each twin.
28. Recognize the changing balance of the twin relationship, including alternating leader-follower patterns.
29. Offer opportunities for the other preschoolers to gain an understanding about twinship.
30. Encourage behaviors and actions that free twins from being compared with one another.
31. Allow twins to be together as long as they want to or seem to benefit.
32. Allow twins as much independence as they are ready for during their early childhood experiences.
33. Develop strategies to maintain motivation of a twin who appears to be second in most activities.

34. Refer to each child by his or her own first name.
35. Honor any supportive checking behaviors between the twins (for example, noting each other's whereabouts and activity involvement).
36. Prepare for gender differences in maturational stages of a boy-girl twin pair.

The PPUNPT inventory of program practices was favorably supported by the expert panel, academics, and preschool teachers who participated in the study I conducted (Arce 2008), which is discussed in the introduction. While all of the practices were considered important, six were identified as most important by the study participants. Of these, three concern acknowledgment of twinship and three concern the interactions and interpersonal activities of twins. The professionals' endorsement may indicate an equally strong support of the practices for supertwins. Even so, application of the practices to supertwins should be undertaken cautiously until specific research findings are available.

Six Program Practices Considered Most Important
The six practices considered most important by the academic respondents, practitioner respondents, and teachers who participated in my study are listed in order of ranking, with the most important listed first. The PPUNPT numbers are provided for reference.

34. Refer to each child by his or her own first name.
27. Acknowledge the characteristics, preferences, abilities, and strengths of each twin.
3. Recognize individual needs of each child and his or her mutual needs as a member of a twin pair.
1. Respect the twins' bond and relationship while encouraging the individuality of each child.
26. Interact with each twin as both an individual and a multiple, respecting differences between them and accepting similarities.
2. Value parental input prior to enrollment and throughout the children's participation in the program.

34. REFER TO EACH CHILD BY HIS OR HER OWN FIRST NAME.

Inclusion of the practice "refer to each child by his or her own first name" initially may seem to be unnecessary. After all, the expectation is that teachers refer to every child by her or his own first name. The participants in my study did not believe this happens consistently. If they had, the practice would not have been substantially supported.

In any setting, but particularly in the preschool setting because of the continuing development of the children, an important task for teachers is to learn children's first names. When multiples enroll in your program, you need to learn their names, be able to distinguish each child, and identify each by his or her name—a little more challenging when the children look very much alike. Remain alert to as many opportunities as possible to use the name of each twin or supertwin, and encourage others to do so too.

As the faculty coordinator of an early childhood education center laboratory, Lorraine Haas observes the students who are meeting their practicum requirement and the laboratory teachers who are modeling teaching strategies while interacting with the children. Lorraine reports that the faculty and teaching staff encourage new student teachers to learn the names of twins. The center teachers suggest that one way to do so is by inserting an inquiry into the conversation with the twin whose name you are trying to identify, such as "Oh, and can you tell me your sister's name?" Other strategies are useful for name identification of twins and supertwins, especially for those who resemble one another. Teachers are encouraged to directly ask a child his or her name, check with other adults, or search for distinguishing physical characteristics.

27. ACKNOWLEDGE THE CHARACTERISTICS, PREFERENCES, ABILITIES, AND STRENGTHS OF EACH TWIN.

Searching for a child's distinguishing characteristics ties in with the importance of acknowledging the individual characteristics of the multiples. "Acknowledge the characteristics, preferences, abilities, and strengths of each twin" suggests to teachers that as they look for the characteristics, preferences, abilities, and strengths of each twin, they notice the child's special traits, interests, and skills. Multiples may have some similar characteristics, such as eye and hair color, and they also may have some differing characteristics, such as the part in their hair, their hair whorls, or the shape of their face. Without labeling the children by these subtle traits, you can discreetly differentiate their distinguishing characteristics and behaviors.

3. RECOGNIZE INDIVIDUAL NEEDS OF EACH CHILD AND HIS OR
    HER MUTUAL NEEDS AS A MEMBER OF A TWIN PAIR.

There is notable gain for twins when teachers value their twin relationship. Twins have individual and mutual needs as members of a twin pair. Accordingly, a third practice ranked among the most important is "recognize individual needs of each child and his or her mutual needs as a member of a twin pair." This practice may also be applicable to supertwins because triplets typically comprise a twin pair and one triplet sibling.

1. RESPECT THE TWINS' BOND AND RELATIONSHIP WHILE
    ENCOURAGING THE INDIVIDUALITY OF EACH CHILD.

Essentially, this practice recommends that teachers recognize the bond between the two in a pair or the members in a supertwin group. Regardless of the apparent strength of the bond or how you perceive it, their relationship is unique. Respect the existing bond and the individuality of each twin and each supertwin.

26. INTERACT WITH EACH TWIN AS BOTH AN INDIVIDUAL AND
     A MULTIPLE, RESPECTING DIFFERENCES BETWEEN THEM AND
     ACCEPTING SIMILARITIES.

This practice, identified by teachers and academics as the fifth most important one, encourages you to respect individuality and group membership by accepting twins' differences and similarities. You can achieve success with this practice by providing special and separate time with each multiple. Such opportunities optimize your insight into each multiple's special temperament, characteristics, and preferences. You become familiar with their similarities and differences.

2. VALUE PARENTAL INPUT PRIOR TO ENROLLMENT AND
    THROUGHOUT THE CHILDREN'S PARTICIPATION IN THE
    PROGRAM.

Of the academics participating in my study, 90 percent considered "value parental input prior to enrollment and throughout the children's participation in the program" to be very important. The teachers who participated responded with 84 percent, ranking the practice as very important. The perceptions of both academics and teachers validate the practice. Positive relationships with families and ongoing collaboration keep programs connected with parents and ultimately contribute to the optimal experiences for the twins and supertwins participating in your program.

Varying Perceptions of Other Program Practices

While the academics and teachers participating in the study mutually supported the practices, there were some differences in their perceptions. The preschool teachers generally thought the most important program practices were those that included references to action with a preschooler, gender differences, and common teaching terms, such as *intervention*. For example, the teachers perceived the relational practice "Develop strategies to maintain motivation of a twin who appears to be second in most activities" as more important than the academics did.

Overall, the academics viewed specific program practices as more important than the preschool teachers did. The practices that the academics considered more important included those related to policy, flexibility, and interaction with families. The academics highly supported the development of flexible policies and procedures sensitive to the special circumstances of families of twins. They approved those practices calling for parental input on preschool enrollment and classroom placement, flexibility in school policies, periodic consultations with parents about enrollment, and classroom placement. The greatest disparity in teachers' and academics' ranking responses was over the tenth practice, "Develop flexible policies and procedures sensitive to the special circumstances of families with twins." The academics ranked this as seventh most important; the teachers ranked it as twenty-third most important. The responses from the teachers and academics were compared to rank their perceptions (Arce 2008).

The differences in the perceptions of the teachers and academics who participated in the study may have been influenced by their familiarity with and access to research-based findings.

Linking Needs of Twins and Supertwins with Program Practices

You have been presented with an introduction to the program practices to meet the UNPT as well as the six practices considered to be most important by academics and preschool teachers who participated in a specific study about twins. The two resources, the UNPT list of needs and the PPUNPT list of practices, offer useful resources as you plan meaningful preschool experiences for twins and supertwins. They also establish practical guidelines. Three core concepts emerge when *both* resources are considered as informational tools for teachers of multiples.

Core Concepts Linking Needs and Practices
Honor the individuality of each child.
Recognize multiples' differences and similarities.
Acknowledge their close relationship.

These core concepts focus attention on the early educational needs of multiples. Consistent with the UNPT and PPUNPT, the first core concept proposes that you honor the individuality of each child; this includes every multiple. The second and third concepts convey the importance of recognizing the differences and similarities of multiples and acknowledging their close relationships. Use the core concepts as you begin to integrate specific information about multiples into the early childhood components at your school.

Both the UNPT and the PPUNPT are divided into three areas: communicational, programmatic, and relational. Review each area to identify specific implementation applicable to the multiples in your program.

Communicational Practices Acknowledging Multiples
The communicational practices acknowledge and recognize twinship. This category frames ideas and concepts for the teacher to use in guiding the preschool experiences of twins, with extended application for supertwins. The nine communicational practices are not prioritized, although they do correlate with the UNPT's communicational practices. Each practice can be applied independently to guide actions as needed for twins and, judiciously applied, for supertwins.

1. Respect the twins' bond and relationship while encouraging the individuality of each child.
2. Value parental input prior to enrollment and throughout the children's participation in the program.
3. Recognize individual needs of each child and his or her mutual needs as a member of a twin pair.
4. Remain receptive to acquiring information and understanding about the development of twins, including their physical maturity, learning readiness, language acquisition, and social-emotional behaviors.

5. Capitalize on the twins' mutual support to facilitate their transitions in early childhood programs.
6. Integrate guidelines for twins into the program enrollment policy.
7. Assess each child to determine individual developmental abilities and potential delays.
8. Utilize the preschool experience as an essential resource for early intervention, as needed.
9. Focus on guiding the twins' development rather than on separation and placement issues.

PERCEPTIONS FROM THE FIELD

With respect to applying the communicational practices, you can utilize the perceptions of other professionals. Those who participated in the study gave consistently high support to the communicational practices. Teachers rated the third practice, "Recognize individual needs of each child and his or her mutual needs as a member of a twin pair," highest in the group of communicational practices. They also considered the seventh practice, "Assess each child to determine individual developmental abilities and potential delays," as essential, rating it as the second most important.

The academics who participated in the study were researchers, professors, physicians, and writers. They rated the first practice, "Respect the twins' bond and relationship while encouraging the individuality of each child," as very important, as well as the third practice, "Recognize individual needs of each child and his or her mutual needs as a member of a twin pair."

Both the teachers and the academics rated the second practice, "Value parental input prior to enrollment and throughout the children's participation in the program," as third most important.

As your insight about multiples expands, you become increasingly acquainted with the importance of the individuality of each twin and supertwin. Their identities become more apparent to you the more you interact with them. The next section explores the importance of the communicational category. The Focused Issue and Teachers Taking Action sections that follow add practical approaches for recognizing and acknowledging multiples. Discussion of the programmatic and relational categories follows.

FOCUSED ISSUE: INDIVIDUAL IDENTITY AND COLLECTIVE IDENTITY

Identity is among the topics of teachers' questions. Often teachers express concerns about the independent behaviors of multiples. For example, teachers have offered comments such as these in workshops.

"They [twins] don't seem to have any differences we can recognize."

"They just seem like the same kid. They look and act the same."

"Most of the teachers at our school do not think the twins know themselves as individuals."

"If they don't see themselves as individuals, how are we suppose to help them?"

Achieving an Individual Identity

Such statements and questions illustrate the need for focused information about identity, particularly how self-identity is achieved by multiples. In the process of achieving self-identity, most children psychologically separate from their mother. This process demonstrates a growing sense of becoming oneself. When twins begin attending preschool, teachers and parents should expect that each child in the pair has his own individual identity. The child's achievement of an identity depends on his stage of maturity.

As with other children, a multiple's process of achieving a sense of self is influenced by her home environment, including family, culture, language, and faith. The family's financial resources, opportunities, stresses, and internal supports further affect the process. The context in which the children develop, especially the dynamics of their multiple group, affects the self-identity and the individuality of twins and supertwins.

Being a twin or supertwin may result in subtle differences concerning awareness of self and others; most apparent is the added awareness of the other twin or supertwins. These differences are not negative and should not suggest that the twins or supertwins suffer from a blurred sense of identity. They do not predict that the personalities of the multiples will be ill formed, and they do not inevitably cause maladaptive behaviors. Closer relationships provide insulating emotional security. For twins and supertwins, close relationships create a social network that offers a partial substitute for reduced parental interaction.

Preschool-age multiples achieve identities separate from their mother and their twin or supertwin. They are probably aware of themselves as individuals and as members of a group.

Among the numerous factors influencing twins' or supertwins' achievement of sense of self is their inherent temperament. The disposition of many infants is apparent when they are very young. Babies' expressions and reactions reveal temperamental behaviors immediately after birth and perhaps even prenatally. Multiples exhibit differing temperaments. Because of their biological makeup, monozygotic (MZ) twins potentially display more similar dispositions than dizygotic (DZ) twins and trizygotic (TZ) triplets. The composition of a multiple group further affects the dynamics among the children and their developing identities. For instance, a triplet group composed of MZ twins and one non-MZ triplet may display different characteristics than triplets who are monozygotic. The MZ pair in the triplet group can be expected to be more like each other than their triplet. In contrast, triplets in a TZ group are distinct, each with different preferences.

Factors that determine any child's identity development are the same for the identity development of multiples, but in addition, the identity formation of multiples is shaped by their extraordinarily close ties, which result from their proximity, contact, and interaction during the prime developmental stages of infancy and toddlerhood. The extent of their closeness increases the likelihood of their displaying similar and complementary behaviors. For example, both children in a twin pair walk with a slight jump on the preschool balance beam, their arms similarly extended. They laugh together as they jump off the balance beam. They have actively played together during infancy and toddlerhood, watched each other, and modeled and imitated one another's movements. They are close. This closeness allows them to anticipate and enjoy each other's movements. Different-age siblings also mimic each other, but their similar behaviors are not as noticeable to teachers because they are usually separated by grade level. You are more likely to notice the similarities and differences of multiples.

Achieving Collective Identity

Some twins and supertwins spend all their time together, while other multiples are enrolled in infant care and have opportunities to interact with other babies their own age. The closeness of twins does not inevitably impede their achieving individual identities. Their sense of collective identity does not keep them from forming a sense of self. Most assuredly, their collective identity allows them to be fully capable of emerging as preschoolers ready for socializing as individuals.

Each pair of twins and group of supertwins determines its own balance in developing self-identity and collective identity. Children who are similar genetically share similar preferences and interests, leading to increased togetherness and closeness. Their similarities also influence other people, primarily their parents, siblings, and grandparents. As their teacher, you reinforce the preferences of supertwins whenever you respond to their requests and needs. Jessie, Jordan, and Jason want to cut strips of adhesive tape. You assist Jessie; he wants green. You provide help to Jordan. He chooses red and orange. You encourage Jason to select the color he wants too. He is looking at the yellow tape. The interest of the three, at least during this one activity period, turns out to be a collective one: cutting and placing adhesive tape on the carpet squares.

Lyla and Leilani play together at home and at preschool. They engage in many activities with the other children at preschool: they enjoy the huge sand area and particularly like using the great variety of rakes, shovels, and buckets. Teacher Rick acknowledges Lyla for creative sand structures and nods at her positively when she gives a shovel to a friend who enters the play area. He also acknowledges Leilani's shoveling skills in the sand area. Leilani receives a smile from Teacher Rick when she invites two friends to help her carry a board to the sand area. They, too, are encouraged and acknowledged. The outcome is that Lyla and Leilani's similarities and interests in particular play activities and mutual interests are reinforced. They are MZ twins fully capable of and comfortable with independent play, and some of their play illustrates their similar preferences.

Close relationships and similar preferences do not cause young children to fail socially and emotionally. Lyla and Leilani are four-year-olds with their own identities. They play together. They play with other children. The intimate ties in a twin pair or in supertwin groups do not prevent the children from achieving individuation. Individuation refers to developing one's own sense of self as an individual.

Being Alert to Atypical Behaviors

The majority of twins develop within the normal range and arrive at preschool with their own individual personalities. In a very few cases, you and program administrators may be alerted to atypical behavior during the initial intake interview. Teacher observation may reveal atypical traits that could indicate the children are not developed socially—for example, twin MZ girls who, after four months of preschool attendance, talk exclusively to one another. Such behavior warrants review and may be considered atypical. Although their teacher requested intervention services, she did not overreact because of the girls' ages. They were three years old when they enrolled and had been burdened by stressful family circumstances. The lack of appropriate parent guidance at that time may have influenced the girls' development. The teachers learned that the girls had been placed with their grandparents, who only rewarded the girls for acting exactly alike. This may have contributed to their inability to act independently and achieve a sense of self. They were responding to the requirements of their home environment, which was not in their developmental interest. The teacher's referral requested services for the twins that included language and behavioral assessments. Situations like this are very rare and should not dictate policy.

Comparing Behaviors

Comparing the behaviors of children neutrally is possible. Developmental milestones provide educators and parents with ranges of expected actions, behaviors, and abilities that can be anticipated in children during particular stages of development. Milestones represent a continuum of development. Achievement of expected skills and typical behaviors occurs over an extended time. Keeping this in mind, know that each twin or supertwin achieves a sense of self at his or her own individual pace and as a unique feature of his or her multiple status. Your focus on the multiples' milestone achievements, both individually and collectively, acknowledges their unique needs and is far more important than just comparing their skills and achievements.

A singleborn child like Brad, for example, illustrates behavior that can be compared with that of his siblings. As the oldest child in his family, Brad responded to his name sooner than his triplet sisters. They are four years younger than Brad, and as triplets, they were born early. Brad enjoyed the exclusive attention of his parents and other adults during the time he was learning language. Brad heard his name used exclusively by his parents. His younger sisters learned their names under different circumstances. They heard all three names. Angela, Natalie, and Vivienne were addressed often and out of necessity in the same sentence. Accordingly, the triplets responded to each other's and their own names later than their older brother had. By the time the triplets began attending school, they were expected to respond to their individual names. However, it was not unexpected that Angela would also respond when the student teacher mistakenly called her Natalie or Vivienne.

Opposite-sex twins do not elicit the same reactions or concerns about their social progress toward individuation. Boy-girl twin pairs begin to interact in different social groups (Thorpe and Gardner 2006). Parents and teachers react to and interact with each of them in different ways because their expectations for each are distinct.

Knowledge about triplets is limited. One study has noted that some teachers believe triplets are overly competitive and dependent. The negative perceptions were based on the teachers' feelings that triplets do not become separate individuals if they are together in a classroom. The researcher notes that the problem lies in the teachers' own inability to see the multiples as individuals (Alin Åkerman 1999). Other teachers in the same study commented on the advantages in interaction of the triplets and found that having them in the same room was an exciting challenge.

TEACHERS TAKING ACTION: SHOULD ONE CHILD BE HELD BACK?

Entry into an early childhood program is a key transition point for multiples. You facilitate their transition by considering their development and by implementing meaningful experiences for them. As you make daily decisions, you also review their progress with special consideration for their individuality, differences and similarities, and close relationships.

Review of developmental progress illuminates the particular issues, questions, and practices that best meet the needs of a multiple. You can link a particular concern raised by staff members or parents to specific needs and practices, and you can be prepared for productive conversations and collaborative decision making with parents. Preparation may include a preliminary review of an issue or question. For your reference, beginning on page 173, a completed Teachers Taking Action form illustrates the applicable UNPT needs and PPUNPT practices related to the question "Should one child be held back?" (See appendix A for the entire UNPT list, and appendix B for the entire PPUNPT list.)

Many decisions you make affecting singleborn children become more complex when you're considering multiples. One decision requiring careful consideration that teachers face is retention, or holding a child back from progressing to another group or class level. Staff members are likely to bring up the decision, and parents are likely to raise it too. Retention in elementary school has not been found to improve progress and, in fact, can negatively affect academic achievement. Retention as an instruction policy can lower children's self-esteem and fail to resolve the problems that keep children from progressing (California Department of Education 1992).

Grouping strategies during the early childhood years require consideration of the children's specific needs. As you follow up with parents and give attention to multiples, you meet their unique needs by recognizing individual and collective needs (**UNPT #2: Recognition of individual and collective needs**). Programs and classrooms with age-specific grouping tend to place burdens on teachers. They must make decisions about the progress of children with a wide range of developmental behaviors and skills. Parents and teachers work collaboratively to establish the needs of the children and the particular opportunities within the program that meet their exact needs. A child may be chronologically young for a particular group experience or developmentally too immature to adjust to a particular group. Decisions regarding group or grade progress become more demanding for the families of twins and supertwins. Providing flexible school and placement policies that accommodate them is one way to meet their unique needs (**UNPT #10: Flexible school and placement policies accommodating the twins' situational needs**).

Although the question of holding back a child may be more complicated for multiples, it does not need to become confrontational. The consideration of another year of preschool for a child, particularly a multiple, invites thoughtful dialog among you, program administrators, and, naturally, parents. Programs that value parents' input prior to the enrollment of their children and throughout their children's participation are more likely to successfully address the particular needs of twins (**PPUNPT #2: Value parental input prior to enrollment and throughout the children's participation in the program**). By attending to each relationship and situation as a cooperative decision made by parents, teachers, and administrators, the unique needs of multiples can be met (**PPUNPT #14: Attend to each relationship and situation as a cooperative decision with parents**).

"Should I hold my one of my twins back?" and "I want one of my twins held back because one is already reading and the other one isn't even interested" are two extremely different issues. One parent is asking for guidance. The second parent is proclaiming that the twins have differing abilities. Some multiple-birth children will have received special intervention services before enrolling in an early childhood program. The developmental effects of premature birth may have been identified early, for example, during an extended stay in the neonatal infant care nursery (NICU). Some developmental delays, such as those affecting hearing and vision, may have become apparent during routine medical visits during infancy and toddlerhood. Physical problems and other disabilities will likely vary for each multiple child in a pair or group (Moskwinski 2002). Depending on the degree of differences among the multiples, their parent will require different information and guidance. It is important to attend to the multiples' unique medical history, home life, and interaction with children outside the twin relationship. Multiples benefit most when parents and educators use the preschool experience as an essential resource for early identification and intervention, should it be needed (**PPUNPT #8: Utilize the preschool experience as an essential resource for early intervention, as needed**). Intervention is especially valuable if one twin, or one or more supertwins, is identified with a delay or impairment (La Trobe Twin Study 1991). You meet the needs of multiples by respecting their developmental progress, individuality, and their identity as multiples. Advance both twins as long as they are developmentally within range to move to another level. Consider the needs of each multiple and their needs as a pair or group. (**PPUNPT #16: Respect individual progress of each twin and advance both twins as long as they are within the same developmental range**). Programs that acknowledge the characteristics, preferences, abilities, and strengths of each multiple meet their specific needs (**PPUNPT #27: Acknowledge the characteristics, preferences, abilities, and strengths of each twin**).

Questions from parents about holding back a child in a group or grade or moving them forward are fairly common. There are no definite answers, but there are suggestions. A starting point is to give each question and situation thorough review. Every child, every twin pair, and every supertwin group is different, and they all deserve to be assessed as individuals and within their relationships. Assessing each child to determine individual developmental abilities and potential delays is another way that you can meet the unique needs of twins (**PPUNPT #7: Assess each child to determine individual developmental abilities and potential delays**). Since more than one preschooler is involved, you need to consider each of their individual and collective needs. As a standard approach, the professional staff should work collaboratively with families. Parents want to be included. As with any decision about a child's development and progress, many factors influence the actions to be taken.

Prepare for the conversations and conferences with parents by using the Teachers Taking Action form. The Teachers Taking Action form is a tool for linking the list of unique needs with the inventory of program practices. (A template for the Teachers Taking Action form is provided in appendix C.)

Begin using the Teachers Taking Action form by synthesizing your concerns into one question. Parents may bring up several issues and concerns at the same time. It is productive for you and the program administrators to synthesize the parents' questions into one inquiry. This provides you time to focus the issue and offer suitable options. After a question is identified, record it on the Teachers Taking Action form. A teacher can individually complete a form and discuss the concerns or issues with the program administrator; the program administrator can initiate a form; or the administrator and the teacher can complete one form together in preparation for a conference with parents. The example that follows illustrates one record. Your actual responses to the same or similar questions depend on your school policies and the particular needs of the multiples. The manner in which you respond also depends on the parents' stated concerns.

The next step is to use the UNPT list of unique needs found in appendix A. Select the needs related to the question posed by a parent or by you or fellow staff members. One or several of the needs may respond to a particular question. Because the needs are not prioritized, you needn't place them on the form in any specific order. The needs selected from the UNPT list apply to the particular situation that initiated the concern or issue. The situation is influenced by the child or children, the family's circumstances, and the school program.

Then you need to identify the program practices related to the question. The selection of the PPUNPT items also depends on the particular question and the circumstances of the children and their family. (The inventory of program practices can be found in appendix B.) Add the date and any comments to the Teachers Taking Action form, either before or after the conference or conversation with the parents. The form is a record of the review process, the parent conference, and the action taken.

Programmatic Practices Relating to Enrollment and Operational Plans

10. Develop flexible policies and procedures sensitive to the special circumstances of families with twins.
11. Consider the needs of each pair of twins.
12. Review enrollment, space, and placement issues that may create challenging conditions for twins and their parents.
13. Regard no rigid policy as applicable to all twins.
14. Attend to each relationship and situation as a cooperative decision with parents.

Teachers Taking Action

Linking Practices to Meet the Unique Needs of Twins and Supertwins

Question, Concern, Issue: *Should one child be held back?*

Related Unique Needs (UNPT list items):
2. *Recognition of individual and collective needs.*
5. *Recognition and encouragement of the child's differences without emphasis.*
8. *Attention to the child's unique medical history, home life, and interaction with children outside the twin relationship.*
10. *Flexible school and placement policies accommodating the twins' situational needs.*
22. *Remaining together as long as the twins want or seem to benefit.*

Relevant Program Practices to Meet the Unique Needs (PPUNPT list items):
2. *Value parental input prior to enrollment and throughout the children's participation in the program.*
7. *Assess each child to determine individual developmental abilities and potential delays.*
9. *Focus on guiding the twins' development rather than on separation and placement issues.*
14. *Attend to each relationship and situation as a cooperative decision with parents.*
16. *Respect individual progress of each twin and advance both twins as long as they are within the same developmental range.*
20. *Schedule periodic consultations to liaison with parents about program placement.*
22. *Reverse a placement decision if it seems stressful for the children.*
27. *Acknowledge the characteristics, preferences, abilities, and strengths of each twin.*
28. *Recognize the changing balance of the twin relationship, including alternating leader-follower patterns.*
31. *Allow twins to be together as long as they want to or seem to benefit.*

Date: May 12, 2009

Comments: Belinda and Irene enrolled August 2008. They were three years and three months at the time of their enrollment. Their parents indicated that tests confirmed the girls are MZ twins. During the intake interview with the program administrator, the parents shared their perceptions of the girls. The parents focused on Belinda's and Irene's height and language. The parents indicated that Irene is "much shorter" and has "very little language."

Teachers have observed Irene throughout the year. Formal observations were recorded in November, January, and April. These indicated that Irene participated in the preschool program activities as expected for preschool girls within this age range. Irene is generally the first to reach and use a trike during outside activity. Irene listens and expresses herself with demonstrative facial responses. When she does respond verbally, her comprehension is apparent, although her sentences are not always complete.

Teachers prepared formal records of the November, January, and April observations. The reports indicated that Belinda generally asks questions during small-group time and provides comments. When she is outside, she usually focuses on the sand area or teacher-guided table activities. She expresses herself with varied eye movements.

Both Irene and Belinda interacted primarily with one another at the beginning of the school year. By the January observation, they routinely expanded their activity participation to introduce other children during most of the preschool session. No apparent language difficulties were reported by the teachers. The girls' language interactions are not exclusive of the other preschoolers. Irene and Belinda appear to be within the range of language development for preschool girls in their first year of preschool attendance, although slightly on the lower end of vocabulary acquisition. Because of the parents' questions regarding the girls' height, their measurements were recorded. Irene measured about two inches shorter than Belinda at the April observation. The difference between the girls is unnoticeable when they are among the other children in their preschool group.

Recommendations: Suggest that Irene and Belinda progress to the prekindergarten group. There is no evidence that their interaction with one another interferes with their development. They appear to have individual abilities and preferences. At this time, retention of one twin or placing the twins in different groups would not benefit them.

Action Taken: An additional conference session with the parents was held to review the observations and recommendation. Both girls would benefit from progressing together to prekindergarten. The parents were invited to observe Irene and Belinda as they actively interacted with other children during preschool sessions. The teacher and program administrator remained accessible to the parents for review. The parents were given resources regarding interaction of multiples and value of the preschool experience for them.

15. Welcome conversation with parents about preschool-age development, highlighting twin information.
16. Respect individual progress of each twin and advance both twins as long as they are within the same developmental range.
17. Establish and maintain a flexible approach to placement.
18. Discuss separation/keeping-together issues with parents, advising them about research findings on the impact of separate placement on twins.
19. Advise parents that no substantial evidence exists for an absolute policy of classroom separation for twins to develop as individuals.
20. Schedule periodic consultations to liaison with parents about program placement.
21. When appropriate, develop procedures for group and room separation, taking into account the circumstances of each twin pair and their family.
22. Reverse a placement decision if it seems stressful for the children.
23. Review supportive methods with parents before reversing placement.
24. Place twins in comparable group settings, subject to the developmental needs of the twins who are placed in separate groups or rooms.
25. Support twins who are placed separately by arranging access to each other and introductions to each others' teachers and to the other children in the group or room.

Programmatic practices—that is, for preschool enrollment and operational plans—suggest ways to facilitate the preschool experience for twins with guidelines that address their particular needs. The practices establish approaches for program administrators and teachers to guide their work with multiples during the preschool experience. The programmatic practices inform school operational policies and guidelines related to twins and their families. With sixteen practices, the programmatic category is the largest in the inventory of the PPUNPT's thirty-six items.

PERCEPTIONS FROM THE FIELD

The program practices organized within the programmatic area have been endorsed by the teachers and academics who participated in my study to identify specific practices that would meet the needs of twins. The teachers rated most of the sixteen practices as very important. Most of the teachers viewed the practice "Review supportive methods with parents before reversing placement" as very important. The other three practices receiving the highest ranking among teachers were "Respect individual progress of each twin and advance both twins as long as they are within the same developmental range," "Consider the needs of each pair of twins," and "Establish and maintain a flexible approach to placement."

"Attend to each relationship and situation as a cooperative decision with parents" was perceived by 100 percent of the academics as very important.

FOCUSED ISSUE: TOGETHER AND APART

"Together and apart" is a topic that consolidates many of the questions about classroom placement that teachers most frequently ask. It appears that educators are equally divided in favor of keeping the children together or placing them apart in groups and classrooms. Some questions imply that assigning twins to different groups and classrooms has been justified and is preferred. For instance, one teacher commented, "We just separate, always, as a matter of policy. But sometimes we don't have a group that can take another child. What we end up doing is moving other children around so that the twins will not be together." Sometimes the inquiries from teachers suggest uncertainty, such as "Should there be a trial period for their separation into different classrooms?" and "What if the school administrators and parents disagree?"

It is not surprising that the most frequently asked questions coming from parents of multiples are about classroom placement. Throughout their children's school years, families with multiples continue to face this dilemma. The issue has led parents of twins into confrontational exchanges with school administrators. Some parents of multiples are not satisfied with mandated policies, especially those requiring separation, but even when they disagree with the decisions, they sometimes defer to administrative decisions because they respect authority. However, when schools inquire about parents' preferences, they discover that the parents are usually divided on the issue: about 50 percent want their children to remain together and about 50 percent favor separation. Parents of MZ twins may be most affected by inflexible mandates because they tend to request that their children remain together more often than parents of DZ twins.

Some schools and school districts have maintained strict rules favoring separate classrooms. They have done so without research to support their arbitrary decision to separate twins (Segal 2003b). Too often administrative decisions continue to mandate separation without regard for the individual needs of the children and their needs as members of a pair or a group.

Concerns about "together and apart" extended beyond the academic hallways when the issue first reached legislative chambers in 2005. Denying one mother of twins the right to have both of her children placed in the same classroom resulted in action. As a legislative aide, the mother encouraged a senator in Minnesota to spearhead the passage of a bill. The bill passed, granting parents the right to provide input about the classroom placement of their multiples. Subsequently, parents of multiples in other states have campaigned for similar legislation to ensure similar rights. Leading the national movement is advocate and mother of twins Kathy Dolan of New York. She supports the campaigns in various states to enact laws to empower parents of twins and supertwins to have the primary voice about classroom placement decisions.

Arbitrary Policies and Alternatives

Some of the arbitrary policies imposed at the elementary school level have seeped into the operations of early childhood programs. In programs where this has taken place, the policies have been imposed in the belief that they have been validated by research-based findings.

The rationale given most often for separating twins in school is fear that they will not otherwise develop their own personalities. Other unsubstantiated rationales claim that keeping multiples together negatively reinforces isolating behaviors, prevents independent behaviors from forming, and causes negative effects on the children's cognitive development. Others who insist on separation believe strongly that keeping children together causes extreme psychological dependency and, for that reason, the educational systems and parents who object must be coerced, using information about the development of individuation, separation, and selfhood (Smilansky 1992).

Some organizations representing the parents of multiples advocate for flexible placement based on individual needs. The Mothers of Supertwins (MOST) strongly encourage placing multiples together for their first school experiences. MOST also encourages teachers and parents to consider alternate options, such as a separate or special setting, especially if the children have different medical or educational needs. They encourage decisions based on the particular needs of the children and family. MOST is one of the groups that does not support specific legislation defining school placement for multiples, especially if the laws give complete authority to one person. The group endorses the distribution of facts to parents to help them make informed decisions about their children's school experiences.

Rationale for Keeping Together

As early as 1970, early childhood educators Sarah Leeper and Dora Skipper concluded that separate classroom assignment was not advisable. They studied twins in first through sixth grades. Applicability of their research to preschool children may be limited by the age of the children in their study as well as the changes that have occurred in the educational systems since that time.

The controversy surrounding classroom placement for multiples continues and has become most contentious in the United States, where the educational system uses rigid, chronologically age-defined school grades. Unfamiliar with the findings from international research about placement or choosing to ignore or dismiss such research, educators have formulated their decisions about "together and apart" on anecdotal experiences and nonacademic publications.

The first longitudinal study examining the effect of separate classrooms on twins established convincing evidence that separation may have unfavorable psychological consequences for some twins (Hay 2004). Hay noted that twins who were separated in the first year of school had more behavioral problems. For the MZ twins in the study, the problems persisted over time. There was some evidence that separated twins experienced more academic problems than twins remaining together. The later-separated MZ twins, but not the early-separated twins, had poorer reading abilities than those kept together (Tully et al. 2004b).

Exploring Effects of Together and Apart

Researchers continue to explore the effects of multiples separated or remaining together in school. The results of a study by Lucy Tully and colleagues provide some evidence that separation negatively affects cognitive performance (Tully et al. 2004b). In another 2007 study, twins who had been separated for at least a year scored lower on average in language when they were assessed in the second grade. Some evidence also indicated that arithmetic scores were slightly lower for twins who had been separated. The researchers identified no effect on cognitive performance of classroom separation in the higher grades. The effect of placement seems to be most pronounced for multiples during the early childhood years (Webbink, Hay, and Visscher 2007).

In contrast, a Dutch study found no differences in academic performance of twins when they were tested. The twins included in the study had been separated at age five. The researchers investigated the long-term effects by measuring the twins' school performances at age twelve. However, more behavior problems were found among the children who had been separated. The study suggests that behaviors that existed before enrollment may have contributed to the differences and that the decision to separate may have been influenced by preexisting behaviors (van Leeuwen et al. 2005).

A more recent study reports that early literacy of twins, on average, is not directly affected by their classroom placement. The study looked at reading ability of twins in kindergarten to second grade in the United States and Australia (Coventry et al. 2009).

Guiding Decisions

Family circumstances should guide decisions about classroom placement. In one study, a mother's interactions with her twin sons were examined. One multiple had normal hearing and the other had a mild hearing loss. The children began preschool at age three at the school where one boy received speech therapy. When the brothers began attending the same school, they were able to see each other during playtime, even though they were enrolled in different classrooms. They were reported by the teachers to be adjusting and progressing normally (Muñoz-Silva and Sanchez-Garcia 2004).

Parental preference is the most important guide for program administrators and teachers when considering group and classroom placement of multiples. Parents are more receptive to information when their requests are respected and when their input is accepted. Working together ultimately leads to the best decision for the multiples. Paulina Alvarado, an executive director of an early childhood program in Bethesda, Maryland, reports that parents now request different rooms for their multiples more often. This is a definite change from what her programs previously experienced. As the numbers of twins and multiples increase, such requests will surely affect more directors, programs, and preschool teachers.

Separation in itself does not speed a child's achievement of independence, individuality, and appropriate social behaviors, nor does it necessarily reduce competition and comparison among multiples. Yet it is one of the two options requested by parents. More parents of DZ twins, especially of boy-girl pairs, request separate placement. With collaborative review, you can assist parents in recognizing whether their children display a readiness for independent experiences. An "apart" option for multiples who are ready for the adjustment may provide opportunities for them, especially if the parents have anticipated the placement. An "apart" placement may be necessitated when one or more of the multiples has differing abilities. A special setting to meet special needs is important. Separate placement in groups and classrooms for a period of time during the day may help the twins adjust without withdrawing them wholly from the support and security of their multiple siblings.

Teachers Relate Reasons

Some teachers say it is simply easier for them to tell the twins apart when they are not in the same classroom. Other educators disagree and find it is easier for them when both children in the twin pair are in the same room, because it forces the teachers to learn the children's personalities and behaviors. When multiples are placed together, a teacher with intrinsic patience finds the extra time required to distinguish between each twin pair and supertwin group.

Teachers have reported that they have separated twins because of what they considered disruptive behaviors. Perceived extreme competitiveness among the twins is a justification teachers give for separating them. Separate placement does not automatically remedy the disruptive or competitive behaviors of preschoolers. By the time they enroll in preschool or advance from infant and toddler child care programs, children have developed behaviors dependent on their age, temperament, and previous family and child care experiences. Review of the behavior, background experiences, and options for guidance is a more effective way to encourage long-lasting prosocial skills.

Teacher Shu-Chen helps the children adjust by providing many opportunities for cross-group activities in the same classroom. She also guides different experiences for multiples when their behaviors warrant separate activities. To encourage separate activities for the multiples in the same classroom, Shu-Chen sets the children's name cards on different tables during snacktime. During weekly walks, Shu-Chen assigns a twin pair to participate in different walk times. Leland walks with the group on Tuesday, and Trevor walks on Thursday with another group.

When children begin attending preschool, they are adjusting to being away from their parents or other primary caregivers. They are moving outside of their core security network. The children may be able to better cope with the adjustment in the presence of their twin or co-supertwins. There may be no substitute or social experience more valuable than a built-in buddy.

Parents Relate Reasons

As teachers and parents are aware, additional logistical conditions influence the classroom placement of their multiple-birth children. The convenience for families is a significant element in their classroom-placement requests. This is particularly so for one-parent and dual-earner families. Many schools have only one classroom placement available. You may think a simple option would eliminate the decision-making dilemma, but apparently this is not so. Teachers in schools with one classroom for each grade have indicated that parents have asked if they should enroll one of the twins in another school, even when that school is miles away. Or parents have asked if they should have one of their twins skip a grade. Such extreme solutions confirm that support for separation has become ingrained.

Another consideration for parents who are deciding whether to keep their twins and supertwins together or apart may be the differences in the quality of teaching. One classroom may meet the educational expectations more effectively. One teacher's style may be a better match for one, both, or all three of the children. Parents can make their decisions most effectively when they have an abundance of information from teachers and program administrations.

Suggestions for Early Childhood Education

Practices relating to the "together and apart" issue suggest that you capitalize on the multiples' mutual support to facilitate their transitions into your early childhood program. Integrate guidelines for multiples into the program's enrollment policy. Develop flexible policies and procedures sensitive to the special circumstances of families with twins and supertwins, and avoid rigid policies. You can do this by attending to each relationship and situation as a cooperative decision to be made jointly with parents.

The programmatic practices primarily concern classroom placement. Preschools that integrate and maintain a flexible approach to placement meet the needs of multiples and may eliminate the issue of "together and apart" by satisfying the children's and families' needs. Discuss the issues directly with parents, advising them about research findings on the impact of separate placement on twins and supertwins (**PPUNPT #18: Discuss separation/keeping-together issues with parents, advising them about research findings on the impact of separate placement on twins**). Advise parents that no substantial evidence exists to endorse an absolute policy (**PPUNPT #19: Advise parents that no substantial evidence exists for an absolute policy of classroom separation for twins to develop as individuals**). Schedule periodic consultation to meet and confer with parents about program placement (**PPUNPT #20: Schedule periodic consultations to liaison with parents about program placement**).

Beginning preschool and kindergarten is a milestone, particularly for children who may not have experienced child care or other activities away from home. Most children who are comfortable and supported adjust positively to a new experience such as school. Children who attend school with their friends adjust more easily than children who attend without another familiar child their own age. The comfort and support provided by a non–family member is no less important for adjustment than the comfort and support twins and supertwins achieve in each other's companionship. Multiples have a built-in advantage for successful adjustment.

Assess, formally or informally, multiple-born children to determine their individual needs. The review helps you determine the best classroom placement. Parents' deliberations are enhanced by information about placement and the developmental needs of their multiples. Develop appropriate and sensitive guidance for group and room separation, taking into account the circumstances of each child and family. Teachers can prepare parents who prefer classroom separation for their twins; they need to be aware of the potential negative reactions of their children. Listening to and accommodating families' wishes are most important. Parents may waver about a placement because it is not what they expected or consider changing a classroom or group assignment. (This issue, reversing placement, is reviewed in the next section and in the Teachers Taking Action form on page 185.)

TEACHERS TAKING ACTION: SHOULD A PLACEMENT DECISION BE REVERSED?

You must routinely make decisions about children's enrollment. You decide which teacher, classroom, and group best fit the developmental needs of each preschooler. You also arrange settings to accommodate children with special needs. You inform, guide, coach, and provide resources to increase parents' understanding of program goals and practices that best serve their children. You also carry out these actions with parents of multiples. In doing this, you enhance your role as a family educator.

Besides sharing age-appropriate expectations to help parents understand each program's intent, you inform them about the specific development of multiples (**PPUNPT #15: Welcome conversation with parents about preschool-age development, highlighting twin information**). You are aware that parents of multiples are confronted with enrollment decisions that parents of singleborn children do not face. With this in mind, collaborate with parents to problem-solve enrollment and placement. Informing parents, listening to them, and accommodating their requests have proven to be most productive. Build flexible enrollment policies into your school handbook. A collaborative relationship will benefit the parents and your program. (**PPUNPT #17: Establish and maintain a flexible approach to placement**).

Children's behaviors and needs change as they mature (**UNPT #2: Recognition of individual and collective needs**). A decision about classroom placement completed in the fall may become obsolete by winter because the needs of the children, one of the multiples, or the expectations of the parents have changed. **(PPUNPT #20: Schedule periodic consultations to liaison with parents about program placement)**. A child's behavior provides insight and clues to his or her readiness for alternative options. Your observations partly determine the necessary adjustments to placement. For example, the placement of Justin and Preston in different classroom groups was a parental decision at the time of the boys' enrollment. The educational staff requested a reconsideration of those placements as a result of documented observations of the boys during their initial three and a half weeks of attendance. Reconsidering a placement is particularly important if the classroom assignment seems stressful for the children or their developmental needs are not being met **(PPUNPT #14: Attend to each relationship and situation as a cooperative decision with parents) (PPUNPT #16: Respect individual progress of each twin and advance both twins as long as they are within the same developmental range) (PPUNPT #22: Reverse a placement decision if it seems stressful for the children)**. Adding new children to a classroom affects the dynamics of the group and may create a need for a review of the placement. In the case of Justin and Preston, the presence of a substitute teacher may have created a mismatch for Justin **(UNPT #5: Recognition and encouragement of the child's differences without emphasis) (PPUNPT #11: Consider the needs of each pair of twins)**, or Justin's and Preston's behaviors must have changed significantly in so short a time that a reassessment of their classroom assignments was warranted.

Programs with adaptable guidelines and open-ended curriculum ease the discourse among teachers about placement **(PPUNPT #17: Establish and maintain a flexible approach to placement)**. Adaptable guidelines set policies that accommodate the needs of the children, families, and teachers.

Prepare for conversations with parents about the placement of their twins and supertwins **(PPUNPT #14: Attend to each relationship and situation as a cooperative decision with parents)** with the Teachers Taking Action form. The form links the Unique Needs of Preschool Twins (UNPT) and the Program Practices to Meet the Unique Needs of Preschool Twins (PPUNPT). (The template for the form is provided in appendix C.)

Synthesize your concerns into one question and place it in the first section on the Teachers Taking Action form. Refer to the UNPT in appendix A and the PPUNPT in appendix B, and determine the needs and practices that relate to a placement decision. These needs and practices establish background information to assist you in preparing a collaborative review of the issue with the parents.

The child or children and the family circumstances influence the selection of particular needs and practices. The example below of Justin and Preston's situation addresses the question "Should a placement decision be reversed?" Comments were added in this example to simulate the process of review. Each review you develop is distinct and refers directly to the circumstances of the children, families, and school.

Teachers Taking Action

Linking Practices to Meet the Unique Needs of Twins and Supertwins

Question, Concern, Issue: *Should a placement decision be reversed?*

Related Unique Needs (UNPT list items):
1. *Acknowledgment and encouragement both as an individual and as a twin.*
2. *Recognition of individual and collective needs.*
4. *Recognition and understanding of twin type.*
5. *Recognition and encouragement of the child's differences without emphasis.*
15. *Periodic (no less frequent than annually) consultation to review group and room placement.*

Relevant Program Practices to Meet the Unique Needs (PPUNPT list items):
3. *Recognize individual needs of each child and his or her mutual needs as a member of a twin pair.*
7. *Assess each child to determine individual developmental abilities and potential delays.*
11. *Consider the needs of each pair of twins.*
14. *Attend to each relationship and situation as a cooperative decision with parents.*
16. *Respect individual progress of each twin and advance both twins as long as they are within the same developmental range.*

17. Establish and maintain a flexible approach to placement.
20. Schedule periodic consultation to liaison with parents about program placement.
22. Reverse a placement decision if it seems stressful for the children.
23. Review supportive methods with parents before reversing placement.

Date: September 25, 2009

Comments: Justin and Preston's parents strongly insisted that their DZ twin sons be placed in separate classrooms when they were enrolled in September 2009. The school has one three-year-old group and one four-year-old group. The parents suggested placing Justin with his age-appropriate group and Preston with the older class. Orientation for the boys included introduction to one another's teacher and time in each other's classroom at the beginning of each day for the first week. They began attending the day after their third birthday. The teachers began observing and recording the behavior of the boys in their separate classrooms. Written observations were also completed by one teacher who was not working directly with the boys and by the program administrator. Additional comments were collected from their classroom teachers and discussed during the staff meetings. Observations noted that Justin routinely asked the teacher about the other classroom with "his brother" and "how much longer until Mommy comes to pick us up?" He participated in some of the activities and engaged in waterplay with other three-year-olds. The observations about Preston indicated that he would usually participate in table activity briefly when he arrived, then would retreat to the book area throughout most of the morning program. He rarely communicated with the teachers or other children verbally. He responded to his teacher's requests; however, he did not appear engaged.

Recommendations: The teachers recommend that the children participate in the same three-year-old classroom for at least six months. Justin's adjustment in the preschool classroom was more apparent, possibly because he was with children within his age range. The teachers asked the program administrator to arrange a conference with the parents to be attended by the teachers and program administrator. Parents will be presented with a summary of the observations and asked to reconsider the placement.

Action Taken: A conference was scheduled with parents to review the specific needs of Justin and Preston and the program practices that would best meet those identified needs. The teachers and program administrator strongly encouraged the parents to approve reversal of the initial placement. The parents agreed and requested that a review of the placement reversal take place with the program administrator prior to school reopening after winter holiday break.

Relational Practices Referring to Multiples' Interaction

Practices categorized as relational practices refer to twin-specific and supertwin interaction or interpersonal activities. The practices emphasize actions that encourage play with other children and opportunities for individual activity. As an early childhood educator, you are acquainted with the value of play and know that it allows time with others and time for individual activity. The relational category offers program practices that positively influence the development of multiples during their play with others and alone.

The relational program practices encourage interaction among the multiples, and they suggest approaches in the preschool setting that meet the specific needs of multiples. The approaches acknowledge each twin's individual characteristics and preferences. Other practices within the relational category include those that recognize the changing balance of behaviors that can be anticipated in multiples. Interaction and interpersonal practices include eleven items.

26. Interact with each twin as both an individual and a multiple, respecting differences between twins and accepting similarities.
27. Acknowledge the characteristics, preferences, abilities, and strengths of each twin.
28. Recognize the changing balance of the twin relationship, including alternating leader-follower patterns.
29. Offer opportunities for the other preschoolers to gain an understanding about twinship.
30. Confirm actions that free twins from being compared with one another.

31. Allow twins to be together as long as they want to or seem to benefit.
32. Allow twins as much independence as they are ready for during their early childhood experiences.
33. Develop strategies to maintain motivation of a twin who appears to be second in most activities.
34. Refer to each child by his or her own first name.
35. Honor any supportive checking behaviors between the twins (for example, noting each other's whereabouts and activity involvement).
36. Prepare for gender differences in maturational stages of a boy-girl twin pair.

PERCEPTIONS FROM THE FIELD

The teachers and academics who participated in my study to identify practices that meet the unique needs of multiples supported the relational program practices. Both the teachers and academics who provided support for the practices agreed that the thirty-fourth practice, "Refer to each child by his or her own first name," is the most important one among those in the relational category. The practice that received the second highest support from teachers and academics was "Acknowledge the characteristics, preferences, abilities, and strengths of each twin." Teachers ranked "Interact with each twin as both an individual and a multiple, respecting differences between twins and accepting similarities," as third highest, and academics ranked it fourth highest among the relational practices.

As you review teachers' and academics' perceptions of the relational category, note the prominence they placed on individual children within relationships. The characteristics, preferences, and abilities of twins and supertwins are important topics and reflect friendship, a common aspect of childhood. Friendship has special connotations for multiples and is presented as the next focused issue.

FOCUSED ISSUE: FRIENDSHIP

Friendship formation for multiples is affected by early interactions with their same-age sibling or siblings. They have intimately interacted with at least one same-age sibling on a daily basis since their birth, even before their parents usually became concerned about their children's success in making friends and participating in events. Parents of multiples commonly expect both or all of their children to be invited to and included in events. You are accustomed to working with numerous same-age children and understand that friendship for young children forms over a period of time. You also understand that invitations during the preschool years are primarily directed by the parents.

Preschool teachers frequently use the word *friend* to refer to a child, and they refer to a group of children as *friends*, saying, for example, "The loft has room for only three friends at one time." Having recognized children as friends does not necessarily indicate that they share a mutually satisfying relationship with a preschool-age peer. The meaning of friendship for young children, at least in the beginning, is characteristically shifting and ephemeral. As they mature through their preschool stages, their social skills equip them to increasingly engage with their contemporaries. Preschool provides opportunities for them to interact with other children, and as they do so, they begin to consider each other's feelings. In elementary school, friendship is a more complex relationship and becomes increasingly so by the time children reach middle school. Nonetheless, the quality of interactions with peers in preschool is predictive of future social and emotional well-being and successful performance in school. Helping preschoolers to be liked by their peers is a worthy aim of early childhood programs.

For almost all young children, active play experiences in the preschool environment commonly place them in close proximity to same-age children. When preschool programs allow children to engage in self-selected activities, they choose experiences and become involved in activities that match their interests. Other children with similar interests become involved in the same activities. Children's social abilities, such as their degree of friendliness, allow them to connect with other children. Nonaggressive behaviors help preschoolers enter into play with other children. When preschoolers become more engaged with other children, they improve their social skills. They do so with your guidance. As their interaction with other children increases, particularly with children who have similar interests, they become more intimate and personal with each other. Their play continues to encourage opportunities for friendship. Play enhances social learning and develops social skills for participating in activities with other same-age children.

The behaviors of children reveal their developing friendships. Their initial interest in other children begins as early as age two. By age four, children verbally use the word *friend*. One-way, or unilateral, friendships are more common; that is, children identify a friend although the friendship may not be reciprocal. Robbie says that he likes Emile. "Emile," he says, "is my friend because I like him." Reciprocal friendships become increasingly possible if the interaction extends over a six-week stretch (Gleason and Hohmann 2006).

Research about Multiples and Friendship Formation

Parents of multiples will be wondering about the friendship formation possibilities for their twins and supertwins. Teachers ask questions about how multiples' relationships influence their ability to make friends at preschool. Teachers want to know how the earlier interaction and close relationship affects their relationships with other children. A number of researchers have asked this question and have gathered data to provide insight for educators.

Information about friendship formation has focused on singleborn children and therefore may be less relevant to multiples. Nonetheless, the notion that the relationships of twins interfere with their developing friends at preschool is not grounded in research. Academic studies are becoming available that directly analyze the friendship development of twins. Recent findings confirm that development of their friendship formation is related to their interdependence and that some factors influence behaviors and future relationships.

The early social interaction of multiples affects the way in which they negotiate friendships later. Some social behaviors contributing to the development of friendship may become apparent earlier for multiples than for some singleborn children. Multiples have already experienced a sustained relationship with another same-age child or children. They were members of an existing group relationship when they began attending early childhood programs. Their relationships necessitated daily social interaction. The interaction most likely required more negotiating, helping, and waiting time. Living each day experiencing routine and special activities together shaped their social skills. For example, observing others receive care and waiting for a turn on her or his mother's or father's lap may positively affect a child's understanding. When the parents of multiples are aware and responsive to developmental stages, their children are likely to develop a sense of empathy from their shared experiences.

For example, when Ramon and Benjamin's mother signed them in on Monday morning, she told the teachers about bandages on both of the boys' knees. She said that after Benjamin fell off his tricycle, Ramon rushed to get Benjamin's special blanket. Then Benjamin insisted that Ramon have a bandage just like his on the same spot. Such unending interactions influence the way the boys adjust their actions, including the blossoming of caring and empathic ways. The boys' interactions lead them to accommodate their behaviors and find ways to conduct themselves with one another and those outside their group, influencing their characteristics and actions.

> Whenever I am with them, whenever I watch and play with them, I learn more about myself. I am beginning to understand why I did what I did and sometimes, even now, why I do what I do. I watch them move, sometimes together, sometimes apart, and in so many ways, they show that they understand they are part of one another. Yet they also know they are their own person . . . probably in the same way their mom and I did. —Olivia, aunt of MZ twin boys and a twin herself

Multiples reared in families in which their needs are nurtured usually acquire qualities of behaviors that enhance friendship, such as empathy and compassion. These and other social skills, such as negotiating, sharing, and turn-taking, are valued abilities in the early childhood setting. Contrary to older views about the close relationship of twins, current research does not see multiples as isolated from others and from forming friendships outside their sibling group (Thorpe 2003).

Their multiple status influences the way twins and supertwins form and sustain friendships with other children. Also, it appears that the multiple status can affect a twin's self-concept. A Korean study showed that twins have a slightly higher self-concept than singleborn children in analysis of self-image. The researchers found similarities in the self-concept of first- and second-born twins. This indicates that birth order had little effect on the outcome of their self-concept (Yoon and Hur 2006). This study of elementary school children is important especially because self-concept has been found to decrease for most children as they enter kindergarten. These findings replicated a study that showed twins have higher adaptive and adjustment capabilities than singleborn children (Pulkkinen et al. 2003).

It is useful for you to review the process of achieving a sense of self as illustrated in Focused Issue: Individual Identity and Collective Identity on page 165. Multiples develop both a self-identity and a collective identity. Doing so prepares them for forming childhood friendships. They have always experienced social settings with their same-age sibling; their friendships are generally formed with their twin present; and they have already experienced a long-term relationship (Thorpe and Gardner 2006).

Another study about twin friendship showed that twin girls influence their social world by continuously navigating everyday social interactions. They navigate friendship differently than singleborn girls. A major difference can be observed in the way twins realign and negotiate their identity with that of their twin (Danby and Thorpe 2006).

Studies cited in chapter 4 illustrate the advantages of boy-girl twin relationships. A novel element is present in the formation of friendships of opposite-sex twins. Boys and girls, including twin pairs, increasingly engage with different groups of children as they mature. In contrast, MZ twins are more likely to remain content with their mutual circle of friends, naturally having more similar interests. Early friendships with preferred playmates provide benefits for children, including multiples. They help children adjust to new people, cope with stressful experiences, facilitate adjustments, and improve their social skills.

A 2003 Finnish study established that opposite-sex twinship contributed to social and emotional behaviors. This included positive outcomes for popularity, leadership, and social competence. The socially active behaviors of the twins were attributed directly to their having interacted with their opposite-sex co-twin. The study of eleven- to twelve-year-old children showed that twin boys were particularly popular among their classmates. The opposite-sex twin pairs were found to have more adaptive behaviors with their classmates (Pulkkinen et al. 2003). Contrary to that study's findings, researchers who focused on preschoolers between the ages of three and six did not find specific socialization advantages for opposite-sex twins, at least during the early childhood years (Laffey-Ardley and Thorpe 2006).

Same Playmates

Another way that friendships form differently for twins and singleborn children is that multiples share friends, especially during the early childhood years. Many twins also have mutual friends as they mature, sustaining long-term and reciprocally close relationships.

Having same-age playmates may influence the children's abilities to interact in social relationships. Because they have a history of cooperating with one or more same-age sibling, twins may be more cooperative and, consequently, more socially engaged in play. There is some indication that MZ twins demonstrate more cooperative behaviors than DZ twins, but their cooperative behaviors do not necessarily transfer to unfamiliar playmates (Segal 1999). A more recent study shows that twins are more social as a result of the time spent with their siblings. Even so, it was also noted that these experiences do not correlate with the experiences of children in child care, where children interact with non-sibling children. The study found that twins who are more accustomed to interacting with a same-age sibling are less likely to engage with unfamiliar peers than singleborn children who experienced child care settings. The twins' interactive skills did not transfer to unfamiliar situations (DiLalla 2006). The behavior of the multiples was consistent with that of the majority of children in the general population. Children tend to select friends who have similar traits and preferences (Guo 2006).

Preschool is where children develop and improve their social skills. Teachers encourage children, both singleborn and multiple, to form friendships with other children. For multiples, the friendships include children outside their multiple groups. Because twins and supertwins may have been encouraged to remain exclusive partners or groups, you may need to let them know it is acceptable to have a special friend other than their twin or supertwin siblings.

Guiding children to acquire social skills raises inquiry about fairness. As a professionally prepared early educator, you are ready to work with groups of same-age children. You are familiar with guidance approaches for preschoolers in small groups and aware that the topic of fairness is routinely deliberated. Fairness, and how it relates to multiples, is the next focused issue.

FOCUSED ISSUE: FAIRNESS

When you acknowledge the value of friendship for twins and supertwins, you guide the children in ways that fulfill their unique needs. Social and emotional development has unexpected challenges. Focusing on children's sociability and emotionality has become accepted and valued in the preschool program. As you guide the development of twins and supertwins in acquiring social skills, including making friends, you will find that opportunities may not always be equal. Experiences, events, and chances are not always fair. While some twins and supertwins experience social interaction earlier than singleborn children, they do not escape the challenge of fairness.

Fairness is an issue at home as well as at preschool. Experiences involve sets of two, three, four, and more preschoolers from one family enrolled at the same time. Parents may inform you that they, too, have faced the fairness dilemma in numerous ways while rearing their children. Twins authority Pat Preedy (1999, 83) notes, "No matter how identical the children are, life cannot provide exactly the same for each child." She writes that teachers who acknowledge that twins have different needs at different stages may ease the teacher's own feeling that twins must be treated in the exact same way. Remember also that from the beginning, twins and supertwins have interacted primarily in multigroup relationships, described here as interactions of twins and supertwins with one another and their family members, including their older siblings and grandparents. The primary caregiver, usually the mother, and at least two children were present in the trio. It may not have been possible for both children to be the first to be picked up or hugged. Trying to alternate who is first, even when they are grown, seems to be the most effective strategy.

Teachers can maintain reasonable fairness when guiding the development and preschool experiences of multiples. The primary methods are to avoid comparison and discourage competition. The UNPT and PPUNPT lists offer clarification for understanding twins, such as providing freedom from comparison with one another (**UNPT #17: Freedom from comparison with the child's co-twin**) and confirming actions that free twins from comparison with one another (**PPUNPT #30: Encourage behaviors and actions that free twins from being compared with one another**). By avoiding comparison and discouraging competition, you support fairness without exaggerating the situations. Excessive emphasis on individual differences may cause a child to feel singled out or distinct from her group, or may discount her collective identity with her twin or supertwin group. A tone of acceptance establishes the welcoming atmosphere for all children (**UNPT #5: Recognition and encouragement of the child's differences without emphasis**) (**PPUNPT #26: Interact with each twin as both an individual and a multiple, respecting differences between twins and accepting similarities**) (**PPUNPT #27: Acknowledge the characteristics, preferences, abilities, and strengths of each twin**) (**PPUNPT #28: Recognize the changing balance of the twin relationship, including alternating leader-follower patterns**).

Encouraging Practices

The topics of competition and comparison assume different meanings when two or more children from the same family participate in the same preschool group. Gender differences require a more elaborate description when the needs of multiples are considered.

Respecting children builds practices that encourage their development fairly. Skillful teachers incorporate meaningful ways to accommodate each child in the classroom. For multiples, this may mean that teachers establish a cubby storage unit for each child, including one for each of the twins and each of the supertwins. Teachers' remarks model their acceptance of each child, further assuring as much fairness as possible. Teachers provide a newsletter and an announcement for each multiple to take home to their families. Twins and supertwins have their own name cards, and during group times, sometimes they enjoy sitting together and at other times they enjoy being placed next to other playmates in the preschool group.

Despite your efforts to establish as much fairness as possible, occasionally you will observe that twins and supertwins experience uneven treatment **(UNPT #1: Acknowledgment and encouragement both as an individual and as a twin) (UNPT #2: Recognition of individual and collective needs) (PPUNPT #1: Respect the twins' bond and relationship while encouraging the individuality of each child) (PPUNPT #3: Recognize individual needs of each child and his or her mutual needs as a member of a twin pair) (PPUNPT #33: Develop strategies to maintain motivation of a twin who appears to be second in most activities)**. Help preschool staff and volunteers recognize multiples as individuals rather than as a unit. Older children are aware of the stigmas associated with their multiple status when, for example, they hear themselves counted as a unit instead of as two second-graders or three fifth-graders. Their parents may have experienced exclusion from activities requiring specific adult-child ratios, and their multiples may be excluded from such events as birthday parties. You can diminish some of the inequities facing multiples, particularly when you and other members of the teaching staff acknowledge the unique circumstances characteristic of twins and supertwins. For example, Teacher Catherine says, "Gwen, I see you have picked a friend to hold your hand while you walk. Gwen, you said this is Brooke. This is not Brooke. Brooke is standing over there. You have picked Maddie." Smiling as she looks gently and approvingly into the child's eyes, Teacher Catherine both validates Gwen's selection and contributes to her learning. Maddie may be accustomed to being addressed as her sister. Teacher Catherine's calming hand on Maddie's back reassures her with a tone of acceptance as she adds, "And Maddie, today Gwen has picked you as her friend."

Recognizing and acknowledging fairness as an issue can help you, as an early educator, guide development more specifically for twins and supertwins. Developmental issues and concerns continually surface. Parents especially want to know about developmental progress. The following Teachers Taking Action provides an example you can use to assist parents in understanding progress and catch-up.

TEACHERS TAKING ACTION: WILL THEIR DEVELOPMENT CATCH UP?

Descriptions of behavior, particularly of young children, are filled with variation. Developmental characteristics are not uniform, even for twins and supertwins. As a teacher, your guidance can alert families to their children's progress. You can gain new perspectives about children by listening to their parents' description of traits, actions, and changing preferences.

Questions from parents and their conversations with one another provide rich detail about their children's actions outside of preschools. Listening to the parents, you hear about the multiples' interactive behaviors. When you monitor exchanges of information between and from parents, you appreciate that parents want to understand their children's developmental progress. They ask, "Are my children okay? Are they like the other children? Will their development catch up?"

Multiples are often born early, and parents may require additional information about their developmental progress. Parents may already know that the majority of multiples born early catch up to expectations for their age range. Yet when the parents enroll their children in a preschool program, concerns resurface. Many are unfamiliar with the developmental range of behaviors typical and expected of all preschoolers. Parental concerns have escalated because of the regimented requirements for learning in many elementary schools. Provide parents with basic information about child growth and development to help them better understand their own children and to enhance what they may already know about multiple-birth children. (Developmental milestones and more specific information about multiples were covered in chapter 3 on physical development, chapter 4 on social and emotional development, and chapter 5 about language and learning.)

Progression in all developmental areas depends on numerous factors, including chronological age, heredity, health, and family circumstances. Too often, chronological age is treated as the only indicator for what should and should not happen during a period of time. Chronological age cannot guarantee a child's performance and achievement of a particular ability. Development occurs in steps, from the general to the specific. Children move forward in some areas, level off, regress in other areas, and then move forward again. For multiples, development includes the constant reference point of either a co-twin or co-supertwins. Remind parents of the importance of gestational age for developmental expectations of multiples.

The activities of two preschoolers—twins attending preschool for the second year—illustrate observable changes in development. This is especially evident because the twins, Will and David, are together most of the time. The togetherness creates a constant reference point to one another event though their parents and teachers avoid comparing the two. Will is climbing the slide rungs quickly. He slides down, jumps up, and is ready to climb again. His brother, David, remains inside the classroom instead. At least today, he prefers to wait his turn at the technology interest center. The previous month, it was David who was leading the tricycle group around the path, agilely and quickly, and it was Will who remained inside, monitoring his headset with the other children participating at the listening picture book center. Children's preferences and abilities may change daily. Their readiness, preferences, and participation in activities may change alternately as they progress. Their activity levels and interest in experiences tend to balance out when observed over a period of time. Because Will and David are together most of the time, their changing and alternating behaviors are apparent to their preschool teachers.

Changing and Alternating Behaviors

Changing and alternating behaviors affect behavioral characteristics as well **(UNPT #6: Recognition of potential for developmental delay without exaggeration) (PPUNPT #28: Recognize the changing balance of the twin relationship, including alternating leader-follower patterns).** Sometimes parents provide information to teachers by saying, "Will seemed to be more dominant after his third birthday. Then it was David. Now it seems as if Will wants to be the leader." Other parents may label one of their children, perhaps inappropriately branding him with a comment such as "He's always the bossy one." Families benefit from your explanations about their children's development, including their changing patterns of behavior. Lyla may be the dominant leader for a while. Leilani may become more assertive outwardly or in other ways, only to be followed by Lyla's insistence on making their decisions as they exchange behaviors again. Children also assume different behaviors in different settings, sometimes because of adults' guidance and sometimes because of adults' expectations. Their reactions may depend on whether they are familiar with the setting and the people. Twins modify their behaviors depending on the time, place, and expectations. Their approaches and actions may alternate, sometimes on a daily basis. Regardless of these changing dynamics (**PPUNPT #28: Recognize the changing balance of the twin relationship, including alternating leader-follower patterns**) (**PPUNPT #33: Develop strategies to maintain motivation of a twin who appears to be second in most activities**), the children's intrinsic characteristics and temperaments are consistent.

Insight from parents can help you make collaborative decisions with them (**PPUNPT #14: Attend to each relationship and situation as a cooperative decision with parents**). Accordingly, you and other colleagues on your teaching staff should encourage parents to avoid comparing their children (**PPUNPT #33: Develop strategies to maintain motivation of a twin who appears to be second in most activities**), whether these are triplets, quadruplets, or larger groups. In helping parents understand the development of supertwins, try to describe their performance and progress in relation to their peer group rather than to each other. (**PPUNPT #7: Assess each child to determine individual developmental abilities and potential delays**).

Parents' concern about developmental progress is addressed in the last question on the Teachers Taking Action form. Parents watching their children grow often knowingly and unknowingly compare them with one another. Encourage parents to avoid comparisons, and provide them with information about typical and expected growth and development (**PPUNPT #4: Remain receptive to acquiring information and understanding about the development of twins, including their physical maturity, learning readiness, language acquisition, and social-emotional behaviors**) (**PPUNPT #8: Utilize the preschool experience as an essential resource for early intervention, as needed**) (**PPUNPT #24: Place twins in comparable group settings, subject to the developmental needs of the twins who are placed in separate groups or rooms**).

This may diminish their concerns and encourage them to focus less on the discernible differences and more on the achievements and progress of their children.

Using the Teachers Taking Action form involves three steps. First, state a question, concern, or issue. Second, align applicable needs to the question. Third, select the program practices that refer to the question and the needs identified. The children and families whose question is under review shape the question. Refer to the UNPT list of needs provided in appendix A and the PPUNPT inventory of practices in appendix B.

The question proposed in the Teachers Taking Action example below is "Will their development catch up?" It reflects parents' concern about development of triplet boys, Allan, Jeff, and Ryan, as it compared with that of singleborn children in the preschool, as well as differences among the triplets. The six needs and nine practices offer discussion points and informative guidelines for collaborative conference with the parents. This example illustrates how to apply the UNPT to triplets. Apply information about twins cautiously until research about supertwins expands.

Teachers Taking Action

Linking Practices to Meet the Unique Needs of Twins and Supertwins

Question, Concern, Issue: Will their development catch up?

Related Unique Needs (UNPT list items):
2. Recognition of individual and collective needs.
5. Recognition and encouragement of the child's differences without emphasis.
10. Flexible school and placement policies accommodating the twins' situational needs.
11. Principals and teachers receptive to acquiring current twin research and information.
16. Description of performance and progress related to the child's peer group.
17. Freedom from comparison with the child's co-twin.

Relevant Program Practices to Meet the Unique Needs (PPUNPT list items):

3. Recognize individual needs of each child and his or her mutual needs as a member of a twin pair.

15. Welcome conversation with parents about preschool-age development, highlighting twin information.

24. Place twins in comparable group settings, subject to the developmental needs of the twins who are placed in separate groups or rooms.

26. Interact with each twin as both an individual and a multiple, respecting differences between twins and accepting similarities.

27. Acknowledge the characteristics, preferences, abilities, and strengths of each twin.

28. Recognize the changing balance of the twin relationship, including alternating leader-follower patterns.

30. Encourage behaviors and actions that free twins from being compared with one another.

33. Develop strategies to maintain motivation of a twin who appears to be second in most activities.

Date: January 25, 2010

Comments: Allan, Jeff, and Ryan were enrolled last week. The intake interview provided the following information. The boys were born early, at 32 weeks. Their parents have carefully monitored the boys' development with continuing guidance from medical staff. The boys are healthy and progressing. Developmental assessments have been conducted every six months. The parents were told at the last developmental assessment that the boys' motor and language development skills lag somewhat behind their cohorts' expectations, even after their corrected age was considered. The deficits vary for each boy. The boys are trizygotic, so genetically they do not have identical genes. Their height and weight vary. Allan is in the 40th percentile for height; Ryan is in the 38th; and Jeff is in the 32nd. The parents want to be sure that the boys' development and behavior will be similar to that of the other boys in their group and age. The parents have repeatedly asked whether their sons' growth will catch up.

Recommendations: Request copies of the developmental assessments conducted externally on the triplets. Invite parents to participate in the classroom, and schedule additional observation time to coordinate with time availability of the program administrator. Schedule follow-up conferences with the parents to review the observations completed by teachers and program administrator.

Action Taken: The developmental assessment data indicated that the boys are developing steadily. Their motor and language skills are individually different. As trizygotic multiples, they display differing and individual growth patterns, abilities, and preferences. The program administrator followed up with the parents in conferences to answer questions regarding the boys' developmental progress. The parents observed other children in the program who demonstrated a wide range of behaviors. The parents responded positively to this information and indicated that it helped them see the differences in their sons' behaviors and individualities. The initial observations of Allan, Ryan, and Jeff that were completed by the teacher and program administrator were combined with resource handouts during the conference with parents. The information established a valuable foundation of information for the parents. Their questions during the conference revealed a sense of satisfaction with the boys' development and their potential for catching up developmentally, particularly after observing the actions and behaviors of the other children.

Parents continue to reach out to early childhood educators for information, confirmation of perceptions, and interpretation of data. Information based on research findings is valuable when it is applicable for parents, particularly when the information helps them understand their multiples. During the early childhood years, the daily presence of parents in the preschool program offers opportunities for you to directly relate to them, and it offers an extraordinary opportunity to have an impact on the lives of their children through informal family education. Teachers are able to interact directly with parents by answering their questions and sharing current findings about developmental progress. Early childhood educators build strong foundations for families and children. One of the ways you accomplish this is by distributing information about development, progress, and the substance of transition to primary grades while the twins and supertwins are still enrolled in the early childhood program. The opportunities change radically for parents once their children enter primary grades.

Guidelines and Transition to Primary Grades

When early childhood educators have access to research-informed knowledge about multiples, they feel enlightened, as one teacher indicated. "Now I understand what one of my parents was trying to explain to me about her twins." The increasing enrollment of multiples in early childhood programs focuses attention on multiples. To help answer teachers' questions, this book offers specific information about the development, relationships, and early education of twins and supertwins. Classroom placement of multiples is one topic that reverberates in questions from teachers. Mandated policies dictating school experiences for multiples motivated some parents to demand a voice in school decisions about their children. Parents want school experiences to respect their twins' and supertwins' unique circumstances.

Teachers' demands for information about twins and supertwins and the parents' advocacy for their children resemble another movement decades ago. Before the implementation of Public Law 91-230, Education of the Handicapped Act of 1970, children who were learning disabled did not receive special services or education (Berger 2005). Teachers and parents embarked together on a goal to provide suitable education for children whose needs were not addressed by the educational system. Today mainstreaming and inclusion are synonymous with quality care and education.

To ensure similar success for twins and supertwins, teachers' preparation must include coursework on twins and supertwins. More research is still needed about multiples and their unique circumstances. When teachers are introduced to research-based findings during their professional preparation as a matter of policy, they will be ready to best serve multiples and their families (Segal and Russell 1992).

Considering Guidelines to Meet the Needs of Twins and Supertwins

Information about the development of twins and supertwins changes practices in early childhood programs. No single policy adequately addresses the needs of all twins and supertwins. No structured list of rules can ensure their well-being. Ideally, school policy is formulated with considerable collaboration between the educators and families, especially families with multiples. Formulating evidence-based guidelines together accommodates and makes use of dual perspectives: yours and parents'.

School policies in the United States have been based on information slanted decidedly in favor of singleborn children. Regulations and standards do not cite information about multiples. Research findings about the developmental needs of twins and supertwins can help you formulate usable guidelines. A comprehensive platform for early childhood education must include information about multiples. Honor the individuality of each child, recognize the differences and similarities among children in a multiple group, and acknowledge their close relationship.

School policy regarding twins and supertwins can consist of one brief statement or thoroughly detailed guidelines. Develop guidelines by assembling questions and central issues that teachers and parents have presented about multiples. For example, one issue may concern denial of enrollment because of limited space for a family with two or more children. To make your guidelines more inclusive of multiples, use steps similar to those you used in crafting other school policies.

1. Collect input and questions from parents and teachers.
2. List the issues and concerns.
3. Review existing preschool policies and guidelines.
4. Articulate proposed changes; review with staff, parents, and advisory board.

5. Establish guidelines; integrate with existing school purpose, guidelines, and policies.

Practical guidelines and policies emerge from discussions with teachers and parents in a collaborative process. Your guidelines should be varied and functional. A single statement could read something like this:

The University Child Development Center acknowledges the special circumstances of twins and supertwins and their families by supporting flexible policies related to their enrollment.

You might consider creating an enrollment addendum to your existing school policies that includes information about twins and supertwins. The list of unique needs and program practices can inform specific guidelines and statements. In programs with high enrollment of multiples, a more thorough list of guidelines may be included. The following list illustrates three examples of flexible guidelines.

The University Child Development Center sets out to respect the relationship among multiples while encouraging their individuality.

The University Child Development Center maintains flexible enrollment policies for twins and supertwins by collaborating with parents in the decision-making process.

The University Child Development Center encourages its staff to interact with each twin as both an individual and as a multiple, respecting the twins' and supertwins' differences and accepting their similarities.

Your particular type of school and program determine what information about twins and supertwins is applicable. The guidelines you develop are particularly pertinent for parents, especially those reviewing your school's suitability for enrollment of their children. Your guidelines might state the following:

The University Child Development Center will remain receptive to acquiring and sharing current twin and supertwin research and information with families.

Establishing guidelines and policies requires staff time. Flexible guidelines fundamentally benefit the children and encourage parents' receptiveness to their children's educational environment. The inclusion of information about twins and supertwins in school guidelines generates a sense of belonging for them and their families. They benefit from additional guidelines concerning the transition process, which particularly affects them. The practices proposed for successful transition from preschool to kindergarten are most useful when joined with the information from the research studies found throughout the previous chapters.

Transitioning to Primary Grades

Cross-culturally and historically, formalized teaching has begun for children between the ages of five and seven years. During this two-year span, all children go through tremendous changes in all developmental areas; these transformations contribute to their increasing receptivity for systematic learning and direction.

Within the five- to seven-year-old range, children make the transition to primary school and traditionally begin attending kindergarten. Some children move directly from home to kindergarten. Some young children move from child care, and many from a variety of early childhood programs. Kindergarten attendance marks a transition for the entire family. When singleborn and multiple children begin attending kindergarten, their daily routines change and contact expands beyond their parents and siblings.

The kindergarten environment introduces many changes for young children: The traditional elementary school classroom can be expected to be more structured than quality early childhood settings. The larger kindergarten classes require children to interact with more adults and more children. Many kindergarten classrooms require children to sit for longer periods of time and to maintain greater self-control than they did in preschool. Some children are required to ride a bus to kindergarten with an unfamiliar adult and older children (Pianta and Cox 2002). These differences present considerable changes for the children transitioning from preschool or home to kindergarten. The transition to primary school is influenced by each child's maturity level and his or her preparation for the new experience.

Educating at Home

Some families choose to educate their children at home. Homeschooling involves direct parental participation in the children's education. It is an alternative to the traditional private and more formalized public school settings. Some parents select homeschooling to ensure a religious-based education, others want to avoid violence in schools, and some want to increase the amount of time they spend with their children (McReynolds 2007). Still others select homeschooling because they are dissatisfied with academic instruction in the school setting. A 2003 survey by the U.S. Department of Education found that parents who homeschool do so primarily because they are concerned about the school environment, including such issues as safety, drugs, and negative peer pressure (World Almanac 2008).

The National Center for Education Statistics reported in 2007 that 1.5 million students were being homeschooled in the United States. The increase from 850,000 in 1999 is dramatic. Increasingly, homeschool families participate in Internet-based instruction and join learning cooperatives and other forms of community-based learning (Bielick 2008). An additional option is part-time school enrollment coupled with homeschooling (McReynolds 2007). Data about families who educate at home identify the number but not the age of children in each household. The number of multiples who are homeschooled is unknown at this time.

Families of twins and supertwins may consider the homeschooling option to avoid contentious dealings with school districts about classroom placement. Parents who do so eliminate the burden of negotiating with the school district or waiting for modification of fixed rules. Some parents of twins and supertwins may choose to homeschool because neighborhood schools cannot accommodate their needs—for example, the kindergarten classroom may have limited openings or be unable to schedule the children in the same session.

Parents who homeschool indicate that they can modify curriculum to accommodate the varying educational levels of their children. Parents of multiples who homeschool can meet the differing learning needs of their twins, triplets, quadruplets, or larger groups without imposing grade-school specific content on them.

Transition Practices That Work

Transition to primary grades is considered complex. Positive relationships among schools and families and supportive activities appear to ease the potential stress of moving from one program to another. Parental involvement in the school and the parents' feelings of self-worth are associated with improved academic results for their children (Rous 2009).

Children who experience positive teacher-child relations, both during and after transitions, are predicted to adjust more soundly to the new school experiences and settings. Children in transition also benefit from programs in which teachers and administrators regard social skills highly and are familiar with the requirements of the children's next school environment (Rous 2009). The quality of the preschool program that children attend influences their transition. Equally important, the family and the peer group influence children's success in their new school setting. How families and schools interact and cooperate is the major factor in a successful transition for young children.

Policies that build bonds and partnerships between preschools and elementary schools contribute to positive transitions for children. Transition-planning teams with representation from both preschools and elementary schools are needed to enhance home-school partnerships. One suggestion emerging from team planning is early contact between the teachers and children and their families. This is preferable to impersonal, group-oriented activities that occur too late to build relationships (Pinata and Cox 2002).

Beneficial practices include inviting primary school teachers to personally call on children before or after school starts. Teachers who visit children's homes and preschool classrooms create valuable transition practices. These are uncommon practices, but they are preferable to mailing form letters that merely list school requirements. Contact by teachers with the children and families is encouraged (Pianta and Cox 2002).

Transitional practices validated in one study emphasized the benefit of communitywide and programwide activities. Information that clearly specified time lines, referral, and enrollment processes was considered valuable. Clearly delineated roles and responsibilities of staff members contributed to the functioning transition process, and staff-to-staff communication across programs was supported. Meetings for the individual child and family were emphasized (Rous 2008). Essentially, researchers recommend that elementary school personnel reach out to families and preschools, connecting with families before the children begin attending kindergarten. Such efforts can range from distributing pamphlets to making personal contact (Bohan-Baker and Little 2004).

READINESS

Transition is considered closely connected to readiness. Readiness of children for a new experience, especially one as important as a new school, is multifaceted. Because readiness is so important, it should be developed over a multiyear period (Bohan-Baker and Little 2004). Readiness for multiple-birth children is influenced by their dynamics of the pair or group and the interactions they may or may not have with them. The type of preschool experiences they have had also contributes to their readiness. By the time multiples are ready to make the transition to primary school, most can group themselves into categories by more than just their age and gender—they also know they are members of a sibling group. Children who are twins identify themselves as twins. Triplets know they are one of three in a group. A group of four understands the label *quadruplets* when it refers to them. Understanding these concepts represents another unique undertaking for multiples.

Readiness to make the transition to kindergarten requires that the children have the necessary skills and capabilities to function in an environment different from their preschool's. As children mature, they become more logical in their thinking. This is important, but readiness for primary grades is multidimensional—what they know is only part of their preparedness for school. Other important elements in school readiness include physical well-being and motor development, language development, social and emotional development, cognition and general knowledge, and the way in which they approach learning (Bruner, Floyd, and Copeman 2005).

As they develop, children become more skilled at categorizing and sequencing, and as their familiarity with people, events, and objects increases, so does their memory. Children who are ready for kindergarten can reverse images and have a better sense of time, using their increasing cognitive skills. Their imagination, language, and listening abilities are improving. Children who are ready for kindergarten have gained mastery over movement skills and may be more socially capable. Essentially, as children become ready to make the transition to kindergarten, they are developing in all areas.

Some assess children to determine acceptance for kindergarten enrollment. The assessments try to evaluate what a child can do and knows. But because young children do not develop at a consistent rate, the effectiveness of this type of evaluation for determining kindergarten admission is unsubstantiated. Ideally, assessment should be used by educators to tailor learning to the specific needs of each child (Rhode Island Kids Count 2005).

The outcome of assessing children's readiness for kindergarten places an exaggerated burden on parents of multiples because the children may be progressing normally but at differing rates of development, as discussed in chapter 3. Evaluation to determine kindergarten readiness may unnecessarily exaggerate the differences between the multiple children and force undesirable comparisons and competitive behaviors.

PREPARATION

You can prepare children for their progress to kindergarten by becoming familiar with the expectations for them at their next school. Knowing expectations can assist you in promoting the children's developmental skills with best practices. Teachers need to guide children within appropriate developmental ranges to achieve success while maintaining high self-regard. You can best prepare preschoolers by giving them opportunities to communicate in the dialect used in kindergarten (Bowman and Moore 2006). Proficiency in language is critical for children's school success (Rhode Island Kids Count 2005). Familiarity with symbols gives them an advantage. Effective transition strategies include working with families to honor the child's home language and culture. Their ability to get along with peers is important and valuable. Social and emotional interactions in the early childhood setting can enhance young children's feelings of security and build behaviors that position them to meet new situations and circumstances with ease.

Quality preschool programs buffer children by establishing opportunities for them to interact and develop responsive and resilient actions. Resiliency creates protective factors that help children deal with new situations and people. Children with outgoing temperaments are more able to control their impulsive behaviors. Children who live in healthy circumstances make the transition to kindergarten successfully (Bowman and Moore 2006). Interestingly, children with resilient behaviors can often name a favorite teacher who was an influential role model (Gullo 2006).

From Preschool to Kindergarten: Transition for Multiples

Twins and supertwins join other kindergartners when they make the transition from preschool, meeting larger groups of children and interacting with a greater number of adults.

The parents of twins and supertwins can anticipate that most primary school teachers have not been provided information about the needs of multiples. Their misinformation or lack of information may lead to undesirable circumstances. A first grade teacher revealed that she simply replicated the book order submitted by six-year-old Bella when her twin, Caroline, was absent from school the day the book order was due. This disappointed Caroline, who had wanted to select her own books, different from those Bella had ordered. The teacher admitted that the experience taught her the importance of respecting each individual child, including each individual twin. Another challenge for families of multiples is locating schools that can accommodate their two, three, four, or more children, especially if the parents request the children's placement in the same classroom.

Some early childhood professionals support parents' decision to delay kindergarten entrance until the children are behaviorally ready. This approach is particularly supported because of the heavy academic pressures in kindergarten, the removal of play from many programs, and children's unfamiliarity with school expectations. Children also begin attending kindergarten with teachers who are not usually familiar with them until they arrive on the first day of class. This is one reason early childhood professionals encourage schools to become ready for the children by reaching out to the families as much as possible before school begins. This action prepares kindergarten teachers to address the varied levels of developmental abilities of the children, including multiples.

The La Trobe Twin Study reported that nearly 25 percent of participating parents postponed their multiples' entrance to kindergarten. The primary reasons given were language delays or social immaturity. Lead researcher and *Twins in School* author David Hay suggests that parents remember that prematurity is more common to twins than single born children. The potential long-term effects of prematurity are major factors in determining readiness, especially when school entry depends on formal age criteria, that is, children's chronological age (Hay 1991).

KINDERGARTEN ADMISSION DATE

Children enrolled in a typical kindergarten classroom in the United States represent a considerable age range, from as young as four and three-quarters years to seven and one-quarter years in some kindergartens. Kindergarten enrollment dates confirm a wide range: as of 2006–2007, five states required that children who enter kindergarten turn five years old on or before August 15, while in four states children had only to be five years old by November 30 or as late as January 1 of the kindergarten school year (Berk 2006). Holding children's enrollment another year, regardless of their birth-date eligibility, is a practice referred to as *redshirting*, a trend that became popular with parents after academic pressures on kindergartners increased (Berk 2006).

One measure that suggests some schools are becoming ready for the children rather than expecting the children to conform to rigid expectations is the adjustment of kindergartens' admission cutoff date. When schools push back their kindergarten entrance date, more children are at least five years old when they begin attending (Kagan and Kauerz 2006). This approach is favorable for all children and may be especially so for twins and supertwins because it better accommodates their range of developmental abilities. Developmental differences can be more apparent during the early childhood years, when even a few weeks make a difference in the progression and attainment of a skill.

Adjusting to Kindergarten and Primary Grades

As children move into kindergarten settings, twins and supertwins experience increased awareness of their multiplehood as a greater number of reactions to their multiplehood become evident. Their adjustment to kindergarten is dependent on several factors. Attendance and participation in a quality preschool that supported their developing social and emotional competency will prepare them for the changing and more rigorous routines in kindergarten. The location of the kindergarten classroom is another factor. Children who make the transition to a prekindergarten and kindergarten situated near their preschool experience more favorable outcomes. They may have met some of the school personnel, become familiar with general routines such as school traditions, and have regularly visited the library "at the big school."

Researcher Britta Alin Åkerman believes that problems may be expected when triplets start kindergarten, because so few examples of triplets exist and so little information is available about them. In contrast, in her study of triplets, she reports that teachers indicated triplets developed identities with good self-concepts and made their own friends. The teachers had thought the triplets would be competitive, subject to more comparisons from others, and too dependent on one another, but instead, the teachers saw advantages in the triplet relationships when the triplets were in class together. The teachers' attitudes influenced the school experience. Some appreciated the convenient contact with parents and same homework routines and projects when the triplets were in the same class. The teachers learned the preferences, interests, and traits of each child in the trio group (Alin Åkerman 1999).

THE QUESTION OF PLACEMENT

Separate placement of triplets is not recommended if it isolates one of the children from the rest of the trio. Although to some parents and teachers it may seem logical to place the MZ twins together and the third triplet in another classroom, doing so is not recommended. In Alin Åkerman's study, the parents who chose different classrooms for their triplets did so because the children possessed significantly different abilities in achievement levels. Schools best benefit children when they are flexible enough to accommodate the many different needs of multiples and their families.

Nancy, a parent of MZ twins, recalls that her sons attended school in separate classrooms for kindergarten and first and second grades. The boys were placed in separate classrooms at their parents' request. When the family moved to a smaller community, the school could offer only one single-grade classroom placement for the twins. Consequently, the boys were enrolled in the same classroom for the first time. Nancy says, "As a parent, I was astounded at the way the teacher treated the boys. Charles would come home to tell me that the teacher said his brother, Robert, did something wrong. She would tell Charles to go home and tell me to come to school to talk about Robert's behavior. You would think," Nancy emphasizes, "that they would have learned something about relating to children and especially something about twins."

Kathy Dolan is the mother of twin boys. Her advocacy began when school personnel informed her that her sons would not be placed in the same classroom, a decision she did not accept. She advocated for nationwide legislation, similar to what had been established in Minnesota, authorizing parental participation in their multiples' education. California attorney and mother of triplets Elizabeth Knutson created a Web site on which supporters could register their opinions about petitions supporting the twins bills. Both Dolan and Knutson encouraged families of multiples to join the efforts to empower parents as the primary voice for their children's school placement, whether together or apart.

As twins and supertwins mature, they have their own opinions about classroom placement. Multiples develop greater understanding of their own status. Their parents may encounter unrealistic pressures from other adults for their children to perform similarly. The constant presence of a same-age sibling or siblings, regardless of classroom placement, causes excessive scrutiny from others, many of whom are unable to avoid concentrating on competition and comparison.

COMPARISON AND FAIRNESS IN PRIMARY GRADES

School-age children begin comparing themselves in terms of their appearances, physical development, and academic achievement. Some parents also emphasize comparisons among the children, even when they are in different classrooms. Unfortunately, comparisons of children by parents occur too often when the children's academic achievement is not progressing similarly. The issue of comparison is addressed in chapter 6, "Freedom from Comparison with the Child's Co-Twin," page 149. Kindergartners, like preschoolers, have the right to be free from comparison. In primary school, comparison may be magnified as the matter of fairness is introduced, especially related to honors and awards. Fairness is not a reason to withhold an honor in order to shield a disappointed twin. Teachers can help develop the abilities of the child who may be second too often. For example, teachers can help parents assist their child to shape a winning science project for the next annual contest (**PPUNPT #33: Develop strategies to maintain motivation of a twin who appears to be second in most activities**). Primary-age multiples desire to be acknowledged for their own characteristics, preferences, abilities, and strengths (**PPUNPT #27: Acknowledge the characteristics, preferences, abilities, and strengths of each twin**) and to attend a school that helps them remain motivated.

Author and school-age twins researcher John Mascazine reports that there are three major issues relating to multiple children. These are competition and comparison by others, working with peers who may not understand the learning styles of multiples, and balancing the expectations of others with their own. Mascazine points out that what may be a simple action or task for singleborn children can be an issue for multiples. Even school photographs can be an issue; for example, one photographer returned a co-twin's photos, thinking he had taken double photographs of the same child (2004).

When Mascazine looked at multiples as learners, considering learning-style factors such as environment, modes of communication, and social interaction, he found that twins share 40 percent of their learning-style factors.

A Powerful Unit

Children in twin and supertwin groups create powerful units. Their unit influences their friendships and determines their playmates. Multiples share many of the same friends during the early childhood years, and some share and exchange best friends throughout adolescence and even adulthood. Sharing playmates affects multiples' inclusion and exclusion from events such as playtimes, sleepovers, birthday parties, and travel invitations—an especially personal concern for twins because they always have a sibling who is in the same setting and participates in most of the same activities. Exclusion and inclusion is far more noticeable for multiples. For example, a parent may extend an after-school playtime invitation to only one of the triplets simply because there is only one car seat or a limited number of seat belts available. Or a parent may not know the invited child has triplet siblings, especially if the multiples do not resemble one another or are in different classrooms. Parents who are informed about the unique needs of multiples can prepare their children to handle circumstances of inclusion and exclusion. Because multiples should be encouraged to make individual friends as they mature, solo invitations may be accepted and supported (**UNPT #18: Encouragement to make individual friends as the child matures**).

Twins and supertwins face issues unique to their status. Some issues are less problematic when teachers and principals become more informed about multiples' unique needs. More sensitive behaviors from teachers and principals translate into practices that help prepare the school-age multiples to balance their status with the perceptions others have about them.

Successful Transition: How Preschools Can Help

Well-prepared teachers in high-quality preschools provide opportunities for children to explore, imagine, and assume self and social responsibility. Preschools purposefully prepare parents for their children's transition to the primary grades by expanding parental awareness of typically developing children and evidence-based research about their twins and supertwins. Teachers and program administrators will be better prepared to respond to the needs of multiples with specific and positive information about twins and supertwins.

Supporting successful experiences during preschool children's transition to the primary grades should include consideration of the maturational differences of multiple children. For example, unique needs specific to preschoolers have relevance for primary-age children. Twins and supertwins making the transition to kindergarten benefit when you recognize and encourage their differences without emphasis, and when you encourage their independence as they are ready (**UNPT #5: Recognition and encouragement of the child's differences without emphasis**) (**UNPT #19: Independence as the child is ready**). Children's experiences while making the transition to kindergarten are most successful when there is a synchronized plan; preschools and school districts create continuity for the children through collaborative planning for transition from one level to another.

Transition to the primary grades includes various types of orientation, including kindergarten roundup, classroom visits, short session attendance, and staggered enrollment. Preschool teachers and primary school teachers who connect with each other during meetings and conferences, even through e-mail, enhance their communication, heightening positive outcomes for children. Staggering children's enrollment eases them into a new situation, a new schedule, and new people. Staggered enrollment schedules the first day of attendance for a few children each day.

Permitting the use of transition materials, such as backpacks with special items from home and from preschool, increases children's comfort levels and adjustment to kindergarten. If transition is difficult for them, or if they are assigned to different classrooms, multiples benefit from opportunities to see and meet one another's teachers before the first day of class (**PPUNPT #5: Capitalize on the twins' mutual support to facilitate their transitions in early childhood programs**).

Children continually develop social skills, and as they do, they may confidently develop positive relationships with their teachers. When children have quality relationships with their teachers, their skills and behaviors are positively enhanced. Positive skills and behaviors also attract other children into their peer group. The social skills also influence their school readiness (Palermo et al. 2007). The type of program and the length of the daily program affect adjustment and transition. Full-day kindergarten may be less effective for children, especially if the classes are large (Zvoch, Reynolds, and Parker 2008). Readiness seems to be dependent for some children on their prekindergarten experiences. Children from diverse ethnic and linguistic backgrounds and those from low-income families achieve gains in prekindergarten programs according to a 2008 study. Although the study was not focused on multiples as a group, its findings demonstrate that enrollment in center-based child care programs and public school prekindergarten programs may contribute to school readiness. The study showed particular gains in language and cognition skills for poor and ethically diverse children (Winsler et al. 2008).

Transition is less stressful for children when kindergarten meets their developmental needs. Children, including those who are twins and supertwins, adjust more successfully to the kindergarten environment and its teachers when their needs are recognized. Teachers who become tuned in to the characteristics and needs of children take action responsively toward the specific children in their classes. They arrange the setting with considerable attention to the lighting, noise level, privacy, size, and arrangement of the room.

Mixed-age classrooms offer an exemplary method for encouraging positive transition. This arrangement is particularly accommodating to multiples, considering that developmental differences of the children in a group from one family are possible. Particularly relevant to primary-age children are the unique needs identified for preschoolers, including being given opportunities for independence as they are ready and for self-responsibility adjusted to each co-twin's level of maturity (**UNPT #19: Independence as the child is ready**) (**UNPT #21: Opportunities for self-responsibility adjusted to each co-twin's level of maturity**). The program practices particularly effective for primary-age children include recognizing their individual needs and their needs as members of a multiple group, capitalizing on their mutual support, interacting with each as an individual and as a multiple, and acknowledging each child's characteristics, preferences, abilities, and strengths (**PPUNPT #3: Recognize individual needs of each child and his or her mutual needs as a member of a twin pair**) (**PPUNPT #5: Capitalize on the twins' mutual support to facilitate their transitions in early childhood programs**) (**PPUNPT #26: Interact with each twin as both an individual and a multiple, respecting differences between twins and** accepting similarities) (**PPUNPT #27: Acknowledge the characteristics, preferences, abilities, and strengths of each twin**). Different levels of achievement are less obvious in groupings that accommodate a wide range of abilities and skills. Comparison and competition are reduced. Primary schools without grade distinctions offer twins and supertwins beneficial opportunities to develop and interact in experiential learning environments.

Meeting Needs with a Flexible Perspective

Teachers and program administrators who are willing to acquire and apply knowledge about twins and supertwins profoundly affect early education. The perspectives of early childhood educators contribute to the development of multiples during their preschool and primary-school experiences.

Twins and supertwins develop in their own unique ways, and developmental variations among the children in twin and supertwin groups occur. Accordingly, preschool and primary school teachers should expect discernible differences between same-age siblings who make the transition from preschool into kindergarten classrooms. Success in primary grades and the possibilities for long-term success in life are dependent on early school experiences.

This book was written especially for you, the early childhood professional. The increasing population of multiples, and the absence of information about them in professional preparatory work, prompted my efforts to promote an understanding of them by presenting information that is relevant to you, program administrators, and the parents of the multiple-born children enrolled in early childhood programs. In writing this book, I identified important themes, including the primary point that twins and supertwins are worthy of study. Research-based findings about their development establish the foundation of knowledge to inform your discipline, which guides and educates children and their families.

A second recurring theme focuses on the unique needs of multiples and the flexible and sensitive program practices that meet their specific circumstances.

Finally, support for parental input on preschool experiences for their twins and supertwins has been a continuous premise. Collaboration between schools and families has lasting significance. The partnership established early with parents empowers them to become advocates for their children's education. The quality of the team relationship with parents is a valuable incentive for you and directly benefits the families of multiple-birth children.

As an early childhood educator, you are best positioned in your profession to offer the most enduring educational foundation for multiples. Enhance the quality early education practices you already honor with a foundation of knowledge about twins and supertwins. Ensure their quality experiences for optimal growth and development with a flexible perspective, one that is filled with sensitive and responsive practices. Honor the practices that meet the needs of multiples as individuals and as members of a group. You can profoundly influence twins, supertwins, and their families by meeting their unique needs with understanding.

Glossary

assisted reproductive technology (ART)
Assisted reproductive technology includes a range of infertility treatments, including ovulation-stimulating drugs, in vitro fertilization, and gamete or zygote transfer.

attention deficit/hyperactivity disorder (ADHD)
Attention deficit/hyperactivity disorder is considered one of the most common childhood disorders. The disorder produces heightened levels of inattention and/or hyperactive and impulsive behavior.

autonomous language
Autonomous language is an incomplete form of adult communication that children in all families can develop. Twins develop autonomous language because they model immature language to one another.

child development center
A child development center provides care and education in a facility based outside of a child's home. It can be located in the community or at a school site. The children served and educated at a child development center can range from infants to approximately two to five years of age. Child development centers include publicly funded, nonprofit, and private-for-profit programs.

conjoined
Conjoined twins are born physically attached in some way. Conjoined twins previously were referred to as Siamese twins.

couple effect
The couple effect refers to the interdependent nature of the twin relationship, in which circumstances are shared and complementary.

dyadic
Dyadic means two. Twins, especially during the early childhood years, interact in a dyadic relationship with their co-twin and a triadic (three-way) relationship with their parent and co-twin.

early childhood program
An early childhood program offers voluntary participation for children usually three to five years old. The programs vary widely in quality, funding, settings, organization, sponsorship, and experiences offered to the children.

epigenetics
Epigenetics is a new science focused on developmental differences that may be related to and caused by how genes are triggered on and off. The exceptional differences between monozygotic (MZ) twins are one focus.

family child care
Family child care offers child care services for small groups of infants and children in home settings other than the child's own. Licensing and qualifications vary widely by state and influence quality of care and opportunities provided for the children.

fraternal, or dizygotic (DZ)
Fraternal, or dizygotic (DZ), twins develop from two eggs and two separate sperm. They are nonidentical. Two-thirds of all twins are dizygotic. Triplets can be nonidentical or trizygotic (TZ) if all develop from different eggs fertilized by different sperm. The term *dizygotic* is more accurate, current, and preferred.

genotype
Genotype refers to genetic makeup, including features and characteristics that may or may not express themselves phenotypically (physically).

gestational age

Gestational age identifies the age of the newborn in weeks of gestation. It is often used to describe multiples to provide a corrected or appropriate age because of their early births.

higher-order multiples

Higher-order multiples (HOM) refers to children who are part of a triplet, quadruplet, quintuplet, sextuplet, septuplet, or octuplet group of multiples born to one woman from a single pregnancy. Higher-order multiples typically are conceived at the same time, are born at the same time, and share some biological makeup.

identical, or monozygotic (MZ)

Identical or monozygotic twins (MZ) develop from a single egg that splits after it is fertilized by a single sperm. Monozygotic twins have the same genes and therefore are more similar than DZ twins. One-third of all twins are MZ pairs. The term *monozygotic* is more accurate, current, and preferred.

identity

Identity is a sense of understanding oneself. Twin and supertwin children develop self-identity as individuals. They also develop a sense of identity as members of a group.

idioglossia

Idioglossia often is the term used to describe the language of twins. Private language among multiples is very rare.

imaginative play

Children's imaginative play is spontaneous and can be enjoyed whenever they have unrestricted time to act alone or with others. Multiples engage in imaginative play like singleborn children when they have time, space, and encouragement.

individuation

Individuation is the process of developing the sense of oneself as an individual.

low birth weight (LBW)
Low birth weight causes measurable differences between multiple and singleborn newborns and indicates that the newborn at birth has not gained the weight expected for that point of development.

milestones
Milestones are the developmental levels that children are expected to achieve during a particular stage of development.

mirror image
Mirror-image twins occurs in approximately 23 to 25 percent of MZ twins. Certain features appear on the opposite sides of each twin's body, making them mirror images of each other.

monozygotic (MZ) quintuplets
Quintuplets who developed from one fertilized ovum are monozygotic (identical). Birth of MZ quintuplets is rare.

multiple type
Multiple type is a description that provides a more accurate alternative to the two outdated labels *identical* and *fraternal*. Multiple type is also referred to as *zygosity* and twin type.

multiples
A multiple-birth child, multiple-birth children, and multiples are a group of two (twins) or more (supertwins) children who typically are conceived at the same time, are born at the same time, and share certain biological makeup.

octuplets
Octuplets are the eight children born to one woman from a single pregnancy. They typically are conceived at the same time, are born on the same day, and share biological makeup, depending on their zygosity.

opposite-sex twins
A boy and girl in a pair are opposite-sex twins. They are DZ twins from separate fertilized ova. They may also be referred to *unlike-sex pairs*.

phenotype

Phenotype refers to apparent physical characteristics, including appearance. (See also *genotype*.)

polyzygotic

Polyzygotic describes the many twinning patterns that compose some supertwin groups. For example, supertwins may be the result of MZ twinning and DZ twinning or only one of these types.

prematurity

Infants born prior to the thirty-seventh week of pregnancy are considered premature. Twins and supertwins are smaller at birth because on average they are born earlier than singleborn children.

PPUNPT

A list identifying the Program Practices to Meet the Unique Needs of Preschool Twins.

quadrazygotic (QZ)

The most common combination of quadruplets is quadrazygotic (QZ) supertwins, who grow from four different fertilized ova.

quadruplets

Quadruplets are the four children born to one woman from a single pregnancy. They typically are conceived at the same time, are born on the same day, and share biological makeup, depending on their zygosity.

quintuplets

Quintuplets are the five children born to one woman from a single pregnancy. They typically are conceived at the same time, are born on the same day, and share biological makeup, depending on their zygosity.

septuplets

Septuplets are the seven children born to one woman from a single pregnancy. They typically are conceived at the same time, are born on the same day, and share biological makeup, depending on their zygosity.

sextuplets
Sextuplets are the six children born to one woman from a single pregnancy. They typically are conceived at the same time, are born on the same day, and share biological makeup, depending on their zygosity.

singleborn
A singleborn child is one child born to one woman, from one pregnancy, and one birth. A singleborn child may have siblings who have different birth dates.

supertwins
Supertwins are multiple births of three or more—including triplets, quadruplets, quintuplets, sextuplets, septuplets, and octuplets—born to one woman from a single pregnancy, on the same day. Supertwins are also referred to as *higher-order multiples (HOM)* and *triplets/+*. *Co-supertwin* is the term used to identify the child who is a member of a supertwin group.

supportive checking behaviors
Supportive checking behaviors provide security to children in new settings. Very young children find comfort in noting the whereabouts of their primary caregiver. Toddlers, exploring a new playground, might walk toward the open door looking back several times for approval from their parent, caregiver, or teacher. In the same way, multiples will locate their sibling to note the sibling's location and activity involvement, achieving comfort and security.

Teachers Taking Action
A planning form intended for teachers and program administrators to use in preparing assessments of multiples. The form may be utilized for parent conferences.

triadic
Triadic means three. Multiples interact together in a three-way (triadic) relationship with one of their parents rather than in the dyadic (two-way) relationship normal for a singleborn child and his or her parent. Triplets interact together in a triadic relationship.

triplets

Triplets are the three children born to one woman from a single pregnancy. They typically are conceived at the same time, are born on the same day, and share biological makeup. They are usually trizygotic but can be the result of a single fertilized ovum that split.

triplets/+

The U.S. Department of Health and Human Services uses the term *triplets/+* to refer to triplets and higher-order multiple births in vital statistical data. In some cases, quadruplets, quintuplets, sextuplets, and other higher-order multiple births are not reported separately or differentiated in the national data set.

trizygotic (TZ)

Trizygotic refers to triplets who grow from three separate fertilized ova.

twin situation

Twins have been studied because of their genetic characteristics. The term *twin situation* refers to exploring and comparing genetic and environmental influences on human characteristics and abilities.

Twin to Twin Transfusion Syndrome (TTTS)

Twin to Twin Transfusion Syndrome is a condition in which one multiple fetus develops as expected and the other does not, probably because of their shared placenta.

twin type

Twin type is a description that provides a more accurate alternative to the two outdated labels *identical* and *fraternal*. Twin type is also referred to as *zygosity* and multiple type.

twins

Twins are the two children born to one woman from a single pregnancy. They typically are conceived at the same time, are born on the same day, and share biological makeup. *Co-twin* is the term used to identify one of the multiples in the pair.

UNPT
UNPT, the Unique Needs of Preschool Twins, is a list of twenty-two needs identified through research to assist early childhood educators and parents in facilitating the growth and development of multiples.

unlike-sex pairs
A boy and girl twin pair is referred to as *opposite-sex twins* or *unlike-sex pairs*. They are DZ twins.

vanishing twin syndrome
A vanishing twin results from a spontaneous fetal reduction, in which one or more of multiple fetuses does not survive. This occurs because one of the gestational sacs does not develop and is absorbed into the uterus or disintegrates. Also referred to as *spontaneous fetal reduction*.

virtual twins
Virtual twins are unrelated children who are the same age and from infancy are reared together in a family as siblings.

zygosity
Zygosity identifies whether the twins developed from one or more fertilized ova. Zygosity helps clarify twin type by describing the type of conception.

Appendix A:
Unique Needs of Preschool Twins (UNPT)

Communicational refers to the preschool teacher's acknowledgment and recognition of twinship. Each twin enrolled in a preschool program has a unique need for the following:

1. Acknowledgment and encouragement both as an individual and as a twin.
2. Recognition of individual and collective needs.
3. Recognition and encouragement of individuality.
4. Recognition and understanding of twin type.
5. Recognition and encouragement of the child's differences without emphasis.
6. Recognition of potential for developmental delay without exaggeration.
7. Recognition of gender differences in maturational stages of a boy-girl twin pair.
8. Attention to the child's unique medical history, home life, and interaction with children outside the twin relationship.

Programmatic refers to the preschool's enrollment and operational plans regarding twinship. Each twin enrolled in a preschool program has a unique need for the following:

9. Policies and practices recognizing twins as a special group with unique family circumstances.
10. Flexible school and placement policies accommodating the twins' situational needs.

11. Principals and teachers receptive to acquiring current twin research and information.
12. Added consideration in preschool admission.
13. Parent conferences and placement procedures sensitive and responsive to twinship.
14. Reevaluation of school practices, such as mandates for classroom separation.
15. Periodic (no less frequent than annually) consultation to review group and room placement.
16. Description of performance and progress related to the child's peer group.

Relational refers to twin-specific interactions and interpersonal activities. Each twin enrolled in a preschool program has a unique need for the following:

17. Freedom from comparison with the child's co-twin.
18. Encouragement to make individual friends as the child matures.
19. Independence as the child is ready.
20. Opportunities for individual participation in activities.
21. Opportunities for self-responsibility adjusted to each co-twins' level of maturity.
22. Remaining together as long as the twins want or seem to benefit.

Appendix B:
Program Practices to Meet the Unique Needs of Preschool Twins (PPUNPT)

Communicational practices refer to the preschool teacher's acknowledgment and recognition of twinship.

1. Respect the twins' bond and relationship while encouraging the individuality of each child.
2. Value parental input prior to enrollment and throughout the children's participation in the program.
3. Recognize individual needs of each child and his or her mutual needs as a member of a twin pair.
4. Remain receptive to acquiring information and understanding about the development of twins, including their physical maturity, learning readiness, language acquisition, and social-emotional behaviors.
5. Capitalize on the twins' mutual support to facilitate their transitions in early childhood programs.
6. Integrate guidelines for twins into the program enrollment policy.
7. Assess each child to determine individual developmental abilities and potential delays.
8. Utilize the preschool experience as an essential resource for early intervention, as needed.
9. Focus on guiding the twins' development rather than on separation and placement issues.

Programmatic practices refer to preschool enrollment and operational plans about twinship.

10. Develop flexible policies and procedures sensitive to the special circumstances of families with twins.
11. Consider the needs of each pair of twins.
12. Review enrollment, space, and placement issues that may create challenging conditions for twins and their parents.
13. Regard no rigid policy as applicable to all twins.
14. Attend to each relationship and situation as a cooperative decision with parents.
15. Welcome conversation with parents about preschool-age development, highlighting twin information.
16. Respect individual progress of each twin and advance both twins as long as they are within the same developmental range.
17. Establish and maintain a flexible approach to placement.
18. Discuss separation/keeping-together issues with parents, advising them about research findings on the impact of separate placement on twins.
19. Advise parents that no substantial evidence exists for an absolute policy of classroom separation for twins to develop as individuals.
20. Schedule periodic consultations to liaison with parents about program placement.
21. When appropriate, develop procedures for group and room separation, taking into account the circumstances of each twin pair and their family.
22. Reverse a placement decision if it seems stressful for the children.
23. Review supportive methods with parents before reversing placement.
24. Place twins in comparable group settings, subject to the developmental needs of the twins who are placed in separate groups or rooms.
25. Support twins who are placed separately by arranging access to each other and introductions to each other's teachers and to the other children in the group or room.

Relational practices refer to twin-specific interaction and interpersonal activities.

26. Interact with each twin as both an individual and a multiple, respecting differences between twins and accepting similarities.
27. Acknowledge the characteristics, preferences, abilities, and strengths of each twin.
28. Recognize the changing balance of the twin relationship, including alternating leader-follower patterns.
29. Offer opportunities for the other preschoolers to gain an understanding about twinship.
30. Encourage behaviors and actions that free twins from being compared with one another.
31. Allow twins to be together as long as they want to or seem to benefit.
32. Allow twins as much independence as they are ready for during their early childhood experiences.
33. Develop strategies to maintain motivation of a twin who appears to be second in most activities.
34. Refer to each child by his or her own first name.
35. Honor any supportive checking behaviors between the twins (for example, noting each other's whereabouts and activity involvement).
36. Prepare for gender differences in maturational stages of a boy-girl twin pair.

Appendix C

Teachers Taking Action

Linking Practices to Meet the Unique Needs of Twins and Supertwins

Question, Concern, Issue: _____

_____

_____

_____

Related Unique Needs (UNPT list items): _____

_____

_____

Relevant Program Practices to Meet the Unique Needs (PPUNPT list items): _____

_____

_____

_____

Date: _____

Comments: _____

_____

_____

_____

Recommendations: _____

_____

_____

_____

Action Taken: _____

_____

_____

Appendix D:
Resources to Support
Multiples and Their Families

Partial List of Internet Resources

Asociación de Nacimientos Múltiples A.C. (ANMMEX)
www.anmgemelos.com/asociacion.html

Association d'entraide des parents de naissances multiples (ANEPNM)
www.naissancesmultiples.asso.be

Australian Multiple Birth Association (AMBA)
www.amba.org.au/

Center for Loss in Multiple Birth (CLIMB), Inc.
www.climb-support.org/

Center for the Study of Multiple Birth
multiplebirth.com

Council of Multiple Birth Organizations (COMBO)
web.mac.com/madcock313/Site/About_COMBO.html

Dutch Association for Parents of Multiples
www.nvom.net

Expecting Twins, Triplets and More
www.askdrrachel.com

Federation francaise des parents de jumeaux et plus
www.jumeaux-et-plus.fr

Finnish Multiple Births Association (FMBA)
www.suomenmonikkoperheet.fi

Hong Kong Mothers of Multiples
www.moms-hongkong.com

International Twins Association (ITA)
www.intltwins.org

Irish Multiple Births Association (IMBA)
www.imba.ie

Japanese Association of Twins' Mothers (JATM)
www.tmcjapan.org/

Minnesota Center for Twin and Family Research
www.mctfr.psych.umn.edu

Multiple Births Canada/Naissances multiples Canada (MBC)
Began as Parents of Multiple Births Association (POMBA)
www.multiplebirthscanada.org

Multiple Birth Foundation of Sri Lanka
infolanka.com/org/twin-registry/MBF.htm

Mothers of Supertwins (MOST)
www.mostonline.org

Multiple Births Foundation (United Kingdom)
www.multiplebirths.org.uk/

National Organization of Mothers of Twins Clubs (NOMTC)
www.nomotc.org

New Zealand Multiple Birth Association
www.nzmba.org

Tvillingforeldreforeningen (Norwegian Organization)
www.tvilling.no/index.php?page_id=1

Swedish Twin Society
www.tvillingklubben.se/

The Louisville Twin Study
http://louisville.edu/medschool/pediatrics/research/child-development-unit/louisville-twin-study.html

Twins Days Festival
www.twinsdays.org

Twins & Multiple Births Association (TAMBA) (United Kingdom)
www.tamba.org.uk

The International Society for Twin Studies
www.ists.qimr.edu.au

The Triplet Connection
www.tripletconnection.org

Twinless Twins Support Group
www.twinlesstwins.org

Twinsight®
www.twinsight.com

Twins and Multiples: Curtin University of Technology
www.twinsandmultiples.org

The Twin to Twin Transfusion Syndrome Foundation
www.tttsfoundation.org

Twin Services Consulting
www.twinservices.org

TWINS Magazine
www.twinsmagazine.com

References

Abbe, Kathryn McLaughlin, and Frances McLaughlin Gill. 1980. *Twins on twins*. New York: Clarkson N. Potter.

Agnew, Connie L., Alan H. Klein, and Jill Alison Ganon. 2005. *Twins! Pregnancy, birth, and the first year of life.* 2nd ed. New York: HarperCollins.

Ainslie, Ricardo C. 1997. *The psychology of twinship.* Northvale, N.J.: Jason Aronson.

Ainsworth, Mary D. Salter, and Silvia M. Bell. 1970. Attachment, exploration, and separation: Illustrated by the behavior of one-year-olds in a strange situation. *Child Development* 41 (1): 49–67.

Alin Åkerman, Britta. 1999. The psychology of triplets. In *Twin and triplet psychology: A professional guide to working with multiples,* ed. Audrey C. Sandbank, 100–118. London: Routledge.

Alin Åkerman, Britta, and Eve Suurvee. 2003. The cognitive and identity development of twins at 16 years of age: A follow-up study of 32 twin pairs. *Twin Research* 6 (4): 328–33.

Ames, Louise Bates. 1970. *Child care and development.* New York: Lippincott.

Arce, Eve-Marie. 2000. *Curriculum for young children: An introduction.* Albany, N.Y.: Delmar Thomson Learning.

———. 2008. A descriptive study of academic and practitioner perceptions identifying program practices meeting the unique needs of twins in center-based preschools. EdD diss., University of La Verne.

Asbury, Kathryn, Judith F. Dunn, Alison Pike, and Robert Plomin. 2003. Nonshared environmental influences on individual differences in early behavioral development: A monozygotic twin differences study. *Child Development* 74 (3): 933–43.

Bamforth, Fiona, and Geoffrey Machin. 2004. Why zygosity of multiple births is not always obvious: An examination of zygosity testing requests from twins or their parents. *Twins Research* 7 (5): 406–11.

Beachamp, Heather M., and Lawrence J. Brooks Jr. 2003. The perceptions, policy, and practice of educating twins: A review. *Psychology in the Schools* 40 (4): 429–37.

Begley, Sharon. 2009. What alters our genes: Was a "fraud" really a discovery? *Newsweek* (September 28): 32.

Belsky, Jay, and Michael J. Rovine. 1988. Nonmaternal care in the first year of life and the security of infant-parent attachment. *Child Development* 59 (1): 57–167.

Belsky, Jay, and Laurence D. Steinberg. 1978. The effects of day care: A critical review. *Child Development* 49: 929–49.

Berger, Kathleen. 2005. *The developing person through the life span.* 6th ed. New York: Worth.

Berk, Laura E. 2006. Looking at kindergarten children. In *Teaching and learning in the kindergarten year,* ed. Dominic F. Gullo, 11–25. Washington, D.C.: National Association for the Education of Young Children.

Bielick, Stacey. 2008. *15 Million Homeschooled Students in the United States in 2007.* National Center for Education Statistics. http://nces.ed.gov/ (accessed August 20, 2009).

Bishop, Dorothy V. M., and S. J. Bishop. 1998. Twin language: A risk factor for language impairment? *Journal of Speech, Language & Hearing Research* 41 (1): 150–60.

Blum, Deborah. 2008. Twin fates: Sharing the womb with a brother may influence a girl's development. *Science News:* 25–28.

Bohan-Baker, Marielle, and Prescilla M. D. Little. 2004. The transition to kindergarten: A review of current research and promising practices to involve families. *Harvard Family Research.* http://www.hfrp.org (accessed July 26, 2009).

Boklage, Charles E. 2006. Reply: Mosaic/chimeras and twinning in the current reproductive genetics perspective. *Human Reproduction* 21 (9): 2461–62.

Bouchard, Thomas J., Jr. 2009. http://www.psych.umn.edu/people/faculty/bouchard.htm (accessed April 29, 2009).

Bowman, Barbara, and Evelyn K. Moore, eds. 2006. School readiness and social-emotional development: Perspectives on cultural diversity. Washington, D.C.: National Black Child Development Institute.

Bruner, Charles, with Sheri Floyd and Abby Copeman. 2005. Seven things policy makers need to know about school readiness. State Early Childhood Policy Technical Assistance Network. Des Moines, Iowa: Child and Family Policy Center.

Bryan, Elizabeth. 1992. *Twins, Triplets and More.* London: Penguin Books.

Bryan, Elizabeth M. 1999. Twins with special needs. In *Twin and triplet psychology: A professional guide to working with multiples,* ed. Audrey C. Sandbank, 7–18. London: Routledge.

Buckler, John M. H. 1999. Growth and development of twins. In *Twin and triplet psychology: A professional guide to working with multiples,* ed. Audrey C. Sandbank, 143–66. London: Routledge.

Butler, Sue, Catherine McMahon, and Judy Ungerer. 2003. Maternal speech style with prelinguistic twin infants. *Infant and Child Development* 12 (2): 129–43.

Byrne, Brian, Sally Wadsworth, Robin Corley, Stefan Samuelsson, Peter Quain, John C. DeFries, Erik Willcutt, and Richard K. Olson. 2005. Longitudinal twin study of early literacy development: Preschool and kindergarten phases. *Scientific Studies of Reading* 9 (3): 219–35.

California Department of Education. 1992. *It's elementary! Elementary grades task force report,* ed. Bill Honig.

Calis, Kristin. 2008. Bundle of three delivered at Ajax-Pickering hospital. News, June 16. DurhamRegion.com. http://newsdurhamregion.com/news/article/128636 (accessed July 7, 2009).

Camilli, Gregory, Sadako Vargas, Sharon Ryan, and W. Steven Barnet. Meta-analysis of the effects of early education interventions on cognitive and social development. *Teachers College Record* 112 (3). http://www.tcrecord.org (accessed May 4, 2009).

Carbonneau, Rene, Lindon J. Eaves, Judy L. Silberg, Emily Simonoff, and Michael Rutter. 2002. Assessment of the within-family environment in twins: Absolute versus differential ratings, and relationship with conduct problems. *Journal of Child Psychology & Psychiatry & Allied Disciplines* 43 (8): 1064–74.

Carfioli, Joanne. 1998. The oral communication skills of identical twins compared to the oral communication skills of fraternal twins between the ages of 2 and 7 years. MS thesis, Texas A&M University.

Caspi, Avshalom, Terrie E. Moffitt, Julia Morgan, Michael Rutter, Alan Taylor, Louise Arseneault, Lucy Tully, Catherine Jacobs, Julia Kim-Cohen, and Monica Polo-Tomas. 2004. Maternal expressed emotion predicts children's antisocial behavior problems: Using monozygotic-twin differences to identify environmental effects on behavioral development. *Developmental Psychology* 40 (2): 149–61.

Cassidy, Sarah. 1999. Twins gain from lifestyle change. *Times Educational Supplement,* July 23, http://www.tes.co.uk/article.aspx?storycode=309244 (accessed February 5, 2009).

Cassill, Kay. 1982. *Twins: Nature's amazing mystery.* New York: Atheneum.

Celizic, Mike. 2009. Octuplet mom defends her 'unconventional' choices. http://www.msnbc.msn.com/id/29038814/ (accessed July 7, 2009).

Chandler, Vicki. 2009. Quiet down over there! The new science of slicing genes. BIO5 Institute. http://bio5.arizona.edu/node/1196 (accessed August 9, 2009).

Children's Hospital. 2009. Arthrogryposis. http://www.childrenshospital .org/az/Site594/ (accessed July 13, 2009).

Colón, Angel R., and Patricia A. Colón. 2001. *A history of children: A socio-cultural survey across millennia.* Westport, Conn.: Greenwood.

Coventry, William L., Brian Byrne, Marreta Coleman, Richard K. Olson, Robin Corley, Eric Willcutt, and Stefan Samuelsson. 2009. Does classroom separation affect twins' reading ability in the early years of school? *Twin Research and Human Genetics* 12 (5): 455–61.

Dale, Philip S., Thomas S. Price, Dorothy V. M. Bishop, Robert Plomin. 2003. Outcomes of early language delay: I. Predicting persistent and transient language difficulties at 3 and 4 years. *Journal of Speech, Language, and Hearing Research* 46 (3): 544–60.

Danby, Susan, and Karen Thorpe. 2006. Compatibility and conflict: Negotiation of relationships by dizygotic same-sex twin girls. *Twin Research and Human Genetics* 9 (1): 103–12.

Day, Ella J. 1932. The development of language of twins. A comparison of twins and single children. *Child Development* 3 (3): 179–99.

Deary, Ian J., Alison Pattie, Valerie Wilson, and Lawrence J. Whalley. 2005. The cognitive cost of being a twin: Two whole-population surveys. *Twin Research and Human Genetics* 8 (4): 376–83.

DiLalla, Lisabeth Fisher. 2006. Social development of twins. *Twin Research and Human Genetics* 9 (1): 95–102.

DiLalla, Lisabeth Fisher, and Rebecca A. Caraway. 2004. Behavioral inhibition as a function of relationships in preschool twins and siblings. *Twin Research* 7 (5): 449–55.

Dionne, Annette, Cecile Dionne, and Yvonne Dionne. 1997. Advice from the Dionne quintuplets. *Time.com.* http://www.time.com/time/printout/0,8816,987457,00.html (accessed July 6, 2009).

Dolan, Kathy. 2006. "Hello and Status," August 4, personal e-mail.

Eberling, Hanna, Tuulikki Porkka, Varpu Penninkilampi-Kerola, Eija Berg, Sari Jarvi, and Irma Moilanen. 2003. Inter-twin relationships in mental health. *Twin Research* 6 (4): 334–43.

Etaugh, Claire, and Spencer A. Rathus. 1995. *The world of children.* New York: Harcourt Brace College.

Farber, Susan L. 1981. *Identical twins reared apart: A reanalysis.* New York: Basic Books.

Farmer, Penelope. 1996. *Two, or the book of twins and doubles.* London: Virago.

Feldman, Ruth, and Arthur I. Eidelman. 2004. Parent-infant synchrony and the social-emotional development of triplets. *Developmental Psychology* 4 (6): 1133–47.

———. 2005. Does a triplet birth pose a special risk for infant development? Assessing cognitive development in relation to intrauterine growth and mother-infant interaction across the first 2 years. *Pediatrics* 115 (2): 443–52.

Feldman, Ruth, Arthur I. Eidelman, and Noa Rotenberg. 2004. Parenting stress, infant emotion regulation, maternal sensitivity, and the cognitive development of triplets: A model for parent and child influences in a unique ecology. *Child Development* 75 (6): 1774–91.

Fierro, Pamela Prindle. 2009. Quintuplets-quints. http://multiples.about.com/od/quintssextuplets/a/quintuplets.htm (accessed August 9, 2009).

Fotheringham, Janine. 2001. Identical twin women: Their experience of twinship. MEd thesis, University of Regina, Canada.

Franklin, Rachel. 2005. *Expecting twins, triplets, and more.* New York: St. Martin's Griffin.

———. 2009. "RE: Twins Early Childhood Book," August 12, personal e-mail.

Gardner, D. Bruce. 1973. *Development in early childhood.* 2nd ed. New York: Harper.

Garitte, C., J. P. Almodovar, E. Benjamin, and C. Canhao. 2002. Speech in same- and different-sex twins 4 and 5 years old. *Twin Research* 5: 538–43.

Gibbons, Jennifer. 1993. "Silent twin" of a study. Obituaries, 29 *New York Times.* http://www.nytimes.com/1993/03/12/obituaries/jennifer-gibbons-29-silent-twin-of-a-study.html (accessed August 11, 2009).

Gielen, Marj, Patrick J. Lindsey, Catherine Derom, Ruth J. Loos, Nicole Y. Souren, Aimee D. C. Paulussen, Maurice P. Zeegers, Robert Derom, Robert Vlietinck, and Jan G. Nijhuis. 2008. Twin-specific intrauterine 'growth' charts based on cross-sectional birthweight data. *Twin Research and Human Genetics* 11 (2): 224–35.

Gleason, Tracy R., and Lisa M. Hohmann. 2006. Concepts of real and imaginary friendships in early childhood. *Social Development* 15 (1): 128–43.

Gleeson, Catherine, David A. Hay, Carl J. Johnston, and T. M. Theobald. 1990. Twins in school: An Australia-wide program. *Acta Geneticae Medicae et Gemellologiae: Twin Research* 39 (2): 231–44. http://0-web.ebscohost.com. (accessed June 22, 2009).

Goldberg, Susan, and Michael Lewis. 1969. Play behavior in the year-old infant: Early sex differences. *Child Development* 40 (1): 21–31.

Goldblatt, Jennifer. 2004. Cheaper by the half-dozen? Hardly. *New York Times.* http://query.nytimes.com/gst/fullpage.html?res=9C04EZD7163AF934A25753C1A9629C8 (accessed December 15, 2009).

Goshen-Gottstein, Esther R. 1981. Differential maternal socialization of opposite-sexed twins, triplets, and quadruplets. *Child Development* 52 (4): 1255–62.

Gregory, Alice M., Fruhling V. Rijsdijk, Jennifer Y. F. Lau, Maria Napolitano, Peter McGuffin, and Thalia C. Eley. 2007. Genetic and environmental influences on interpersonal cognitions and associations with depressive symptoms in 8-year-old twins. *Journal of Abnormal Psychology* 116 (4): 762–75.

Gromada, Karen Kerkhoff, and Mary C. Hurlburt. 2001. *Keys to parenting multiples.* 2nd ed. Hauppauge, N.Y.: Barron's.

Guilherme, Romain, Severine Drunat, Anne-Lise Delezoide, Camille Le Ray, Jean-Francois Oury, and Dominique Luton. 2008. *Twin Research and Human Genetics* 11 (6): 648–55.

Gullo, Dominic E., ed. 2006. *Teaching and learning in the kindergarten year.* Washington, D.C.: National Association for the Education of Young Children.

Guo, Guany. 2006. Genetic similarity shared by best friends among adolescents. *Twin Research and Human Genetics* 9 (1): 113–21.

Hall, Judith G. 2003. Twinning. *Lancet* 362 (9385): 735–43. http://0-web.ebscohost.com (accessed June 18, 2008).

Hankins, Gary V. D., and George R. Saade. 2005. *Paediatric and Perinatal Epidemiology* 19 (Suppl. 1): 8–9.

Hay, David A. 1991. *Twins in school.* Melbourne, Australia: La Trobe Twin Study and Australian Multiple Birth Association Inc.

———. 1999. Adolescent twins and secondary schooling. In *Twin and triplet psychology: A professional guide to working with multiples,* ed. Audrey C. Sandbank, 119–42. London: Routledge.

———. 2004. Together or apart? *Twin Research* 7 (2): iii–iv.

Hay, David A., Kellie S. Bennett, Florence Levy, Joseph Sergeant, and James Swanson. 2007. A twin study of attention-deficit/hyperactivity disorder dimensions rated by the strengths and weaknesses of ADHD-symptoms and normal-behavior (swan) scale. *Biol Psychiatry* 61 (5): 700–705.

Hay, David A., Kellie S. Bennett, Michael McStephen, Rosanna Rooney, and Florence Levy. 2004. Attention deficit-hyperactivity disorder in twins: A developmental genetic analysis. *Australian Journal of Psychology* 56 (2): 99–107.

Hay, David A., C. Clifford, P. Derrick, J. Hopper, B. Renard, T. M. Theobald. 1990. Twin children in volunteer registries: Biases in parental participation and reporting. *Acta Genet Med Gemellol (Roma)* 39 (71): 71–84.

Hay, David A., and Pauline J. O'Brien. 1983. The La Trobe Twin Study: A genetic approach to the structure and development of cognition in twin children. *Child Development* 54 (2): 317–30.

Hay, David A., and Pat Preedy. 2006. Meeting the educational needs of multiple birth children. *Early Human Development* 82 (6): 397–403.

Hay, David A., M. Prior, Simon Collett, M. Williams. 1987. Speech and language development in preschool twins. *Acta Geneticae Medicae et Gemellologiae* 36 (2): 213–23.

Hayashi, Chisato, Kazuo Hayakawa, Chika Tsuboi, Keiko Oda, Yukiko Atnau, Yoko Kobayashi, and Kenji Kato. 2006. Relationship between parents' report rate of twin language and factors related to linguistic development: Older sibling, nonverbal play and preschool attendance. *Twin Research and Human Genetics* 9 (1): 165–74.

Hayiou-Thomas, Bonamy Oliver, and Robert Plomin. 2005. Genetic influences on specific versus nonspecific language impairment in 4-year-old twins. *Journal of Learning Disabilities* 38 (3): 222–32.

Iervolino, Alessandra, Melissa Hines, Susan E. Golombok, John Rust, and Robert Plomin. 2005. Genetic and environmental influences on sex-typed behavior during the preschool years. *Child Development* 76 (4): 826–40.

Institute for Behavioral Genetics. 2008. Specific twin studies http://ibg
.colorado.edu/research/sts.html (accessed November 2009).

Jackson, Donna M. 2001. *Twin tales: The magic and mystery of multiplebirth.*
Boston: Megan Tingley Books.

Jensen, Arthur. 2000. Twins. In *Encyclopedia of psychology,* ed. Allan E.
Kazden, 132–35. New York: Oxford University Press.

Kagan, Jerome. 1979. Family experiences and the child's development.
American Psychologist 34 (10): 886–91.

Kagan, Sharon L., and Kristie Kauerz. 2006. Making the most of kindergarten trends and policy issues. In *K today: Teaching and learning in
the kindergarten year,* ed. Dominic F. Gullo, 161–70. Washington, D.C.:
National Association for the Education of Young Children.

Katz, Lilian G. 1998. Twins in school: What teachers should know. http://
ceep.crc.uiuc.edu/pubs/katzsym/intro.html.

Kids Count Data Center. 2009. The Annie E. Casey Foundation http://
www.kidscount.org/datacenter/ (accessed March 3, 2009).

Klitsch, Michael. 1995. Why so many twins and triplets? *Family Planning Perspectives* 27 (2): 52.

Koch, Helen L. 1966. *Twins and twin relations.* Chicago: University of
Chicago Press.

Koeppen-Schomerus, Gesina, Frank M. Spinath, and Robert Plomin. 2003.
Twins and non-twin siblings: Different estimates of shared environmental
influence in early childhood. *Twin Research* 6 (2): 97–105.

Kovas, Yulia, Marianna E. Hayiou-Thomas, Bonamy Oliver, Dorothy V. M.
Bishop, Philip S. Dale, and Robert Plomin. 2005. *Child Development* 76
(3): 632–51.

Laffey-Ardley, Sioban, and Karen Thorpe. 2006. Being opposite: Is there advantage for social competence and friendship in being an opposite-sex twin?
Twin Research and Human Genetics 9 (1): 131–40.

La Trobe Twin Study. 1991. *Twins in school.* Melbourne: La Trobe University
and the Australian Multiple Birth Association.

Leblanc, Nancy, Michel Boivin, Ginette Dionne, Mara Brendgen, Frank
Vitaro, Richard Tremblay, and Daniel Perusse. 2008. The development
of hyperactive-impulsive behaviors during the preschool years: The predictive validity of parental assessments. *Journal of Abnormal Child Psychology* 36 (7): 977–87.

Levy, Florence, David Hay, Michael McLaughlin, Catherine Wood, and Irwin Waldman. 1996. Twin-sibling differences in parental reports of ADHD, speech, reading and behavior problems. *Journal of Child Psychology and Psychiatry* 37 (5): 569–78.

Luke, Barbara, and Tamara Eberlein. 2004. *When you're expecting twins, triplets or quads: Proven guidelines for a healthy pregnancy.* Rev. ed. New York: HarperResource.

Luke, Barbara, Morton B. Brown, Mary L. Hediger, Rata B. Misiunas, and Elaine Anderson. 2006. Perinatal and early childhood outcomes of twins versus triplets. *Twin Research and Human Genetics* 9 (1): 81–88.

Luke, Barbara, S. Leurgans, L. Keith, D. Keith. 1995. The childhood growth of twin children. *Acta Geneticae Medicae et Gemellologiae* 44: 169–78.

Lyons, Susanne, ed. 2001. *Finding our way: Life with triplets, quadruplets and quintuplets.* Ontario: Triplets, Quads & Quints Association.

Lytton, Hugh, Dorice Conway, and Reginald Sauvé. 1977. The impact of twinship on parent-child interaction. *Journal of Personality and Social Psychology* 35 (2): 97–107.

MacDonald, Alison M. 2002. Bereavement in twin relationships: An exploration of themes from a study of twinship. *Twin Research* 5 (3): 218–26.

Malmstrom, Patricia Maxwell, and Janet Poland. 1999. *The art of parenting twins.* New York: Skylight Press.

Malmstrom, Patricia, and Marilyn N. Silva. 1986. Twin talk: Manifestations of twin status in the speech of toddlers. *Journal of Child Language* 13 (2): 293–304.

Martin, Joyce A., Brady E. Hamilton, Paul D. Sutton, Stephanie Ventura, Fay Menacker, and Sharon Kirmeyer. 2009. Births: Final data for 2006. *National Vital Statistics Reports* 57 (7): 1–102. Hyattsville, Md.: National Center for Health Statistics.

Martin, Joyce A., Brady E. Hamilton, Paul D. Sutton, Stephanie J. Ventura, Fay Menacker, Sharon Kirneyer, and Martha L. Munson. 2007. Births: Final data for 2005. *National Vital Statistics Reports* 56 (6): 23–25. Hyattsville, Md.: National Center for Health Statistics.

Martin, Joyce A., and Melissa M. Park. 1999. Trends in twin and triplet births: 1980–97. *National Vital Statistics Reports* 56 (6): 11–15. Hyattsville, Md.: National Center for Health Statistics.

Martin, Neilson C., Florence Levy, Jan Pieka, and David A. Hay. 2006. A genetic study of attention deficit hyperactivity disorder, conduct disorder, oppositional defiant disorder and reading disability: Aetiological overlaps and implications. *International Journal of Disability, Development and Education* 53 (1): 21–34.

Mascazine, John. 2004. *Understanding multiple-birth children and how they learn: A handbook for parents, teachers, and administrators.* Bloomington: AuthorHouse.

Masters, Coco. 2007. A new kind of twin. *Twin.com.* http://www.time.com/time/hearlth/article/0,8599,1603799,00.html (accessed August 9, 2009).

McDougall, Megan R., David A. Hay, and Kellie S. Bennett. 2006. Having a co-twin with attention-deficit hyperactivity disorder. *Twin Research and Human Genetics* 9 (1): 148–54.

McGregor, Karl K., and Nina C. Capone. 2004. Genetic and environmental interactions in determining the early lexicon: Evidence from a set of tri-zygotic quadruplets. *Journal of Child Language* 31 (2): 311–37.

McReynolds, Kate. 2007. Homeschooling. *Encounter* 20 (2): 36–41.

Medland, Sarah E., David L. Duffy, Margaret J. Wright, Gina M. Geffen, and Nicholas G. Martin. 2006. Handedness in twins: Analysis of data from 35 samples. *Twin Research and Human Genetics* 8 (1): 46–53.

Medland, Sarah E., John C Loehlin, Gonneke Willemsen, Peter K. Hatemi, Mathew C. Keller, Dorreet I. Boomsma, Lindon J. Eaves, and Nicholas G. Martin. 2008. Males do not reduce the fitness of their female co-twins in contemporary samples. *Twin Research and Human Genetic* 11 (5): 481–87.

Meijer, Chantal. 2007. My twins have separate birthdays. *TWINS* (March–April): 29.

Mogford-Bevan, Kay. 1999. Twins and their language development. In *Twin and Triplet Psychology: A Professional Guide to Working with Multiples,* ed. Audrey C. Sandbank, 7–18. London: Routledge.

Moskwinski, Rebecca E., ed. 2002. *Twins to quints: The complete manual for parents of multiple birth children.* Compiled by National Organization of Mothers of Twins Clubs (NOMOTC). Nashville: Harpeth House.

Mothers of Supertwins. 2009. *Supertwin statistics-general facts about multiple births.* http://www.mostonline.org/facts.outsidersources.htm (accessed January 26, 2009).

Mowrer, Ernest R. 1954. Some factors in the affectional adjustment of twins. *American Sociological Review* 19 (4): 468–71.

Multiple Births Canada/Naissances multiples Canada. 2008. History Time-line. *Multiple Moments* 2–3.

Multiple Births Canada/Naissances multiples Canada. 2009. Resources higher order multiples support. http://www.multiplebirthscanada.org (accessed January 26, 2009).

Muñoz-Silva, Alicia, and Manuel Sanchez-Garcia. 2004. Maternal distancing strategies toward twin sons, one with mild hearing loss: A case study. *American Annals of the Deaf* 149 (2): 360–64.

National Geographic. 2009. *In the womb: Identical twins.* DVD. Pioneer Productions for National Geographic Channel.

New York Times. 2002. Sextuplets born in Kansas. http://www.nytimes .com/2004/oz/04/07/us/sextuplets-born-in-kansas.html (accessed July 6, 2009).

Noble, Elizabeth. 2003. *Having twins and more: A parent's guide to multiple pregnancy, birth and early childhood.* Boston: Houghton Mifflin.

Nussbaum, Debra. 2009. Triplet nation. *New York Times* http://www .nytimes.com/2005/10/23/nyretion/nyrggioja12/23nTRIPLET.html?_r=1 (accessed February 10, 2009).

Oliver, Bonamy R., and Robert Plomin. 2007. Twins' early development study (TEDS): a multivariate, longitudinal genetic investigation of language, cognition, and behavior problems from childhood through adolescence. *Twin Research and Human Genetics* 10 (1): 96–105.

Palermo, Francisco, Laura D. Hanish, Carol Lynn Martin, Richard A. Fabes, and Mark Reiser. 2007. Preschoolers' academic readiness: What role does the teacher-child relationship play? *Early Childhood Research Quarterly* 22 (4): 407–22.

Parisi, Paolo. 2004. Twin research, and its multiple births and expressions: A short, personal voyage through its scope, history, and organization. *Twin Research* 7 (4): 309–17.

Parker, Neville. 1968. Twins and twin relations. *Journal of Sociology* 4 (1): 74–75.

Pearlman, Eileen, and Jill Alison Ganon. 2000. *Raising twins from birth through adolescence: What parents want to know (and what twins want to tell them).* New York: HarperCollins.

Pianta, Robert, and Martha Cox. 2002. Transition to kindergarten. *Early Childhood Research & Policy Briefs* 2 (2): 2–5. http://www.ed.ncedl.org (accessed July 29, 2009).

Piontelli, Alessandra. 1999. Twins in utero: Temperament development and intertwin behaviour before and after birth. In *Twin and triplet psychology: A professional guide to working with multiples,* ed. Audrey C. Sandbank, 7–18. London: Routledge.

Preedy, Pat. 1999. Meeting the educational needs of pre-school and primary aged twins and higher multiples. In *Twin and triplet psychology: A professional guide to working with multiples,* ed. Audrey C. Sandbank, 7–18. London: Routledge.

Posthuma, Daniëlle, Eco J. C. De Geus, Nico Bleichrodt, and Dorrett I. Boomsma. 2000. Twin-singleton differences in intelligence? *Twin Research* 3 (2): 83–87.

Pulkkinen, Lea, Inka Vaalamo, Risto Hietala, Jaakko Kaprio, and Richard J. Rose. 2003. Peer reports of adaptive behavior in twins and singletons: Is twinship a risk or an advantage? *Twin Research* 6 (2): 106–18.

Rector, Joe. 2008. The Brentz twins . . . a story of loss and inspiration. *TWINS* (November–December): 16–17.

Resnick, Steven J., Robin Corley, and JoAnn Robinson. 1997. A longitudinal twin study of intelligence in the second year. *Monographs of the Society for Research in Child Development* 62 (1), serial no. 249.

Rhode Island Kids Count. 2005. *Getting ready: Findings from the national school readiness indicators initiative. A 17 state partnership.* Providence: National School Readiness Indicators Initiative.

Robin, Monique, Denis Corroyer, and Irene Casati. 1996. Patterns of mothers of twins during the first year. *Journal of Child Psychology and Psychiatry* 37 (4): 453–60.

Robin, Monique, Gaid Le Maner-Idrissi, and Denis Corroyer. 1998. Mothers' representations of their 13-month-old twins and child raising attitudes. *Infant Mental Health Journal* 19 (1): 1–19.

Rocha, Alana. 2008. Kansas sextuplets turn six. *Kansas—the CW Channel.* http://www.kansascw.com/global/sotry.asp?s=8126442&ClientType (accessed July 6, 2009).

Rommelse, Nanda, N. J., Marieke E. Altink, Ellen A. Fliers, Neilson C. Martin, Cathelijne J. M. Buschgens, Catharina A. Hartman, Jan K. Buitelaar, Stephen V. Faraone, Joseph A. Sergeant, and Jaap Oosterlaan. 2009. Comorbid problems in ADHD: Degree of association, shared endophenotypes, and formation of distinct subtypes. Implications for a future "dsm." *Journal of Abnormal Child Psychology* 37 (6): 793–804. http://www.eric.ed.gov/ERICWebPortal/Home.portal:jsessionid=HhY fzsWyTyJpLnMKN2 (accessed February 2, 2010).

Rooney, Rosanna, David Hay, and Florence Levy. 2003. Small for gestational age as a predictor of behavioral and learning problems in twins. *Twin Research* 8 (1): 46–54.

Rous, Beth. 2008. Recommended transition practices for young children and families: Results from a national validation study. Technical Report #3. Lexington: University of Kentucky, Human Development Institute, National Early Childhood Transition Center http://www.hdi.uky.edu/nectc/ (accessed July 29, 2009).

Rous, Beth. 2009. Review of transition research. April Transition Alert. National Early Childhood Transition Center http://www.hdluky.edu/libraries/NECTC (accessed July 29, 2009).

Sandbank, Audrey C., ed. 1999. *Twin and triplet psychology: A professional guide to working with multiples.* London: Routledge.

Santrock, John W. 1993. *Children.* 3rd ed. Madison, Wisc.: Brown & Benchmark.

Scheinfeld, Amram. 1967. *Twins and Supertwins.* Baltimore: Penguin.

Segal, Nancy L. 1985. Monozygotic and dizygotic twins: A comparative analysis of mental ability profiles. *Child Development* 56 (4): 1051–58.

———1999. *Entwined lives.* New York: PLUME.

———2000. Virtual twins: New findings on within-family environmental influences on intelligence. *Journal of Educational Psychology* 92 (3): 442–48.

———2003a. Spotlights; Research samplings; literature, policies, photography and athletics. *Twin Research* 6 (1): 72–81.

———2003b. Between twins; research summaries; in the real world. *Twin Research* 6 (6): 498–501.

———2005a. Education issues; twin study summaries; famous twin babies and famous twins. *Twin Research and Human Genetics* 8 (4): 409–14.

———2005b. *Indivisible by two: Lives of extraordinary twins.* Cambridge: Harvard University Press.

———2006. SuperQuads: A day in the life; research reviews: color-number association, finger-length ratios, twinning diets, athletic pairs. *Twin Research and Human Genetics* 9 (4): 609–14.

———2008. Twins and politics: Political careers and political attitudes/twin research reviews: pair-bonding; facial expressivity in reared apart twins; educating multiples/stories that move and amaze us: A military funeral; a twins' reunion; Egyptian septuplets; rare occupations. *Twin Research and Human Genetics* 11 (6): 656–60.

Segal, Nancy L., and Jean M. Russell. 1992. Twins in the classroom: School policy issues and recommendations. *Journal of Educational and Psychological Consultation* 3 (1): 69–84.

Shere, Marie Orr. 1956. Socio-emotional factors in families of the twin with cerebral palsy. *Exceptional Children* (February): 197–208.

Siemon, Mari. 1980. The separation-individuation process in adult twins. *American Journal of Psychotherapy* 34 (3): 387–400.

Smilansky, Sara. 1992. *Twins and their development: The roles of family and school.* Rockville, Md.: BJE Press.

Soucy, Jean-Yves, with Annette Dionne, Cecile Dionne, and Yvonne Dionne. 1995. *The Dionne quintuplets' own story.* New York: Berkley Books.

Steinman, Gary D., and Christina Verni. 2007. *Womb mates: A modern guide to fertility and training.* New York: Baffin Books.

Stewart, Elizabeth A. 2000. The comparative constitution of twinship: Strategies and paradoxes. *Twin Research* 3 (3): 142–47.

———. 2003. *Exploring twins: Towards a social analysis of twinship.* London: Palgrave Macmillan.

Sutcliffe, Alastair G., and Catherine Derom. 2006. Followup of twins: Health, behavior, speech, language outcomes and implications for parents. *Early Human Development* 82 (6): 379–86.

Swanson, Patricia B., Robert T. Kane, Jillian G. Pearsall-Jones, Carl F. Swanson, and Maxine L. Croft. 2009. How couples cope with the death of a twin or higher order multiple. *Twin Research and Human Genetics* 12 (4): 392–402.

Thomas, Diane. 1986–87. Preschool challenges. *Twinline Reporter* (Winter. ed.) Patricia Malmstrom. Berkeley, Calif.: Twin Services.

Thompson, Ross A. 2008. Connecting neurons, concepts, and people: Brain development and its implications. *Preschool Policy Brief.* National Institute for Early Education Research, issue 17.

Thorpe, Karen. 2003. Twins and Friendship. *Twin Research* 6 (6): 532–35.

———. 2006. Twin children's language development. *Early Human Development* 82 (6): 387–95.

Thorpe, Karen, and Susan Danby. 2006. Compromised or competent: Analyzing twin children's social worlds. *Twin Research and Human Genetics* 9 (1): 90–94.

Thorpe, Karen, and Karen Gardner. 2006. Twins and their friendships: Differences between monozygotic, dizygotic same-sex and dizygotic mixed-sex pairs. *Twin Research and Human Genetics* 9 (1): 155–64.

Thorpe, Karen, Michael Rutter, and Rosemary Greenwood. 2003. Twins as a natural experiment to study the causes of mild language delay. II: Family interaction risk factors. *Journal of Child Psychology and Psychiatry* 44 (3): 342–55.

Tinglof, Christina Baglivi. 2007. *Parenting school-age twins and multiples.* New York: McGraw Hill.

Tomasello, Michael, Sara Mannle, and Ann Cale Kruger. 1986. Linguistic environment of 1-2-year-old twins. *Developmental Psychology* 22 (2): 169–76.

Torgersen, Anne Mari, and Harald Janson. 2002. Why do identical twins differ in personality? Shared environment reconsidered. *Twin Research* 5 (1): 44–52.

Trias, L. Tuulikki, Hanna E. Ebeling, Varpu Penninkilampi-Derola, Ann M. Kunnelius, Tina T. Tirkkonen, and Irma K. Moilanen. 2006. How long do the consequences of parental preference last: A study of twins from pregnancy to young adulthood. *Twin Research and Human Genetics* 9 (2): 240–49.

Trouton, Alexandra, Frank M. Sinath, and Robert Plomin. 2002. Twins early development study (TEDS): A multivariate, longitudinal genetic investigation of language, cognition and behavior problems in childhood. *Twin Research* 5 (5): 444–48.

Tully, Lucy A., Louise Arseneault, Avshalom Caspi, Terrie E. Moffitt, and Julie Morgan. 2004a. Does maternal warmth moderate the effects of birth weight on twins' attention deficit/hyperactivity disorder (ADHD) symptoms and low IQ? *Journal of Counseling and Clinical Psychology* 72 (2): 218–26.

Tully, Lucy A., Terrie E. Moffitt, Avshalom Caspi, Alan Taylor, Helena Kiernan, and Penny Andreou. 2004b. What effect does classroom separation have on twins' behavior, progress at school, and reading abilities? *Twin Research and Human Genetics* 7 (2): 115–24.

TWINS. 1997. *Multiples in the News* 13 6 (11). Ed. Susan Alt. Centennial, Colo.: The Business Word.

Twins and Multiples. 2006. Curtin University of Technology. http://www.twinsandmultiples.org/facts_figures/index.htm (accessed August 8, 2006).

Twins and Multiples. 2006a. A model for relationships between multiples. Curtin University of Technology. http://www.twinsandmultiples.org/preschool/p4a.htm (accessed August 11, 2007).

Twin Research and Human Genetics. 2006. Table of contents. 9 (6): i–vi.

Twin Services Reporter. 1989. *Twins: Unique developmental aspects,* ed. Patricia Malmstrom. Berkeley: Twin Services.

Tymms, Peter, and Pat Preedy. 1998. The attainment and progress of twins at the start of school. *Educational Research* 40 (2): 243–49.

University of Louisville. 2009. Louisville twin study. http://louisville.edu/medschool/pediatrics/research/child-developement-unit (accessed April 29, 2009).

University of Virginia Health System. 2004. *High-risk pregnancy: Multiple pregnancy.* http:www.hsc.virginia.edu/uvahealth/peds-hrpregnant/multiple.cfm (accessed February 2010).

van Leeuwen, Marieke, Stéphanie M. van den Berg, Toos C. E. M. van Beijsterveldt, and Dorret I. Boomsma. 2005. Effects of twin separation in primary school. *Twin Research and Human Genetics* 8 (4): 384–91.

Vandell, Deborah Lowe, Margaret Tresch Owen, Kathy Shores Wilson, and V. Kay Henderson. 1988. Social development in infant twins: Peer and mother-child relationships. *Child Development* 59: 168–77.

Wadsworth, Sally, John C. DeFries, Richard K. Olson, and Erik G. Willcutt. 2007. Colorado longitudinal twin study of reading disability. *Annals of Dyslexia* 57 (2): 139–60. http://www.proquest.com.leopac.ulv.edu (accessed July 14, 2009).

Walker, Sheila O., Stephen A. Petrill, Frank M. Spinath, and Robert Plomin. 2004. Nature, nurture and academic achievement: A twin study of teacher assessments of 7-year olds. *British Journal of Educational Psychology* 74 (3): 323–42.

Webbink, Dinand, David Hay, and Peter M. Visscher. 2007. Does sharing the same class in school improve cognitive abilities of twins? *Twin Research and Human Genetics* 10 (4): 573–80.

Willcutt, Erik G., and Bruce F. Pennington. 2000. Comorbidity of reading disability and attention deficit/hyperactivity disorder: Differences by gender and subtype. *Journal of Learning Disabilities* 33 (2): 179–91.

Wilson, Ronald S. 1977. Twins and siblings: Concordance for school-age mental development. *Child Development* 48 (1): 211–16.

———. 1983. The Louisville twin study: Developmental synchronies in behavior. *Child Development* 54 (2): 298–316.

Winsler, Adam, Henry Tran, Suzanne C. Hartman, Amy L. Madigan, Louis Mantra, and Charles Bleiker. 2008. School readiness gains made by ethnically diverse children in poverty attending center-based child-care and public school pre-kindergarten programs. *Early Childhood Research Quarterly* 23 (3): 314–29.

Withrow, Rebecca, and Valerie L. Schwiebert. 2005. Twin loss: Implications for counselors working with surviving twins. *Journal of Counseling and Development* 33 (1): 21–29.

Wood, John. 2007. A dad deals with his twin son's unique medical needs. *TWINS* (July–August): 15.

World Almanac. 2008. Homeschooled students. World Almanac & Book Facts. http://0-web.ebsohost.com.leopac.ulv.edu/ehost/delivery?vid=25vhi d=107&sid=27aa3595 (accessed August 3, 2009).

Wright, Lawrence. 1997. *Twins and what they tell us about who we are.* New York: John Wiley.

Yokoyama, Yoshie. 2003. Comparison of child-rearing problems between mothers with multiple children who conceived after fertility treatment and mothers with multiple children who conceived spontaneously. *Twin Research* 6 (2): 889–96.

Yokoyama, Yoshie, Masako Sugimoto, and Syuichi Ooki. 2005. Analysis of factors affecting birthweight, birth length and head circumference: Study of Japanese triplets. *Twin Research and Human Genetics* 8 (6): 657–63.

Yokoyama, Yoshie, Masako Sugimoto, Karri Silventoinen, and Jaakko Kaprio. 2008. Weight growth charts from birth to 6 years of age in Japanese triplets. *Twin Research and Human Genetics* 11 (6): 641–47.

Yokoyama, Yoshie, Saeko Wada, Masako Suimoto, Miyuki Saito, Miyoko Matsubara, and Jun Sono. 2007. Comparison of motor development between twins and singletons in Japan: Population-based study. *Twin Research and Human Genetics* 10 (2): 379–84.

Yoon, Young-Soon, and Yoon-Mi Hur. 2006. Twins have slightly higher self-concepts than singletons in the elementary school period: A study of South Korean twins and singletons. *Twin Research and Human Genetics* 9 (2): 233–39.

Zvoch, Keith, Ralph E. Reynolds, and Robert P. Parker. 2008. Full-day kindergarten and student literacy growth: Does a lengthened schoolday make a difference? *Early Childhood Research Quarterly* 23 (1): 94–107.

Index

brain weight, 60

C

caregiving, 80–81, 84
See also parenting, high-quality
caring and empathic behaviors, 190–191
Carley, Lucy, 32
Castor and Pollux, 34
catch-up, in developmental progression, 114, 124–126, 196–202
Center for the Study of Multiple Birth, 38
cerebral palsy, 21
childbirth, delayed, and triplet births, 28–29
child care, 84–85, 97
chorionicity, and placentation, 19
classroom placements
    decision-making about, 146, 147, 179–181
    decision reversals, 183–187
    of multiple-birth children, 203
    programmatic practices, 182–183
    separation, mandated, 177, 178–179
    of triplets, 213
    See also separation of multiple-birth children
Clink, Edward and Elsie, 38
closely coupled twins, 96
clothing, as logistical issue, 75
cognitive development
catch-up in, 114
critical thinking skills, 64
    environmental factors in, 113
    imaginative play and, 110
    language development and, 129
    triplets and delays in, 59, 112
collaboration, between schools and families, 218–219
collective identity, balance with self-identity, 166–167
Colorado Longitudinal Twin Study of Reading Disability, University of Colorado at Boulder, 71
color blindness, 17
Comedy of Errors (Shakespeare), 34–35
communication
    about unacceptable behaviors, 102–103
    of discontent by toddlers, 102
    in early childhood, 116–129
    opportunities for, and early literacy, 127–129
    of parents to multiple-birth vs. singleborn children, 120–121
    See also language development

communicational needs of preschool twins, 139, 142–145, 229
communicational program practices, 156–157, 163–172, 231
community programs, and supertwin families, 32
comparisons of children, 149, 168–169, 194, 214
competitiveness, 94, 181, 194
co-multiple-birth children, defined, 12
confidence, secure attachment and, 84–85
conjoined twins, 23, 35–36
Conway, Dorice, 42
cooperative behaviors, 99, 101, 109, 193
core concepts linking needs and practices, 163
co-supertwins, defined, 12
co-twins, defined, 12
couple effect, 44, 86
critical thinking skills, 64
cryptophasia, 123
cultural narratives, dual relationships in, 33–34

D

date of birth, 76
Day, Ella J., 41
death of a co-twin, 103–104
depression, 68, 69
developmental progression
    brain, 108
    catching up, 114, 124–126, 196–202
    delays in, 59, 68, 112, 115, 144, 197
    differences in early childhood years, 212
    information-sharing with parents, 201–202
    neonatal, of twin girls vs. boys, 57
    personality, 88–89
    reviews of, 148
    variations among multiple-birth children, 218
    vulnerabilities in, 58–59
    See also cognitive development; language development; physical development; social development
"Development of Language in Twins" (Day), 41
dichorionic twins, 19–20
Dilley, Keith and Becky, 37
Dionne quintuplets, 17, 36, 37
disabilities in multiple-birth children, 67–68

dizygotic (DZ) twins
    connection between, 15
    defined, 18
    as percent of twin population, 22
    placentas of, 20
    similarities and differences in, 59–60
    temperaments of, 166
    as twin type, 13
Dolan, Kathy, 177, 213
Doublemint Twins, 35
dressing alike and differently, 73–74
dual relationships in cultural narratives,
    33–34

E

education
    birthrate of multiple-birth children and,
        29
    early childhood, 156–159, 182–183
    programs for families, 152–153
Education of the Handicapped Act (1970),
    203
Eidelman, Arthur, 31, 45, 59
emotional and behavioral problems,
    102–103
emotional competence, and self-esteem,
    100
emotional development, 80–83
empathy, 102
Eng and Chang of Siam, 35–36
enrollment and operational plans, 172–187,
    205
environmental factors, individualizing
    effect of, 55–56, 97, 113
epigenetics, 17
Esau and Jacob, 33–34
exclusion and inclusion, multiple-birth
    children and, 215
experiments, destructive, 44
exposure and celebrity status, 37
extrasensory perception (ESP), 116
extreme individual twins, 96

F

fairness, 195–196
families
    bulletin boards for, 153
    and caregiving, 80–81, 84
    education programs for, 152–153
    and intellectual functioning, 115
    and language development, 126
    linking to resources and advocacy,
        153–154

of multiple-birth children, 96–99
    See also parents of multiple-birth
    children
Families of Supertwins Bill of Rights, 31
Farber, Susan, 41
fathers, 84, 97, 104
    See also parents of multiple-birth
    children
Feldman, Ruth, 31, 45, 59
festivals, 38, 39
*Finding our Way: Life with Triplets,
    Quadruplets and Quintuplets* (Lyons), 32
fingerprints, 61
Fisher quintuplets, 37
focused issues
    fairness, 193–196
    individual identity and collective
        identity, 165–169
    together and apart, 176–183
fraternal twins, 12–13, 18
    See also dizygotic (DZ) twins
free play, 100
friendship development, 47, 99–100, 149,
    188–190, 191–192

G

Galton, Sir Francis, 40
gender differences
    and ADHD, 70, 90, 92
    in language development, 112, 122
    in left-handedness, 62
    and maturity, 77, 91
    recognition of, in maturational stages,
        145
gender identity, 77–78, 90–91
genes, and intelligence, 111
genotype, 15
gestational age, for multiple-birth vs.
    singleborn children, 56, 57–58
Gibbons, June and Jennifer, 36
Gill, Frances McLaughlin, 36
girls, with boy-twin partners, 77–78, 91–92
glossary, 221–228
Good Housekeeping magazine, 36
Gosselin, Kate and Jon, 37
growth charts, individualized vs.
    population-based, 58
guidelines to meet the needs of twins and
    supertwins, 204–209
Guttensohn quintuplets, 37

milestones in, 116–118
in multiple-birth vs. singleborn children, 114–115, 117–119, 126
and transition to kindergarten, 210–211
in twins, 41, 42, 45, 107, 123–124
language disorders, in MZ vs. DZ twins, 122
La Trobe Twin Study of Behavioral and Biological Development (Hay), 43, 45, 112, 211
learning, 68, 109–116
See also cognitive development
Leeper, Sarah, 178
left-handedness, 62
Levy, Florence, 71
Lewis, Jim, 43–44
longitudinal studies on twins, 41–44, 46
Longitudinal Twin Study of Early Literacy Development: Preschool and Kindergarten Phases (Byrne et al.), 46
loss of a co-twin, 103–104
Loss of Multiples Support Network, 104
Louisville Twin Study, 42
low birth weight (LBW), 58, 113, 115
lyonization, 17
Lyons, Susanne, 32
Lytton, Hugh, 42

M

mainstreaming and inclusion, 203
Malmstrom, Patricia, 2, 38–39
Mascazine, John, 45, 214–215
mature dependent twins, 96
maturity differences between boys and girls, 77, 91
McCaughey, Bobbi and Kenny, 37
media stories, 48
Mengele, Josef, 44
milestones
achievement of, by multiple-birth children, 168–169
beginning preschool and kindergarten, 182–183
in language development, 116–118
in learning, 108
in physical development, 55–62
preschool attendance as, 133
in social and emotional development, 80–83
Minnesota Study of Twins Reared Apart (MISTRA), 41, 43
mirror-image twins, 20–21, 22, 23, 62
Mirsky, Bracha, 32
misconceptions, 48–50

mixed-age classrooms, 217
modeling empathy, 102
modeling speech, 128
monochorionic twins, 19–20
monozygotic (MZ) twins
cooperation by, 100
couple effect in, 86
defined, 18
differences in, 14–15, 59
frequency of, 15
as percent of twin population, 22
placentas of, 20
similar worldviews of, 113
stressful events and, 97
temperaments of, 166
as twin type, 24
motherhood, triadic, 98
mother-infant relationships, 45, 59
mothers and mothering, 28–29, 92, 112, 121
See also parents of multiple-birth children
Mothers of Supertwins (MOST), 31, 178
Mowrer, Ernest R., 42
multiple-birth children
overview, 11
acknowledgment of, 136, 138, 160
adaptability of, 88–89
assumptions about, 48–50
and attachment, 84–86
characteristics of, 59–62, 80–81, 87, 136, 160
defined, 12–13
major issues relating to, 214–215
rates of, 26–30
and relationships, 45, 59, 98, 101, 216
self-image of, 191
separation of, 40–41, 44
as term, 2
types of, 25
See also relationships among multiple-birth children; twins and twin types
multiplehood, 30–31
Multiples Canada, 69
myth, fiction, and reality, 33–39
myths, popular, 48–50

N

name identity, 89–90, 160
Naperville, Illinois, triplet births in, 27
National Association for the Education of Young Children (NAEYC), 4
National Center for Education Statistics, 207

National Organization of Mothers of Twins Clubs (NOMOTC), 38, 69
national twin registries, 40
Native Americans, twin births among, 29
Nebraska, triplet births in, 27–28
needs of multiple-birth children
  overview, 136–137
  guidelines for meeting, 204–209
  identification of, 134–136
  individual and collective, recognition of, 143, 161
  linking program practices with, 163
  primary school teachers and, 211
  summary concepts of, 138
  See also Unique Needs of Preschool Twins (UNPT)
neonatal development, of twin girls vs. boys, 57
neonatal intensive care unit (NICU), 68–69
neonatology, 59
neurological outcomes, of singleborn vs. multiple-birth children, 113
newborn multiple-birth children, 45, 59, 80, 109, 117
New Jersey, multiple-birth children in, 27–28, 29–30
Nonshared Environmental Influences on Individual Differences in Early Behavioral Development: A Monozygotic Twin Differences Study (Asbury et al.), 46

O

octuplets, 25, 38
opposite-sex twins
  gender identity in, 90–91
  and independent experiences, 47
  and individuation, 169
  language development in, 45, 122
  social skills of, 192

P

parent-child interactions
  and early development, 42
  with multiple-birth children, 96–97, 118–119, 126
  with multiple-birth vs. singleborn children, 96–97, 120–121
  negative disciplinary expressions, 46
parent conferences, 147
parenting, high-quality, 80–81, 84, 119–120

parents of multiple-birth children
  advocacy by, 153–154
  attitudes of, and behavior of children, 98
  depression in, 69
  expectations of, based on children's birth order, 76
  expression of emotions by, 104
  information sharing with, regarding developmental progression, 201–202
  input by, 161, 177
  and language acquisition by children, 126
  preferences in classroom placement, 180, 181–182
  resources for, 71–72, 150–154, 237–239
  as resources for information, 31–32, 45, 49, 51
  and shared child care workload, 97
  sharing research with, 128
  transition practices for, 208
Parent Trap (film), 35
perceptions from the field
  on communicational program practices, 164–169
  on programmatic program practices, 162, 176
  on relational program practices, 188–193
Perinatal and Early Childhood Outcomes of Twins versus Triplets, 47
personality development, multiple-birth children and, 76, 87, 88–89
phenotypes, 15, 17
physical development
  and critical thinking skills, 64
  factors in, 55–56
  large-motor, 63–65
  patterns in, 56–59
  skills acquisition, 62–67
  small-motor, 65–67
  variations in, among multiple-birth children, 60, 73–74
play, 99, 100, 109, 110, 189
playmates, 110–111, 192–193, 215
polarity, in personality characteristics, 87
polyzygotic (PZ) supertwins, 24
PPUNPT. See Program Practices to Meet the Unique Needs of Preschool Twins (PPUNPT)
Preedy, Pat, 20, 95–96
pregnancies, stressful, and female embryo survival rate, 29

About the Author

Dr. Eve-Marie Arce remains active in professional organizations. She held the office of state president for the Association for the Education of Young Children in California and numerous positions advising and consulting on child development and instruction. She entered the field as a Head Start teacher, directed a state preschool and a university lab, and established child development centers on nine college campuses before teaching college for twenty years. Currently she consults and presents on topics related to twins in preschool, the focus of her doctoral dissertation. She holds an EdD in organizational leadership, a BA in child development, and an MA in early childhood education and human and family development. She was the academic editor for *Perspectives: Early Childhood Education* and authored *Curriculum for Young Children: An Introduction*. She is married and still takes pleasure in her own twin daughters (now thirty-two years old) and especially delights in her two-and-a-half-year-old twin grandsons.